Migration, Diasporas and Citizenship Series

The Migration, Diasporas and Citizenship series covers three important aspects of the migration progress. Firstly, the determinants, dynamics and characteristics of international migration. Secondly, the continuing attachment of many contemporary migrants to their places of origin, signified by the word 'diaspora', and thirdly the attempt, by contrast, to belong and gain acceptance in places of settlement, signified by the word 'citizenship'. The series publishes work that shows engagement with and a lively appreciation of the wider social and political issues that are influenced by international migration.

Also published in Migration Studies by Palgrave Macmillan

Rutvica Andrijasevic
MIGRATION, AGENCY AND CITIZENSHIP IN SEX TRAFFICKING

Gideon Calder, Phillip Cole and Jonathan Seglow
CITIZENSHIP ACQUISITION AND NATIONAL BELONGING
Migration, Membership and the Liberal Democratic State

Huub Dijstelbloem and Albert Meijer (*editors*)
MIGRATION AND THE NEW TECHNOLOGICAL BORDERS OF EUROPE

Thomas Faist and Andreas Ette (*editors*)
THE EUROPEANIZATION OF NATIONAL POLICIES AND POLITICS OF IMMIGRATION
Between Autonomy and the European Union

Thomas Faist, Margit Fauser and Peter Kivisto (*editors*)
THE MIGRATION–DEVELOPMENT NEXUS
A Transnational Perspective

Thomas Faist and Peter Kivisto (*editors*)
DUAL CITIZENSHIP IN GLOBAL PERSPECTIVE
From Unitary to Multiple Citizenship

Martin Geiger and Antoine Pécoud (*editors*)
THE POLITICS OF INTERNATIONAL MIGRATION MANAGEMENT

John R. Hinnells (*editor*)
RELIGIOUS RECONSTRUCTION IN THE SOUTH ASIAN DIASPORAS
From One Generation to Another

Ayhan Kaya
ISLAM, MIGRATION AND INTEGRATION
The Age of Securitization

Marie Macy and Alan H. Carling
ETHNIC, RACIAL AND RELIGIOUS INEQUALITIES
The Perils of Subjectivity

George Menz and Alexander Caviedes (*editors*)
LABOUR MIGRATION IN EUROPE

Laura Morales and Marco Giugni (*editors*)
SOCIAL CAPITAL, POLITICAL PARTICIPATION AND MIGRATION IN EUROPE
Making Multicultural Democracy Work?

Aspasia Papadopoulou-Kourkoula
TRANSIT MIGRATION
The Missing Link Between Emigration and Settlement

Prodromos Panayiotopoulos
ETHNICITY, MIGRATION AND ENTERPRISE

Vicky Squire
THE EXCLUSIONARY POLITICS OF ASYLUM

Lucy Williams
GLOBAL MARRIAGE
Cross-Border Marriage Migration in Global Context

Migration, Diasporas and Citizenship
Series Standing Order ISBN 978–0–230–30078–1 (hardback) and 978–0–230–30079–8 (paperback)
(*outside North America only*)

You can receive future titles in this series as they are published by placing a standing order. Please contact your bookseller or, in case of difficulty, write to us at the address below with your name and address, the title of the series and the ISBN quoted above.

Customer Services Department, Macmillan Distribution Ltd, Houndmills, Basingstoke, Hampshire RG21 6XS, England

---

The Migration–Development Nexus

A Transnational Perspective

Edited by

Thomas Faist
Bielefeld University, Germany

Margit Fauser
Bielefeld University, Germany

Peter Kivisto
Augustana College, USA

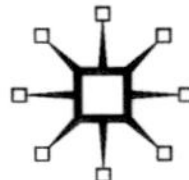

First published 2011 by
PALGRAVE MACMILLAN

Palgrave Macmillan in the UK is an imprint of Macmillan Publishers Limited, registered in England, company number 785998, of Houndmills, Basingstoke, Hampshire RG21 6XS.

Palgrave Macmillan in the US is a division of St Martin's Press LLC, 175 Fifth Avenue, New York, NY 10010.

Palgrave Macmillan is the global academic imprint of the above companies and has companies and representatives throughout the world.

Palgrave® and Macmillan® are registered trademarks in the United States, the United Kingdom, Europe and other countries.

ISBN 978–0–230–22857–3 hardback

This book is printed on paper suitable for recycling and made from fully managed and sustained forest sources. Logging, pulping and manufacturing processes are expected to conform to the environmental regulations of the country of origin.

A catalogue record for this book is available from the British Library.

A catalog record for this book is available from the Library of Congress.

10 9 8 7 6 5 4 3 2 1
20 19 18 17 16 15 14 13 12 11

Printed and bound in Great Britain by
CPI Antony Rowe, Chippenham and Eastbourne

The editors would like to thank the Center for Interdisciplinary Research (ZiF) at Bielefeld University for sponsoring a ZiF research group from October 2008 to February 2009. The contributions to this book are based on research carried out within the framework of the ZiF research group.

Contents

Part III Outlook

List of Tables and Figure

Tables

Figure

Preface

Some issues in the social sciences keep reappearing with some regularity. Migration and development seems to be one of the nexuses which have been on and off the agenda of both development and migration research since the 1960s. The current enthusiasm around migrants as agents of development reflects a paradigm which holds that migration can produce beneficial outcomes for both emigration and immigration countries. This enthusiasm, however, reflects little memory of previous debates. In particular, scant systematic thought is given to what the continuities in this debate are and what is 'new' this time around. This book shows various ways in which a transnational perspective, broadly understood, may answer these questions and triggers new research questions and perspectives around the migration–development nexus. In particular, a transnational perspective recognizes the emergence of a new agent in development discourse, variably called 'migrants', 'diaspora' or 'transnational community'. Such a lens captures both the cross-border ties and engagements these actors sustain and the role played by institutions on the local, national and global level, including international organizations such as the World Bank, national states and organizations in development cooperation.

The chapters of this book are grouped loosely into two sections. In the first part, the emphasis is on the variety of paradigms which have characterized the debates around the migration–development nexus (chapters 2 and 3). The second part deals with new theoretical approaches and research questions which emerge from organizations, networks and states (chapters 4 to 7). The book is framed by an introductory essay that connects the strands of the debate (Chapter 1) and an outlook which reflects upon both the role of social scientists in public debates and policy-making around the migration–development nexus, as well as the conceptual advances and empirical results presented by the chapters in this book (chapters 8 and 9).

A multidisciplinary book project like this one always risks ending up as a compilation of disconnected essays. We have attempted to reduce this danger by engaging all the authors in an intensive process of debate during an initial conference as well as in subsequent rounds of elaboration and revision of the chapters. The project started as a ZiF

Cooperation Group at the Centre for Interdisciplinary Research (ZiF) at Bielefeld University between October 2008 and February 2009. The Cooperation Group 'Transnationalisation and Development(s): Concepts and Venues for Research' under the guidance of Thomas Faist organized several workshops which entailed intensive discussions of selected topics around the migration–development nexus, such as interdisciplinary perspectives on the nexus; transnational citizenship; social protection and mobility; and the social sciences and public policy. The group's efforts concluded with a final authors' workshop.

Apart from the authors and editors, several other persons have been involved in this project and have contributed to its successful conclusion. Listing them and their locations shows how producing this book on the migration–development nexus from a transnational perspective was itself a transnational process. Several colleagues provided comments at an authors' workshop: Gudrun Lachenmann (Bielefeld), Boris Nieswand (Göttingen), Nicola Piper (Swansea) and Phil Triadafilopoulos (Toronto). At the Centre for Interdisciplinary Research (ZiF) at Bielefeld University, Britta Padberg and Barbara Jantzen were pivotal in the administration of the ZiF cooperation group and its follow-up. In Toronto, Edith Klein carefully edited the manuscript for book publication. The Palgrave Macmillan team has also been very supportive. We are grateful to all of them.

Thomas Faist, Margit Fauser and Peter Kivisto

Notes on Contributors

Humberto Márquez Covarrubias currently serves as Research Professor in the Academic Unit of Development Studies at the Autonomous University of Zacatecas, Mexico. He is a member of the National System of Researchers (SNI), the International Network on Migration and Development (INDM) of the Mexican Association for Rural Studies (AMER) and faculty in migration and development. Among his recent publications are *Espejismos del río de oro. Dialéctica del desarrollo y la migración entre México y Estados Unidos*, Miguel Ángel Porrúa Publishers (co-authored with Raúl Delgado Wise) (in press) and *Desarrollo desigual y migración forzada*, Miguel Ángel Porrúa Publishers (co-authored with Raúl Delgado Wise) (in press).

Raúl Delgado Wise is Professor and Director of the Doctoral Program in Development Studies at the University of Zacatecas, Mexico and Executive Director of the International Migration and Development Network. He is the author/editor of 14 books and more than 100 essays. He has been a guest lecturer in Canada, the United States, Germany, the Netherlands, Denmark, Belgium, Switzerland, Great Britain, Italy, Spain, Ghana and various Latin American countries. He received the annual 'Maestro Jesús Silva Herzog' prize for economics research in 1993. He is a member of the Mexican Academy of Sciences, the National System of Researchers, and several scholarly associations in Canada, the United States, Latin America and Europe. He is the editor of the book series on 'Latin America and the New World Order' for Miguel Angel Porrúa Publishers and the chief editor of the journal *Migración y Desarrollo.*

Thomas Faist is Professor of Transnational Relations and Sociology of Development at the Department of Sociology, Bielefeld University, Germany. His research focuses on migration, citizenship and transnationalisation. Recent book publications include *Citizenship: Discourse, Theory and Transnational Prospects* (co-authored with Peter Kivisto, Blackwell, 2007), *Beyond a Border: the Causes and Consequences of Contemporary Immigration* (co-authored with Peter Kivisto), and *Diasporas and Transnationalism: Concepts, Theories and Methods* (co-edited with Rainer Bauböck). He is currently working on a book dealing with the transnational social question.

Margit Fauser, PhD, is a Lecturer and Researcher at the Department of Sociology at Bielefeld University, Germany. Her research fields are international migration, transnationalization, urban studies and development. She received her PhD in Sociology with a study on migrant organizations in the new immigration cities of Madrid and Barcelona. Her publications include 'Selective Europeanization: Europe's Impact on Spanish Migration Control' (in Thomas Faist and Andreas Ette [eds] *Between Autonomy and the European Union: The Europeanization of National Immigration Policies and Politics*, Palgrave Macmillan, 2007) and *Migrants and Cities. The Accommodation of Migrant Organizations in Europe* (forthcoming).

Nina Glick Schiller is Director of the Cosmopolitan Cultures Institute and Professor of Social Anthropology at the University of Manchester, UK. Her fields of interest include transnational migration, diasporic connection, long-distance nationalism, and comparative perspectives on city rescaling and migration. The founding editor of the journal *Identities: Global Studies in Culture and Power*, her books include *Towards a Transnational Perspective on Migration* and *Nations Unbound* (both with Linda Basch and Cristina Szanton Blanc), *Georges Woke Up Laughing* (co-authored with Georges Fouron) and *Locating Migration* (co-edited with Ayşe Çağlar). Her research has been conducted in Haiti, the United States and Germany, and she has worked with migrants from all over the globe.

Peter Kivisto is the Richard Swanson Professor of Social Thought and Professor and Chair of Sociology at Augustana College, USA. His research focus has shifted over time from the last great wave of immigration a century ago to contemporary immigration. In addition to empirical studies, he has been engaged in work on theoretical developments in immigration and race relations. Among his 22 books are *Citizenship: Discourse, Theory, and Transnational Prospects* (with Thomas Faist); *Intersecting Inequalities: Class, Race, Sex, and Sexualities* (with Elizabeth Hartung); and *Incorporating Diversity: Rethinking Assimilation in a Multicultural Age*. He is currently working on a theoretical examination of Jeffrey Alexander's idea of the civil sphere.

Jean-Baptiste Meyer is a Senior Researcher at the *Institut de Recherche pour le Développement* and is associated with the doctoral programmes of the University of Montpellier 1 and of the *Facultad Latino Americana de Ciencias Sociales* in Buenos Aires. His work deals with issues of knowledge and development and especially with the mobility of highly qualified personnel from the South to the North. He is the author of numerous articles, chapters and books on diaspora networks which aim to contribute to their countries of origin through their skills and abilities. Selected publications include 'Knowledge Diasporas for Development: a Shrinking Space for Scepticism' (co-authored with Eric Leclerc, *Journal of Asian Population Studies*, 3 [2], 2007), 'Policy Implications of the Brain Drain's Changing Face' (*SciDev* website, edited by *Science* and *Nature* and the TWAS, 2003); and *Diasporas scientifiques/Scientific Diasporas* (co-edited with R. Barre, V. Hernandez and D. Vinck, IRD Editions, 2003).

Lothar Smith is Assistant Professor at the Department of Human Geography, Radboud University, Nijmegen, the Netherlands. In research and education Lothar Smith takes a special interest in the globalization–development nexus for the global South, notably where this concerns the mobility of people. Research themes include: transnational flows; migration, development and diasporas, South–South migration; and migration, economics, and climate change. Among his recent publications are 'Constructing Homes, Building Relationships: Migrant Investments in Houses' (co-authored with Valentina Mazzucato, *Tijdschrift voor Economische en Sociale Geografie*, 100 [5], 2009) and *Tales of Development: People, Power and Space* (co-edited with Paul Hebinck and Sef Slootweg, van Gorcum, 2008).

Nicholas Van Hear is Deputy Director of the Centre on Migration, Policy and Society (COMPAS), at the University of Oxford, UK. He works on forced migration, development, conflict, diaspora, transnationalism and related issues, and has field experience in Africa, the Middle East, South Asia and Europe. Before joining COMPAS on its launch in 2003, he held posts at the Refugee Studies Centre in Oxford (1990–2000) and at the Danish Centre for Development Research in Copenhagen (2000–2003). His books include *New Diasporas, The Migration–Development Nexus* (International Organisation for Migration, 2003), and *Catching Fire: Containing Forced Migration in a Volatile World* (co-edited with Christopher McDowell, 2006).

1

The Migration–Development Nexus: Toward a Transnational Perspective

Thomas Faist and Margit Fauser

The nexus between migration and development has once again found entry into public debate and academic research in connection with the mobility of persons and issues of economic and socio-political development. This is to say, interest in the topic is currently resurging after peaking twice previously, in the 1960s and the 1980s. The current enthusiasm around migrants as agents of development reflects a paradigm which holds that migration can produce beneficial outcomes for both emigration and immigration countries. Current discussions, however, often reflect little memory of previous debates. In particular, scant systematic thought is given to what is 'new' this time around.

The contributions to this book argue that the current enthusiasm about the migration–development nexus should be approached from a transnational perspective that recognizes the emergence of a new agent in development discourse, variably called 'migrants', 'diaspora' or 'transnational community'. A transnational perspective, thus, is one which captures both the cross-border ties and engagements these actors sustain and the role played by institutions on the local, national and global level, including international organizations such as the World Bank, national states and organizations in development cooperation. Increasingly, the cross-border ties of geographically mobile persons and collectives have been receiving great attention with respect to development cooperation. Governments and inter- and supra-national organizations seek to co-opt and establish ties with these agents, who are engaged in sustained and continuous cross-border relationships on a personal, collective and organizational level. Addressing this new type of development agent from a decidedly transnational perspective allows us to look at what is usually called 'development' in both the North and the South. Instead of repeating the 'new mantra' (Ratha, 2003) of migration and development, which is simply a rehash of previous debates in familiar terms, it is necessary to seek a deeper understanding of current constellations. Two dimensions seem crucial here: first, the macro-structural factors and paradigms in which current debates and new policies are embedded, and second, the meso-level phenomena of transnational actors and associated transfers beyond the limited but dominating focus on financial remittances. This book thus offers an analysis of new agents in various fields of transnational activities such as knowledge networks, post-conflict and development engagement of diasporas, migrant organizations and transnational business activities, and the structures and ongoing social transformations in which agency is embedded.

New enthusiasm and open questions

The new enthusiasm around migration and development rests on a number of strong claims and thereby raises relevant questions which are hardly discussed. These claims can be summarized in the statement that migration and the resultant remittances migrants send 'back home' (that is, the flows of money, knowledge, and universal ideas) can have a positive effect on what is called development. Obviously, this is not a new insight. It has been part of familiar debates that have been on the public and academic agendas on and off at least since the 1960s. However, this positive evaluation of the nexus between migration and development has gained great appeal in the past few years. The first claim is that financial remittances carry a huge potential for poverty reduction and local business and infrastructure investment. This statement is supported by the observation that remittances very often are resistant or even counter-cyclic to economic recession. Several studies have suggested that remittances often keep on flowing from immigration to emigration contexts despite recession in the country of immigration (such as Ratha, 2003). Even more strikingly, the amount of remittances transferred to developing countries through officially sanctioned channels, such as banks or money transfer services, has increased sharply over the past several years – from about US$40 billion in 1990 to US$167 billion in 2005, up to US$338 billion in the year 2008 (IOM, 2005, p. 270; World Bank, 2009). Although in 2008 total net official development assistance (ODA) from members of the OECD's Development Assistance Committee (DAC) reached its highest figure ever recorded – at US$119.8 billion (OECD, 2009), officially recorded remittance flows are still three times higher.

Second, despite the fact that financial remittances still stand at its core, in this new round of enthusiasm strong emphasis has been placed on the transfer of skills, knowledge, and social remittances from the North to the South. With such a shift in perspective, the perception of the costs and benefits of migration has also changed. Over the course of many years, in particular during the 'brain drain' of the 1970s, the loss of skilled personnel educated and trained in emigration countries in the South and their movement to the North without proper compensation, was one of the main concerns of development agencies and emigration-side governments. In the 1990s and 2000s the consequences of knowledge transfer have been re-coined into 'brain gain'. Nowadays, there are supposedly more win-win situations for mobile persons, states and societies on the different sides of the migratory process (Doyle, 2004). In addition, current debates hinge upon the newer concept of 'social' remittances, referring to the flow of ideas and practices (Levitt, 1998). In this interpretation social transfers shall promote development given that they are 'good' since they are related to modernity and modern development, reflected in human rights, gender equity, and democracy, to name only the most obvious ones. Third, part of the 'new mantra' is the desirability of temporary labour migration based on the expectation that temporary migrants will constitute no loss in human capital and furthermore transmit a higher percentage of their income than permanent immigrants. This view was prominently propounded by the Global Commission on International Migration in its 2005 report (GCIM, 2005). Recent efforts have taken this notion further, in particular with the United Nations High-Level Dialogue on International Migration and Development in 2006, and the recent report of the United Nations Development Programme (UNDP 2009).

Cutting across all forms of remittances, it is not only recent labour migrants who are thought to remit but also settled migrants. Moreover, there has been a shift from considering return to the country of origin as the best way of contributing to development, to other perspectives on migrants settled in immigration countries who return temporarily on short or extended visits – for example, professionals in the scientific realm who transmit their knowledge. Overall, these three broad claims are tied to migration management and control. It is the hope expressed in many policy documents and official statements by political institutions such as the European Commission (2005) that, in the long run, economic growth supported in part by financial, knowledge and social remittances will reduce 'migration pressure' in the sending countries. Yet, even a cursory glance at this new enthusiasm casts doubt on this optimistic agenda and points to at least two broad questions.

The first question is: what has changed in the thinking about the migration–development nexus? In fact, after decades of research, there is a consensus regarding the consequences of migration on development, at least among economists: while the economic impacts undoubtedly 'have positive effects' for receiving countries, and most powerfully for OECD countries, it is also agreed that the benefits for sending countries are less clear-cut and heavily contested among both agents in the field of development cooperation and in academic research (cf. Delgado Wise and Márquez Covarrubias, Chapter 3 in this volume). Most studies analysing socio-economic changes in emigration regions conclude that development in the countries of origin is not a result of migration and resultant remittances and investments by migrants. Rather, development – along with the right political and institutional conditions – is a prerequisite for migrants to invest and to remit meaningfully (Castles and Delgado Wise, 2008). Given the fact that current knowledge does not allow for simple and uniform conclusions about the potentials of migration for developing countries, the question arises as to what is peculiar in this phase of the thinking on the nexus compared to previous ones.

The second question concerns the structural–political constellations which explain the recent rise in attention and literal euphoria on the migration–development nexus at this particular point in time. What are the broader structural factors behind this new enthusiasm? How is it connected to changing paradigms in development thinking and the regulation of international migration? How does it relate to the trinity of the market, the state, and the community/civil society? What role is played by changing geo-political formations and new concerns for security and migration control following the demise of the Cold War? And how does this new thinking materialize in relation to different fields and actors related, for instance, to post-conflict reconstruction, knowledge transfer and transnational business?

Three phases of thinking on the migration–development nexus

The fundamental claims associated with the migration–development enthusiasm presented in current academic and policy discourses are not as new as they appear. Looking at the past 60 years, that is, when development became established as a policy field and as a discourse in both the developed, industrialized world on the one hand and the developing, technologically modernizing and often decolonizing states on the other hand, considerable similarities but also some important shifts in thinking can be observed. From a simple cost-benefit point of view, the original idea posits that the flow of emigrants and the accompanying brain drain are partly or wholly compensated for by a reverse flow of money, ideas and knowledge. Over time, this perspective was challenged by more critical evaluations rejecting the potentials of migration for development. With a slightly different emphasis and with new political instruments, the positive view on potentials has returned. It is not surprising that the conceptualization of the nexus between migration and development mirrors the dominant development paradigms and their changes over the decades with migration always playing an important but changing role. The following three phases can thus be distinguished:

Phase 1: Migration and development – remittances and return

In phase 1, during the 1950s and 1960s, public policy emphasized the need to fill 'labour gaps' in the North with migrant workers and thereby also contribute to 'development' in the South. The latter was supposed to result from financial remittances, return migration and the subsequent transfer of skills and knowledge that this involved (Kindleberger, 1967). This view corresponded to overall economic modernization concepts in development thinking and to a belief that state capacity could shape economic growth as well as control migration according to national needs. Moreover, it was congruent with the textbook mantra in economics, which suggests that the emigration of surplus labour from underdeveloped areas leads to a new equilibrium between capital and labour (see Lewis, 1954): if labour goes North, labour scarcities in the South should then attract inflow of capital and, eventually, lead to economic development in the South (cf. Hamilton and Whaley, 1984). This academic thinking was mirrored in policies: both sending and receiving states of migrant workers articulated the need for temporariness and return based on the expectation that returnees brought new knowledge and qualifications with them. Nonetheless, retrospectively, critical voices asked whether the magnitude of international migration was high enough to have a significant impact in creating labour scarcities in the emigration countries and thus a need for the introduction of more advanced technologies. In addition, it seemed questionable whether financial remittances were of a scale that went beyond consumption and added to an increase in productivity and economic growth (cf. Hermele, 1997).

Phase 2: Underdevelopment and migration – poverty and the brain drain

In phase 2, during much of the 1970s and 1980s, the term 'development' came to be replaced by 'dependency' as a structural condition of the periphery dominated by the centre, and 'underdevelopment' was seen as its inevitable result. During this period – in which dependency theory and later on world systems theory (Wallerstein, 1974) criticized developmentalist modernization theory – the nexus was conceptualized in the reverse. Rather than working from migration to development the assumed causality moved from underdevelopment to migration (see, for example, Portes and Walton, 1981). Brain drain was one of the most important concerns in this period. In a dependency perspective, underdevelopment led to the loss of the well-educated and most qualified persons, who migrated from the periphery to the centres in the dependent world and, above all, into industrialized countries. This out-migration, in turn, was thought to contribute to even more underdevelopment and increased migration flows through asymmetric distribution of benefits and resources working in favour of the economically developed centres. At the same time, from the early 1970s most European countries started to cut off official recruitment and closed their main gates, keeping only side doors open for selected categories of immigrants. Since less skilled workers found it increasingly difficult to enter the economically advanced countries because of more restricted recruitment schemes, academic and policy attention focused even more on the implications of highly skilled migration.

Although current assessments tend now to highlight positive linkages, evidence for the brain drain thesis is easy to spot nowadays as well. For example, in 2005, between one-third and one-half of the so-called developing world's science and technology personnel lived in OECD countries. Even those views which give a nuanced account of the positive effects through return, investment and educational benefits, observe 'brain strain hotspots' where out-flow is not balanced by counter-flows and thus severely hampers socio-economic development (Lowell, Findlay and Stewart, 2004). This is the case, for instance, for greater parts of the health sector in sub-Saharan Africa where the World Health Organization warned of the damaging effects of this 'care drain' (for example, Stilwell, 2004). In stark contrast to many African countries suffering from brain drain, countries developing quickly along economic lines, such as Taiwan, South Korea and the People's Republic of China, have increasingly managed to re-attract students and experts from abroad and thus could change the situation into 'reverse brain drain' (Zweig, 2006). These stand at the centre of public attention in this third phase.

Phase 3: Migration and (co)development – the celebration of transnational circulation

We are now observing a third phase which has been underway since the 1990s. In this phase the idea of what in French policy circles has been called *co-développement* best describes the dominant public policy approaches. This idea puts the migrant at the centre of attention identifying him or her as the development agent par excellence. In this phase the migrant has been constituted as an element of development cooperation. Along with it goes a reversal of the nexus taking us back to a more optimistic view, akin to the 1960s. Again, nowadays, international migration is supposed to fuel development. Most emphasis is placed on financial remittances and many attempts aim at facilitating and channelling individual and collective money transfers. In addition, skills, flows of knowledge and social remittances have also gained significance (Maimbo and Ratha, 2005). Current initiatives thus cover a wider range of topics around the circulation of people, money and ideas. First, temporary and circular migration are presented as the ideal combination contributing to economic development by way of remittances while at the same time curtailing brain drain through early return and re-insertion. Such perspectives are reflected in many recent policy recommendations, for example those of the Global Commission to increase opportunities for short-term labour migration (GCIM, 2005). Second, temporary return and brain circulation are among the allegedly new measures. Not only permanent return migration but also temporary stays, shorter visits, and other forms of mobility promoting knowledge transfer are thought to address development issues. For instance, 'diaspora knowledge networks' (Meyer, Chapter 7 in this volume) composed of scientists and R&D personnel, innovative business start-ups (cf. Rauch, 2001), and professionals working for multinational companies (Kuznetsov, 2006) are supported by states, development agencies and international organizations such as UNDP's Transfer of Knowledge through Expatriate Nationals (TOKTEN) programme or the Migration for Development in Africa (MIDA) programme of the International Organization for Migration (IOM). Third, this recent approach addresses the circular transactions of established migrant groups and diasporic communities in community development and post-conflict reconstruction (De Haas, 2006; Van Hear, Chapter 4 and Fauser, Chapter 6 in this volume). In this phase, new actors are being heavily promoted by sending and receiving, developing and developed states as well as through inter- and supra-national agencies. Thus, acknowledgement of ties and movements across national state borders enters the picture, hence transnationalization.

Toward a transnational perspective

While in phase 1 policy-makers and researchers principally looked on remittances and return migration as a way of transferring resources across borders, in phase 2 the overcoming of development was seen as more critical. Now in phase 3, the landscape of alternatives has widened in an era of 'globalization', 'network society' or 'world society'. What we observe is an ever-increasing emphasis on transnational circulation. All of the new initiatives point to the importance of new transnational agents, that is, 'diasporic' actors. The now prevalent paradigm of phase 3 presumes that migrants and other geographically mobile persons, and those with whom they associate, may be engaged in sustained and continuous cross-border practices.

The emergence and activities of these new transnational actors and initiatives require a transnational perspective. Most globalization theories, world system theory and the world polity approach share a perspective on world-spanning structures and world-wide dynamics and thus are helpful in conceiving social structures beyond the national state as part of larger processes. They provide insights into the broader political, economic and cultural opportunity structures within which the relevant agents move. However, they exclusively focus on top-down processes and generally neglect agency, that is, how global processes materialize in local situations and how actors span cross-border networks (Faist, 2010).

Globalization approaches generally share a bird's-eye view. They take world spanning structures as a point of departure and ask how such structures and associated processes impact and shape lower-level structures and dynamics, for example, on the level of national states and below. In these accounts, the nexus of migration and development is hardly addressed. Even more, migration itself often does not receive great attention and many of the frequently cited works pay scant attention to the mobility of people (Albrow, 2007; Castells, 1996). If they do, they often portray it in a somewhat romantic way, depicting migrants as smooth interlocutors of cosmopolitan lifestyles (Beck, 2007). With the exceptions of David Held and his collaborators in their sweeping account of global transformations (Held et al., 1999), there is an odd silence on the mobility of persons in general and on migration in particular, and their role for concomitant – global and local – societal changes.

In the world polity theory of John W. Meyer and the Stanford School, the global diffusion of ideas, norms and values, that is, world culture, is the starting point. The diffusion of world culture is exogenous to local contexts, worldwide, and based on the premises of modern rationalization in Max Weber's sense (Meyer et al., 1997). This world culture is rationalistic and the related values and norms constitute cognitive models, such as the three-tiered school system or institutions of development cooperation, which expand world-wide. No account is given to the possibility that models may float only very superficially and provoke contestation and diverging interpretations. Non-governmental organizations, including diaspora associations, often adopt interpretations of development favoured by international organizations such as the World Bank or UNDP. Although actors accept such cognitive models, they may not be ready to act according to the standards prescribed. Needless to say, this also applies to the notions of development and their manifold critiques (Pieterse, 2001). In essence, world polity theory prioritizes the rational orientation of agents and organizations regarding organizational models. Yet there is no account of how agency modifies the function of such schemes.

In contrast to the globalization and world polity approaches, world systems theory explicitly considers migration and development. Building upon dependency theory (such as Cardoso and Faletto, 1969) world systems theory seeks to delineate the genesis and reproduction of the modern capitalist world economy in successive periods from a macro-perspective. The world system can be conceived as a set of mechanisms which redistributes resources from the periphery to the core. In this view, the core is composed of the economically developed part of the world, while the periphery is constituted by its underdeveloped part. There is a fundamental and institutionally stabilized 'division of labour' between core and periphery: while the core has a high level of technological development and manufactures complex products, the role of the periphery is to supply raw materials, agricultural products and cheap migrant labour for the dominating economies of the core. This economic exchange takes place on unequal terms, based on a deeply entrenched power asymmetry: the periphery is forced to sell its products at low prices, but has to buy the core's products at comparatively high prices (Wallerstein, 1974). The statuses of core and periphery are not, however, mutually exclusive and fixed to certain geographic areas; instead, they are relative to each other and shifting. There is a zone called 'semi-periphery', which acts as a periphery to the core, and a core to the periphery. In the 21st century, this zone would comprise, for example, Eastern Europe, China, India, Brazil and Mexico. A crucial insight to be derived from world systems theory for the analysis of processes across borders is that transnational flows of people, money and goods emerging in the context of migration strongly coincide with the economic and derivative political power asymmetries of the world economy. Dense and continuous transnational flows build upon migration systems (Kritz et al., 1992) which in turn are structured by core–periphery relations. Yet such asymmetries are not sufficient to account for the emergence and reproduction of transnational spaces in which migrants and other agents move.

All of these accounts of social processes beyond the nation-state offer top down views, which define the properties of lower-order systems. Little room is given to local autonomy and agency in this thinking. Moreover, according to such views, it is modern organizations and networks which rule the societal world, which is a functionally differentiated world, while social formations such as families, tribes, clans and communities play a negligible role, if at all. For instance, world polity theory maintains that cognitive models shape the actors although it is also plausible that agents shape the world polity. The very fact that the World Bank has championed the diaspora model of development and the huge amounts of remittances migrants contribute have very real consequences for conceiving development. Nonetheless different agents hold divergent notions of development which change over time (Glick Schiller, Chapter 2 in this volume). In essence, it is not clear why some patterns are more universal than others, while still others are not at all. We can list many local or national patterns which do not necessarily go back to global models. For example, states in the OECD countries historically have employed very different models of incorporating migrants at the national level, ranging from assimilationist to multicultural models. Moreover, there are divergent assessments of migrants' transnational ties – they can be considered beneficial regarding development cooperation, but often also viewed suspiciously by immigration states when it comes to political activities. While former colonial powers with long experience in penetrating developing countries have seized quickly upon the idea of co-development and the engagement of diasporas for development, others, often characterized by historically less intense international ties, have only recently started to think about such models. Examples for the former category are national states such as France, the UK, Spain and the Netherlands, for the latter Germany, Austria and Sweden.

Hence, manifold new forms and assessments of transnational circulations reaching across state borders have emerged. Accordingly, a transnational perspective is required to link both development and migration studies. Such a perspective has to account for processes of cross-border transactions which may concatenate in transnational fields or spaces. These consist of combinations of social and symbolic ties and their contents, positions in networks and organizations, and networks of organizations that cut across the borders of at least two national states. In other words, the term refers to sustained and continuous pluri-local transactions crossing state borders. Most of these formations are located in between the life-world of personal interactions on the one hand, and the institutionalized fields of the economy, polity, law, science and religion on the other hand. The most basic element of transnational social formations is transactions, that is, bounded communications between social agents such as persons. More aggregated levels encompass groups, organizations and firms. From this perspective, it is an empirical question whether such transnational transactions are of global or regional reach.

Transnational approaches in and beyond migration scholarship certainly do not form a coherent theory or set of theories. Nonetheless they share a focus on migrant agency (Basch et al.,1994), transnational social structures (Smith and Guarnizo, 1998), such as transnational communities (Portes et al., 1999) or diasporas (Bauböck and Faist, 2010). A transnational perspective looks beyond the nation-state without assuming its demise. It is thus able to account for the shaping and differentiating role of state borders for mobility, migration and transnationalization. In so doing, a transnational perspective is suitable for looking both at new social formations *sui generis*, such as transnational social spaces (see Faist, 2000), and at how old national institutions acquire new meanings and functions in the process of cross-border transformation. Here, we take a broad transnational view. The contributions to this volume look bottom up as well as at the macro-structures and opportunities setting the frames of transnational action, its causes and consequences, including a global view on unequal dynamics and asymmetric power structures. While some contributions concentrate on macro-structural processes and institutions (Delgado Wise and Márquez Covarrubias, Chapter 3 and Glick-Schiller, Chapter 2 in this volume), others focus on local structure and agency (Smith, Chapter 5 and Fauser, Chapter 6 in this volume). The aim of this book is not an integrated transnational perspective that coherently connects both macro- and meso-oriented views. Instead, we strive for a critical appraisal of the state of the art in shedding light on the nexus from different vantage points which concern transnational circulations.

Structural transformation and the new migration and development paradigm

The recent discovery of migrants as transnational development agents is embedded in and accompanied by broader structural changes and a paradigmatic shift in relation to the thinking on development and on migration and migrant communities. The macro-structural conditions of this current phase of the migration and development nexus shifted significantly. In addition, the changes in the political and discursive structures need to be considered: first, the constitution of the relationships between the state, the market, and civil society and community established in development thinking; second, geo-political changes since the end of the Cold War and the new political role of diasporas; and, third, the securitization of migration accompanying the discourses and measures favouring circulatory migration and migrants' transnational engagement. The elements of this new paradigm are also reflected in the agency of organizations, networks and other actors and the ways states deal with these.

Structural transformation

The chapters take different views on how structural transformation can be imagined rather than following a uniform approach. What all of them hold in common is a historical view (Delgado Wise and Márquez Covarrubias, Chapter 3 and Glick Schiller, Chapter 2 in this volume). A socio-historical transformation perspective, inspired by classical works such as Karl Polanyi's ([1944] 1968) *The Great Transformation* (implicitly) underlies most contributions. What is particularly inspiring in this work on European transformations from the 18th to the 20th centuries is its viewpoint on broad changes based upon a historical analysis of the political and economic macro-processes ending up in the catastrophe of Nazism. Here, social transformation refers to a fundamental shift in the way societal life is organized. This shift goes beyond the continual processes of incremental social change that are always at work. It refers to a kind of change in which all existing social patterns are questioned and many reconfigured. Polanyi took the rise of market liberalism in the 19th century as his point of departure. In the 21st century, economic but also political and cultural globalization and new patterns of international political and military power are reshaping the world. Taking this work as inspiration, the contributions to this volume revolve around the present global reconstitution of capital and structures of power, migration and development.

The chapters by Raúl Delgado Wise and Humberto Márquez (3) Covarrubias and by Nina Glick Schiller (2) both offer alternative readings to the current migration–development discussion which ignores the ways in which it is linked to global political-economic transformations. Both contributions emphasize the importance of the neo-liberal transformation of the world economy based on a critique of imperialism by Delgado Wise and Márquez Covarrubias and from a 'global power perspective' by Glick Schiller. Delgado Wise and Márquez Covarrubias start with a portrait of uneven development and seek to place the migration–development nexus within an interpretation of accumulation. They contend that labour migration plays a crucial role in the destruction of national accumulation patterns and the evolution of a global accumulation regime. According to this view the emergence of a huge surplus population results in structurally 'forced migration'. This surplus pool for migrants is an inevitable product of the globalization of capital accumulation. The massive transfer of human resources from emigration to immigration regions is in no way compensated for by financial remittances. The current enthusiasm for migrant remittances renders invisible the prior and much more substantial resource transfer. In their view this imbalance becomes evident in the US–Mexican case in which instruments such as maquila investments and production simply paper over the fact that the import of most parts used in maquila production is an 'indirect export of labour'. The indirect export results in a net transfer of profits to the US economy. All of this further dismantles the productive apparatus in Mexico. Regarding the direct export of labour, they point out the deleterious effects on the Mexican countryside through a receding infrastructure due to depopulation. In stark contrast to the current enthusiasm, Delgado Wise and Márquez Covarrubias do not regard migrants as active agents of transformation per se in this global accumulation regime. In their view, only by connecting migrant associations to those organizations promoting a social transformation agenda can the paradoxes of the current migration–development nexus be unveiled.

Nina Glick Schiller is more sanguine about the possibilities of migrant agency since she also looks at practices in everyday life. She considers the current dynamics of the migration–development nexus not as a top-down process in which macro-structural constraints determine local agency but as the mutual constitution of the local and the global. She starts with an interpretation of global discourses around migration and development which privilege interpretations along nation-state perspectives. As an alternative she introduces a 'global power perspective'. This entails looking at migrant remittances in the frame of neo-liberal restructuring of national economies; for example, remittances may fill voids left by cutbacks in social services and protection. At the same time, attention must also be focused upon migrants who form networks across borders and establish trans-locally specific patterns of remittance-sending, which result in changing patterns of winners and losers in the global remittance economy. Glick Schiller goes a step beyond political-economic considerations and conceptualizes the cultural dimension by pointing out, for example, that the 'dehumanization' of migrant activities in the informal sector and the concomitant focus on circular and contract labour further contributes to the neo-liberal transformation of the labour regime through a politics of difference between 'us' and 'them'. The dehumanization goes even further, as evidenced by a 'politics of fear' which portrays migrants as a security risk to entities such as the European Union. Glick Schiller argues that the more states in both North and South are hollowed out as delivering infrastructural needs to their citizens, the more they are keen to provide national identity.

Underlying the new paradigm: changing concepts of statehood, market and civil society

Below the level of macro-structural transformations, this phase also involves shifts concerning the relationship between state(hood), market and civil society/community.

The criticism of the 'civil religion' of development from the 1980s onward has called into question the idea of a homogeneous Third World, notions of progress (Rist, 1996) and, most important for our inquiry, relations between the state and civil society and community (Schuurman, 2000). The changing conceptualizations of the state, the market and civil society over the past 50 years in the development debate may signal a transnationalization of these terms. This can be usefully illustrated in the relationship between, first, the state and civil society and community and, second, the market and civil society and community (Faist, 2008). Overall, development thinking has moved from a focus on the national state to more emphasis on local government and international institutions. Therefore, we have to broaden our concepts and speak not simply of 'the state' but of 'statehood' on various levels. Moreover, as the enthusiasm over the concepts of diasporas and transnational communities indicates, civil society also has to be conceptualized as a *transnational* civil society.

Statehood and civil society

Throughout the 1950s and 1960s modernization theory guided a belief in the central role of the national developmental state. Strong state bureaucracies and developmental dictatorships were the privileged actors in promoting industrialization, modern education, literacy and modernist thinking. A partial shift throughout the 1970s toward basic needs strategies targeting increasing poverty and malnutrition brought more attention to still rather diffuse notions of community and civil society in the search for grass-roots and self-help initiatives. In addition, lower levels of government have gained importance here as well. In the face of decentralization and its attendant slogans, such as 'ownership' and 'stakeholder-ship', local governments, along with civil society and community, have assumed a greater role.

It has been in this context that migrants were introduced in the 1990s as a civil society or community actor, either as individuals remitting funds or as migrant associations in the form of diasporic or transnational communities. In immigration states such as France vis-à-vis West African states, the aforementioned idea of co-development in phase 3 of the migration–development nexus sees migrants as their own development agents regarding sending countries. From this perspective, migrants and their diasporas alleviate poverty and help to solve conflicts, especially if local governments work with diaspora groups to deliver better results. Beyond France, examples can be found in Spain and Italy, but also in the UK and the Netherlands. This focus on local authorities and diasporas has come to be especially relevant in situations where decentralization, community development, and civil society participation have generally gained importance, whether as a result of new policies or as a reflection of the fact that many national states in the 'Third World' had barely managed to establish territorial domination and the rule of law, to institutionalize democracy, or to launch sustained economic development. Here, hope is invested in the prospect of non-governmental organizations and local governments working in a synergetic collaboration with diasporas.

The market and transnational civil society

Not only have statehood–civil society relations changed but so, too, have the linkages between the market and civil society. Communities and civil society are becoming more and more a complement to liberal economic approaches in the era of the post-Washington Consensus. The notion of social capital as touted, for example, by the World Bank, is the very fusion of market-oriented with civil society thought: Social resources, such as trust and networks of reciprocity, are seen as economically and politically productive elements. Two fundamentally different views are to be found – liberal economic thought on the one hand, and participatory approaches on the other. Yet both favour migrant agency for development. The first line emphasizes the 'market' migrant, the second the 'political' migrant. Liberal economic thought would suggest that migrants are their own best development agents. A UK House of Commons report (2004) touting diasporas as development agents approvingly cites John Kenneth Galbraith (Galbraith, 1979, p. 7), who described migration as 'the oldest action against poverty'. The commitment of transnational migrants to their regions of origin is seen as compatible with the concept of the 'market citizen,' who is not necessarily a political citizen. This focus on the economically entrepreneurial citizen in the market is opposite to the politically active citizen in grassroots perspectives. This second 'political' approach is reflected in the fact that participatory approaches, as expressed, for example, by a UNDP report (2002, p. 1), focus on collective remittances. In line with this, migrants' collectives in all forms – hometown associations, diaspora knowledge networks, businesspersons' networks and even religious congregations – are addressed by governments. These broader changes, and public discourses on the migration–development nexus in particular, are thus a decisive element of how the linkage of migration-development has gained ground in policy debates (Faist, Chapter 8 in this volume).

Geo-political changes: the new role of diasporas

Migrants' opportunities to voice political viewpoints concerning their homelands changed dramatically after the end of the Cold War. In the 1960s, lobbying activities of diasporas mainly took the form of protests against the domestic policies of governments in the homelands (Armstrong, 1976). Cold War rivalries largely dictated the effectiveness of these diasporic anti-government campaigns (Shain and Barth, 2003). During the Cold War, Western countries maintained fairly open refugee policies (compared to the post-Cold War era) and supported diaspora groups who formed opposition to unfriendly regimes, such as the support of the US government for Cuban exile groups. Currently, although national liberation diasporas (Kurds, Tamils, Palestinians and so forth) are still ongoing, their activities have become more varied; for example, some diasporas have portrayed themselves as carriers of human rights. Even in the context of armed conflict and civil wars, diasporas have assumed a more visible role. Increasingly, 'diasporas' are acknowledged actors in financial, economic, political and social support in post-conflict reconstruction, peace building and (re)democratization in their homelands from which they had once fled – as is the case with Afghanistan, for instance (von Carlowitz, 2004). This is embedded in a broader shift in the perspectives on conflict held by development agencies. Conflicts along with the refugee movements and diasporas these produced are now seen as an opportunity to rebuild political and economic structures without carrying the burden of previous malfunctioning structures, while bringing new concepts and experiences from the stable and democratic host countries (Van Hear, Chapter 4 in this volume). The new propensity of international organizations such as the World Bank to see the opportunities rather than the risks of post-conflict reconstruction seems to be somewhat reminiscent of Schumpeter's 'gales of creative destruction' (Schumpeter, 1976 [1942]).

The coupling of migration control and development aid

The debates around the migration–development nexus are also connected to concerns for security, migration control and a coupling of migration management and development aid. One of the fundamental ideas at the core of the current debates and efforts is that an increase in development leads to a decrease in migration. The current efforts to control migration flows and borders in Europe are thus reflected in this debate. A number of initiatives on bilateral and multilateral levels, in particular within the European Union, closely bring together development cooperation; cooperation in the management of migration between countries of origin, destination and transit; the fight against irregular migration; return and re-admission agreements; and the synergies of migration and development, in particular with regard to remittances (Fauser, 2008). Since the European Council's Presidency Conclusion of the Tampere summit in the year 1999 the collaboration of third countries in the management of migration is closely linked to international cooperation, trade and aid. In general, partnerships with third countries, in particular at the European periphery, are based on policies which make development aid conditional upon their willingness to collaborate in combating irregular migration (Faist and Ette, 2007). The Cotonou Agreement, for instance, regulating the partnership of the European Union with the African, Caribbean and Pacific countries in matters of development cooperation, economic trade and political dimensions foresees the return and readmission 'of any of its nationals who are illegally present on the territory of a Member State of the European Union, at that Member State's request and without further formalities' (Council of the European Union, 2005). Moreover, in this phase, development cooperation is tied to migration management not only on the international level, but also to local initiatives involving local governments and migrant communities (Fauser, Chapter 6 in this volume).

New paradigms – organizations, networks, states

The activities of organizations and the positioning of agents within networks constitute a strategic research site in which we see social transformation at work. The constitution of diaspora as development agents, and the interface of migrant associations with development organizations and with local, state and international agencies thus present an opportunity to observe the impact of structural changes in the migration–development nexus. There is no single logic which structures this field. Yet we can see that states and organizations on various levels seize upon opportunities to engage in connecting international migration to development cooperation.

Many emigration states have repositioned themselves due to global changes since the late 1980s. Public policies and the corresponding semantics have changed. A prominent example of the transformed political semantics involves the discursive and institutional changes that the People's Republic of China has implemented. Discursively, the slogan to 'serve the country' (*wei guo fuwu*) has replaced the previous motto, 'return to serve' (*huiguo fuwu*) (Cheng Xi in Nyíri, 2001, p. 637). Such rhetoric has been complemented by public policy changes. Examples abound including adaptations through mechanisms such as dual citizenship for emigrants and immigrants (Faist and Ette, 2007), voting rights for absentees, tax incentives for citizens abroad, and co-optation of migrant organizations by local, regional and state governments for development cooperation. Instead of permanent return migration, temporary returns, visits and other forms of transactions have moved to the centre of attention. As already shown, in this third phase of the nexus, the perspective of migrants' return as *the* asset to development has been complemented by the idea that even if there is no eventual return, the commitment of migrants living abroad could be tapped through business incentives, hometown associations, or 'diaspora knowledge networks' (Barré et al., 2003; Meyer, Chapter 7 in this volume). Such measures also include the channelling of remittances into productive investment and infrastructure development. The most prominent example in this respect is the Mexican federal government's *tres-por-uno* (3x1) programme, in which each 'migra-dollar' sent back by migrants living abroad is complemented by three dollars from various governmental levels to go toward regional development projects. More recently, Mexican banks have joined the fray and announced 4x1 programs (Maimbo and Ratha, 2005). In addition to the efforts by migrant-sending countries to attract investment of their citizens abroad, receiving states have also discovered migrant communities and diasporas as development agents.

Engaging with the diaspora for the benefit of development has thus become an important strategy of many immigration states (De Haas, 2006). Cooperation with the diaspora in post-conflict reconstruction and peace-building has moved onto the agendas of development agencies, where previously skepticism and fear as to their conflict-fuelling role had dominated (Van Hear, Chapter 4 in this volume). In the same line, co-development policies address migrant communities and organizations in order to support their transnational engagements for their hometowns and countries (Fauser, Chapter 6 in this volume). These initiatives by development agencies, national governments and local authorities are intended to promote the observed engagement of migrants themselves.

Throughout the past two decades, scholars have also observed a growth in transnational initiatives by migrant collectives and individuals living abroad. A growing number of knowledge networks by highly skilled migrants have come into existence (Meyer, Chapter 7 in this volume). There is a spread of hometown associations, best documented for the Mexican communities located in the United States (Goldring, 2002; Orozco, 2004), but also among established Turkish immigrants in Germany, where transnational organizations are newly emerging (Çağlar, 2006), and similar dynamics can be observed in relation to many migrant groups in recent immigrant places in Southern Europe (Fauser, Chapter 6 in this volume). Moreover, migrants engage in transnational activities not only in such formally organized ways. On an individual level transnational networks emerge between emigrants and those at home. These are not restricted to family and kinship networks, but may involve a variety of relationships considered useful or necessary for the establishment of local and transnational businesses. Such enterprises are, moreover, not only initiated by migrants abroad, but also constitute a strategy activated by those 'at home' (Smith, Chapter 5 in this volume).

The chapters of this book dealing with the changing paradigms and organizational activities cover a wide range of related issues, yet all of them speak to the efforts of how collective agents – migrant associations and diasporas – situate themselves within the changing landscape of opportunities offered by the migration–development nexus: diaspora organizations in post-conflict settings (Van Hear, Chapter 4 in this volume), migrant associations in co-development policies (Fauser, Chapter 6 in this volume), diaspora knowledge networks (Meyer, Chapter 7 in this volume) and networks of relatives and friends in economic entrepreneurship (Smith, Chapter 5 in this volume). These case studies span a multitude of endeavours which constitute distinct facets of transnational spaces in the migration–development nexus.

The contributions by Nicholas Van Hear and Jean-Baptiste Meyer (chapters 4 and 7) both deal with diaspora options with respect to migration and development. While Van Hear discusses the function of diaspora in post-conflict development, Meyer appraises the 'diaspora option' in contrast to an assumed 'return option', that is, emigrants returning 'home'. Van Hear's analysis refers to the broad political and economic transformations which characterize the rather optimistic evaluation of diasporas' potential for mediation and reconstruction in 'conflict-ridden' societies. First, as he argues, geo-political changes and interventions of external powers into the politics of 'failing' and 'failed' states have contributed to the perception of diaspora in its new role as a mediator. Second, Van Hear argues that the policy priorities of international organizations such as the World Bank have somewhat shifted from a neo-liberal agenda epitomized by the Washington Consensus to what he calls a 'liberal agenda'. Rather than exclusively demanding the implementation of market principles, emphasis is now put on providing institutions appropriate for implementing these principles, such as the drive toward good governance. Along these lines, development organizations now embrace the idea that 'post-conflict settings' offer chances for socio-economic and political reconstruction and development. In this context perspectives on diaspora have also shifted in governments and international organizations. Previously the emphasis had been largely on the flight of unwanted people and their conflict-spurning role from abroad. Now, international agents frequently consider them a means for economic and political stability and an instrument of social security across borders. Diaspora then becomes an element of (transnationalizing) civil society. These positive evaluations of diaspora on development are also at the core of Meyer's analysis. He seeks to account for the differential success of so-called Diaspora Knowledge Networks (DKN), the importance and effectiveness of some networks, and the precarious life of others. Meyer draws on examples from around the world (India, China, South Africa and Colombia) to specify the role of DKN as brokers or mediators for the promotion of development from abroad. They not only provide a bridge between expatriates and the home country – they also constitute transnational formations in their own right. Taking this perspective, Meyer investigates their contribution for national development schemes. In addition, Meyer suggests that DKNs reflect global transformations affecting the organization of economic and scientific knowledge in a globalized world.

The chapters by Lothar Smith and Margit Fauser (5 and 6 respectively) look primarily at one of the two sides of transnational resource chains – the former on on transnational resource flows in the emigration context and the latter on transnationally active migrant associations in an immigration country. In a detailed analysis of migrant organizations' practices in Madrid and Barcelona, Margit Fauser looks for the various ways in which migrant associations are constituted as new agents in the realm of migration and development, called co-development. Local–local transactions across borders provide the mainstay of such activities. Of prime importance is her finding that migration and development policies on the one hand and incorporation policies on the other hand form intricate webs. These efforts envision incorporation into the receiving society both a pre-condition and a result of migrants' engagement with their home towns resulting from the institutional exchange, knowledge, skills and self-esteem acquired through this endeavour. This new constellation not only adds to more complicated social and political entanglements across borders and thus also speaks to the networks of migrants and their associations (see also Glick Schiller, Chapter 2 in this volume), but is also evidence that a transnational perspective is called for. This insight also guides Lothar Smith's analysis of transnational business in the case of Accra in Ghana. In developing a typology of transnational business, he starts with the economic opportunity structure created by neo-liberal structural adjustment policies which gave a boost to small-scale business activities. Smith points to the situatedness of migrant entrepreneurship beyond the structural dimension: he offers an analysis of the role and involvement of (relatively immobile) urban actors as business partners of migrants abroad. Not only do the networks which connect both reach beyond family and kinship circles; transnational business is also not only an investment of migrants in the event of return. Urban actors often took the first step initiating the business relationship. One of the insights gained from both Fauser and Smith is the need to pay more attention to the role of non-migrant actors and institutions as they contribute to transnationalization.

Conclusion

A transnational perspective calls into question central assumptions which have re-appeared in the newest round of the migration–development nexus, for example, that migration is one of the central keys to removing structural constraints to economic growth, social well-being and stronger democracy. The results of the myriad studies on the consequences of remittances are inconclusive at best. Going further, the migration–development nexus is part of the ongoing structural transformation of politics, economics and culture worldwide. On the basis of the scepticism arising from these findings the contributions to this volume collectively emphasize the need to rethink the assumptions underlying the migration–development nexus and a careful analysis of both structural changes and agency.

In doing so the chapters to follow examine both (macro-)structural constraints in which migration and development processes are tied, such as the reorganization of the global economy along with national economies, and meso-level agency in networks and organizations. The goal is to paint various parts of a picture which captures changing paradigms in national, local and global institutions, both institutional and discursive. A transnational perspective, which focuses attention on the interlocking webs of international and national development organizations, international organizations, national states and migrant associations and networks, provides a roadmap for this wide-ranging terrain of structural transformation. Eventually, the migration–development nexus can be seen as a specific instance of the 'transnational social question' which reflects the perception of stark social inequalities around the world – within and across the borders of nation-states (Faist, 2009). All perspectives taken in the field of migration and development, including such a transnational optic, need to be self-reflexive about their role beyond academia and particularly in public discourse. Thomas Faist (Chapter 8 in this volume) reminds us that most researchers one-sidedly focus on the question of how to influence policy either by consulting politicians or supporting social movements. In general, the question has been whether and in what ways social scientific research may form a basis for rational political decisions. Faist argues that such questions are misleading. Social scientific research may instead offer crucial stimuli for describing, understanding and explaining the migration–development nexus. This means that sociological analysis of the theory–praxis link should go beyond the focus on research and policy and bring in much more productively social scientists' role in the public sphere. It is through ideas as conduits for thinking and policy that researchers have the greatest impact in public life.

In his conclusion to this book Peter Kivisto (Chapter 9) argues that theories of development have reflected not only general theoretical trends (such as functionalism in the 1950s and 1960s) but also the political contexts of their time. Quite strikingly, ideas and theories of development after World War Two not only occurred in the fight against Communism during the World War but also constituted an effort to reshape the relations to (former) colonies. Moreover, they harboured Eurocentric concepts of development which held that the historical patterns in the West would be the routes to economic, political and social development for rest of the world. Concepts linking development and migration in the 1960s followed this pattern in that they reinforced dominant representations of modern vs. traditional societies. For example, migrants were not only supposed to remit money but also acquire the right kind of work ethic while working abroad. Yet while we already have some knowledge of the discourses around the migration–development nexus, we are only at the start of understanding the economic, political and cultural outcomes for the regions and groups involved.

References

Albrow, M. (2007) *Das globale Zeitalter* (Frankfurt am Main: Suhrkamp).

Armstrong, J. A. (1976) 'Mobilized and Proletarian Diasporas', *American Political Science Review*, 70 (2), 393–408.

Bauböck, R. and Faist, T. (eds) (2010) *Diaspora and Transnationalism: Concepts, Theories and Methods* (Amsterdam: Amsterdam University Press).

Barré, P., Hernandez, V., Meyer, J. B. and Vinck, D. (eds) (2003) *Diasporas scientifiques: Comment les pays en développement peuvent-ils tirer parti de leurs chercheurs et de leurs ingénieurs* (Paris: IRD Editions).

Basch, L., Glick Schiller, N. and Szanton Blanc, C. (1994) *Nations Unbound. Transnational Projects, Postcolonial Predicaments, and Deterritorialized Nation-States* (London: Gordon and Breach Publishers).

Beck, U. (2007) *Weltrisikogesellschaft* (Frankfurt am Main: Suhrkamp).

Çağlar, A. (2006) 'Hometown Associations, the Rescaling of State Spatiality and Migrant Grassroots Transnationalism', *Global Networks*, 6 (1), 1–22.

Cardoso, E., and Faletto, E. (1969) *Dependencia y desarrollo en América Latina* (Mexico, D.F. and Buenos Aires: Siglo Veintiuno Editores).

Castells, M. (1996) *The Rise of Network Society* (Oxford: Blackwell).

Castles, S. and Delgado Wise, R. (eds) (2008) *Migration and Development: Perspectives from the South* (Geneva: International Organization for Migration [IOM]).

Council of the European Union (2005) *Contonou Agreement – Council Decision 2005/599/EC* (Brussels: European Community).

De Haas, H. (2006) 'Engaging Diasporas: How Governments and Development Agencies Can Support Diaspora Involvement in the Development of Origin Countries' (Oxford: International Migration Institute, University of Oxford).

Doyle, M. W. (2004) 'The Challenge of Worldwide Migration', *Journal of International Affairs*, 57 (2), 1–6.

European Commission (2005) *Commission Communication (2005) 390 final. Migration and Development: Some Concrete Orientations* (Brussels: Commission of the European Communities).

Faist, T. (2000) *The Volume and Dynamics of International Migration and Transnational Social Spaces* (Oxford: Oxford University Press).

______ (2008) 'Migrants as Transnational Development Agents: An Inquiry into the Newest Round of the Migration-Development Nexus', *Population, Space and Place*, 14 (1), 21–42.

______ (2009) 'The Transnational Social Question: Social Rights and Citizenship in a Global Perspective', *International Sociology*, 24 (1), 7–35.

______ (2010) 'Towards Transnational Studies: World Theories, Transnationalization and Changing Institutions', *Journal of Ethnic and Migration Studies*, iFirst article, 1–26.

______ and Ette, A. (eds) (2007) *The Europeanization of National Policies and Politics of Immigration: Between Autonomy and the European Union* (Basingstoke: Palgrave Macmillan).

Fauser, M. (2008) 'New Trends – Transnationalization from Below and Above', in A. Warnecke and J. Sommer (eds), *The Security–Migration Nexus. Challenges and Opportunities of African Migration to EU Countries*, Bonn: Bonn International Center for Conversion, brief 36, 61–6.

Galbraith, J. K. (1979) *The Nature of Mass Poverty* (Cambridge, MA: Harvard University Press).

GCIM (2005) *Migration in an Interconnected World: New Directions for Action* (Geneva: Global Commission on International Migration [GCIM]).

Goldring, L. (2002) 'The Mexican State and Transmigrant Organizations: Negotiating the Boundaries of Membership and Participation', *Latin American Research Review*, 37 (3), 55–99.

Hamilton, B., and Whaley, J. (1984) 'Efficiency and Distributional Implications of Global Restrictions on Labour Mobility', *Journal of Development Economics*, 14 (1), 61–75.

Held, D., McGrew, A., Goldblatt, D. and Perraton, J. (1999) *Global Transformations: Politics, Economics and Culture* (Stanford: Stanford University Press).

Hermele, K. (1997) 'The Discourse on Migration and Development', in T. Hammar, G. Brochmann, K. Tamas and T. Faist (eds), *International Migration, Immobility and Development* (Oxford: Berg).

House of Commons (UK), International Development Committee (2004) *Migration and Development: How to Make Migration Work for Poverty Reduction*. Sixth Report of Session 2003–04 (London: The Stationery Office).

IOM (2005) *World Migration: Costs and Benefits of International Migration* (Geneva: International Organization for Migration [IOM]).

Kindleberger, C. P. (1967) *Europe's Postwar Growth: The Role of Labour Supply* (Cambridge, MA: Harvard University Press).

Kritz, M. M., Lim, L. L. and Zlotnik, H. (eds) (1992) *International Migration Systems: A Global Approach* (Oxford: Clarendon Press).

Kuznetsov, Y. (ed.) (2006) *Diaspora Networks and the International Migration of Skills: How Countries Can Draw on Their Talent Abroad* (Washington, DC: World Bank).

Levitt, P. (1998) 'Social Remittances: Migration Driven Local-Level Forms of Cultural Diffusion,' *International Migration Review*, 32 (4), 926–948.

Lewis, A. W. (1954) *Theory of Economic Growth* (London: Unwin).

Lowell, L. B., Findlay, A. and Stewart, E. (2004) 'Brain Strain: Optimising Highly Skilled Migration from Developing Countries,' Asylum and Migration Working Paper No. 3, Institute for Public Policy Research, London.

Maimbo, S. M. and Ratha, D. (eds) (2005) *Remittances: Development Impact and Future Prospects* (Washington, DC: World Bank).

Meyer, J. W., Boli, J., Thomas, G. W. and Ramirez, F. O. (1997) 'World Society and the Nation-State', *American Journal of Sociology*, 103 (1), 144–181.

Nyíri, P. (2001) 'Expatriating Is Patriotic? The Discourse on "New Migrants" in the People's Republic of China and Identity Construction among Recent Migrants from the PRC', *Journal of Ethnic and Migration Studies*, 27 (4), 635–654.

OECD (2009) International Development Statistics online, 'Development aid at its highest level ever in 2008', at: www.oecd.org (accessed: 10 April 2009). Organization for Economic Co-Operation and Development (OECD).

Orozco, M. (2004) 'Mexican Hometown Associations and Development Opportunities', *Journal of International Affairs*, 57 (2), 31–49.

Pieterse, J. N. (2001) *Development Theory: Deconstructions/Reconstructions* (London: Sage).

Polanyi, K. (1968) [1944] *The Great Transformation: The Political and Economic Origins of Our Time*. 9th printing (Boston: Beacon Press).

Portes, A., and Walton, J. (1981) *Labour, Class, and the International System* (New York: Academic Press).

______ Guarnizo, E., and Landolt, P. (1999) 'The Study of Transnationalism: Pitfalls and Promise of an Emergent Research Field', *Ethnic and Racial Studies*, 22 (2), 217–237.

Ratha, D. (2003) 'Workers' Remittances: An Important and Stable Source of External Development Finance', *Global Development Finance 2003* (Washington, DC: World Bank).

Rauch, J. E. (2001) 'Business and Social Networks in International Trade', *Journal of Economic Literature*, 34, 1177–1204.

Rist, G. (1996) *Le développement: Histoire d'une croyance occidentale* (Paris: Presses de Sciences Po).

Schumpeter, J. A. (1976[1942]) *Capitalism, Socialism and Democracy* (New York: Harper & Row).

Schuurman, F. J. (2000) 'Paradigms Lost, Paradigms Regained? Development Studies in the Twenty-First Century', *Third World Quarterly*, 21 (1), 7–20.

Shain, Y. and Barth, A. (2003) 'Diasporas and International Relations Theory,' *International Organization*, 57 (3), 449–479.

Smith, M. and Guarnizo, L. (eds) (1998) *Transnationalism from Below (*New Brunswick: Transaction Publishers).

Stilwell, A. (2004) 'Managing Brain Drain and Brain Waste of Health Workers in Nigeria', *Bulletin of the World Health Organization*, 82, 595–600.

UNDP (2002) *Human Development Report 2001: Making New Technologies Work for Human Development (*New York: United Nations Development Programme [UNDP]).

______ (2009) *Overcoming Barriers: Human Mobility and Development* (New York: United Nations Development Programme [UNDP])

von Carlowitz, L. (2004) 'Migranten als Garanten? Über die Schwierigkeiten beim Rechtsstaatsexport in Nachkriegsgesellschaften,' HSFK Standpunkte 6 (Frankfurt am Main: Hessische Stiftung für Friedens- und Konfliktforschung).

Wallerstein, I. (1974) *The Modern World System: Capitalist Agriculture and the Origins of the European World-Economy in the Sixteenth Century* (New York: Academic Press).

World Bank (2009) 'Migration and Remittance Trends 2009', *Migration and Development Brief* 11 (Washington, DC: World Bank).

Zweig, D. (2006) 'Learning to Compete: China's Efforts to Encourage a "Reverse Brain Drain"', in C. Kuptsch and P. Eng Fong (eds), *Competing for Global Talent* (Geneva: International Labour Organization [ILO]).

Part I

Paradigms – Methodological and Conceptual

2
A Global Perspective on Migration and Development*

Nina Glick Schiller

On a phone booth in Manchester, England – where I now live as a transmigrant – I saw an advertisement that read: 'Send money home from closer to home.' It went on to announce that you can send funds to locations around the world from any British Post Office. The Post Office, whose sales operations have now been privatized, has joined businesses around the world that seek to profit from migrant remittances. Spanish banks extend mortgages to migrants living in Spain who are building houses 'back home' in Ecuador and elsewhere in Latin America, while appliance stores in Brazil process orders for customers whose source of payment comes from family members living abroad (Lapper, 2007a). Migrants' money transfers, purchases of costly commodities, and homeland investments figure large in the recent policies of powerful globe-spanning financial institutions, such as the World Bank, which have proclaimed migrant remitters as the new agents of international development (De Haas, 2007; Fajnzylber and Humberto López, 2008; Lapper, 2007b; World Bank, 2006). Meanwhile, researchers of development and migration, while noting the possibilities and contradictions of migrant remittances on sending and receiving localities, take for granted that migrants are both local and transnational actors (Faist, 2008; Fauser, Chapter 6 in this volume). Yet at the same time that the transnationality of migrants is being both routinely documented and celebrated, politicians and the mass media in Europe and the United States are focusing their concern primarily on questions of 'integration', portraying migrants' transnational ties as threats to 'national security'. In these discourses, migrants are attacked for their supposed lack of loyalty to their new homeland. Politicians, demagogic leaders and media personalities blame migrants for national economic problems, including the growing disparity between rich and poor, the shrinking of the middle class, the reduction in the quality and availability of public services and education, and the rising costs of health care and housing. Calls for tightening borders and ending the influx of migrants are widespread, and countries around the world are shutting their doors in the faces of people desperately trying to flee war, rape and pillage. In the meantime, rates of deportation are rising dramatically.

Within these anti-migration discourses, little is said about migrants' provision of vital labour, services and skills to their new land or their role in the reproduction of workforces – including their sustenance, housing, education and training – in countries around the world. It is true that there is some appreciation for one current in the migrant stream. States as diverse as Singapore and Germany welcome 'global talent' in the form of professional and highly skilled immigrants. Yet this differentiation only serves to reinforce the viewpoint that most migrants are undesirable and that migration should cease.

What is the response of migration theorists to the present contradictory positions on migration whereby migrant remittances are defined as a vital resource, and yet those who send remittances are castigated and increasingly denied the right to move across borders? To date, migration scholars have not, I would argue, established a critical perspective that can adequately make sense of the contradictions. They have not developed a global perspective that can place within the same analytical framework debates about international migration and development, national rhetorics on migration and refugee policies, and migration scholarship. Instead, migration scholars have adopted the perspective of their respective nation-states.

Much of the European and US scholarship on migration confines itself to questions such as: 'How well do they fit into our society?'; 'What are the barriers that keep them from fully joining us?'; or 'Which cultures or religions do not fit in?'. In the United States, migration scholars who see themselves as pro-immigration increasingly embrace what I call 'born-again assimilationism' to show that migrants do indeed become part of the national fabric and contribute to it (R. C. Smith, 2006; Waldinger and Fitzgerald, 2004). New assimilationists and integrationists distinguish themselves from the old by updating what they mean by immigrants becoming an integral part of their new society (Alba and Nee, 2003; Heckmann, 2003; Joppke and Morawska, 2002; Morawska, 2003). Although these scholars accept the persistence of ethnic identities, home ties and transnational networks as in some cases compatible with integration, they continue to see migration as a potential threat to the nation-state. They believe that international migration warrants investigation because it is fundamentally problematic for the social cohesion of the 'host society'. For example, Michael Bommes and Andrew Geddes (2000, p. 6) are concerned that 'migration can be taken as part of a process that erodes the classical arrangement by which welfare states provide an ordered life course for the members of the national community, i.e., for their citizens in exchange for political loyalty'. As Bommes (2005) has noted, 'assimilationists conceptualise ... society as a big national collective'. In Europe, the term used is 'integration', which is often differentiated from assimilation (Esser, 2003, 2006). Whether the concept being deployed is integration or assimilation, however, most scholars of migration reflect and contribute to an approach to the nation-state that depicts a nation and its migrants as fundamentally and essentially distinct – both socially and culturally.

It is likely that future scholars will demonstrate that the revival of the assimilationist theory and the 'new' integrationism at the beginning of the 21st century, rather than representing an advance in social science, reflected the neo-liberal project of the restructuring of nation-states. Rescaled but not replaced in relation to regional and global reorganizations of economic and political power, nation-states began, as they did at the turn of the 20th century, and with the assistance of migration scholars, to build national identities at the expense of immigrants. Even scholars of transnational migration, including those who highlight the role of migrants in transnational development projects, are now concluding their articles with reassurances that migrants' transnational activities are relatively minimal or contribute to their integration into the nation-state in which they have settled (Guarnizo et al., 2003; R. C. Smith, 2006). They have not provided a perspective on migration that explains why major global financial institutions, which portray migrants as agents of development through remittances that sustain impoverished communities, seem unconcerned that these very same people are increasingly disdained and excluded in their countries of settlement.

In this chapter, I build on the work of those scholars who advocate an institutional analysis of contemporary migration policies and discourses, but I continue the argument further by proposing a 'global power perspective' that can link contemporary forces of capitalist restructuring to the specific localities within which migrants live and struggle. After a postmodern period in which any attempt to use or develop globe-spanning perspectives was dismissed as a 'grand narrative', scholars in an array of disciplines, and with very different politics, have once again tried to connect the local and particular with an analysis of broader forces. Contemporary globe-spanning trends have been approached as globalization (Mittleman, 1996), network society (Castells, 1996), and empire (Hardt and Negri, 2000). Yet, ironically, many migration scholars who study cross-border population movements remain inured to concepts of society and culture that reflect historic nation-state building projects. These projects obscure the past and contemporary transnational fields of power that shape political and economic development.

A global power perspective on migration could facilitate the description of social processes by introducing units of analysis and research paradigms that are not built on the methodological nationalism of much migration discourse. It would allow researchers to make sense of local variation and history in relation to transnational processes and connections. Such a framework would allow us to identify contradictions and disjunctures in contemporary scholarship, as well as forms, spaces, ideologies and identities of resistance to oppressive and global relations of unequal power.

One chapter cannot, of course, do more than outline such an alternative analytic framework. In sketching a different approach to migration and development that builds on a global power perspective, this chapter briefly (1) offers a critique of methodological nationalism; (2) addresses neo-liberal restructuring of localities of migrant settlement and ongoing connection; (3) situates the topic of remittances within transnational social fields of uneven power; and (4) analyses the countervailing hegemonic processes that are encapsulated in state migration policies and development discourses.

I want to be clear from the very beginning that by eschewing methodological nationalism and establishing a global framework for the study of migrant settlement and transnational connection, I am not saying – and have never argued – that the nation-state is withering away. I am asserting that to understand the restructuring of globe-spanning institutional arrangements, including the changing role and continuing significance of states, we need a perspective that is not constrained by the borders of the nation-state. This is because nation-states are positioned and transformed within global fields of power, and consequently these fields affect the migration process, including movement, settlement and transnational connection. At the same time, through their connections between places and their actions that affect places, migrants are active agents of contemporary transformations on local, national and global scales. My particular interest is the way in which migrants' settlement and transnational connections both shape and are shaped by the contemporary restructuring of capital and the scalar repositioning of specific localities (Glick Schiller et al., 2006; Glick Schiller and Çağlar, 2009, 2010).

Tracing the lineages of methodological nationalism in migration scholarship

A growing number of social theorists have argued that methodological nationalism has been central to much of Western social science (Beck, 2000; Martins, 1974; A. Smith, 1983; Wimmer and Glick Schiller, 2002a, 2002b). Methodological nationalism is an ideological orientation that approaches the study of social and historical processes as if they were contained within the borders of individual nation-states. Nation-states are conflated with societies, and the members of those states are assumed to share a common history and set of values, norms, social customs and institutions. Some writers label this orientation the 'container' theory of society to highlight that most social theorists, including Emile Durkheim, Max Weber and Talcott Parsons, have contained their concept of society within the territorial and institutional boundaries of the nation-state (Basch et al., 1994; Urry, 2000; Wolf, 1982). A methodological nationalist perspective in migration scholarship led to the separation of development studies from the study of immigrant incorporation into a new country. To reject methodological nationalism requires migration scholars to recover an approach to migration that does not use nation-states as units of analysis but rather studies the movement of people across space in relationship to forces that structure political economy. These forces include states but are not confined to states and their policies. Furthermore, national and international policies are considered within the same analytical lens (Nye, 1976).

I am calling for scholars to recover rather than develop a global perspective on migration, since aspects of this approach were widespread during the period of globalization that took place from the 1880s to the 1920s. At that time, there was broad interest in the diffusion of ideas and material culture through the migration of people. Scholars such as Friedrich Ratzel (1882) treated all movements of people over the terrain as a single phenomenon linked to the distribution of resources across space. Ratzel's writing reflected the assumptions of his times, namely, that the movements of people were normal and natural. The fact that migrants came and went and maintained their ties to home by sending back money to buy land, initiate businesses, and support families and village projects – all this was understood as a typical aspect of migration. Workers migrated into regions in which there was industrial development and returned home or went elsewhere when times were bad. England, Germany, Switzerland, France, the United States, Brazil and Argentina built industrialized economies with the help of millions of migrant labourers, who worked in factories, fields, mills and mines. In general, during that era of globalization and imperial penetration, most European countries abolished the passport and visa system that they had installed in the first half of the 19th century (Torpey, 2000). The United States did not restrict migration from Europe and required neither passports nor visas.

This period of unequal globalization was shaped by fierce competition among many states for control of far-reaching transnational commercial networks. The wealth and workforce of many nations were produced elsewhere, and colonial projects were the basis of the accumulation of nationally based capital. Governmental regimes increasingly deployed the concepts of nation, national unity and national economy in ways that obscured the transnational basis of their nation-state building projects. The people who lived in these states faced increasing pressure to use a single national language, to identify with a national history, to understand their practices and beliefs to be part of a national culture, to equate concepts of blood and nation, and to be willing to sacrifice their lives for the nation's honour.

Both international migrants and citizens of migrant-receiving states sought explanations for the rapid changes they were experiencing. Political theories and social movements that could speak to global transformations flourished, including international socialism, anarchism, pan-Africanism, feminism, nationalism, scientific racism and anti-imperialism (Bodnar, 1985; Gabaccia and Ottanelli, 2001; Gilroy, 1992; Potts, 1990; van Holthoon and van der Linden, 1988). However, state officials, politicians and intellectuals supported nationalist ideologies that portrayed individuals as having only one country and one identity. In so doing, they contributed to the view that immigrants embodied cultural, physical, and moral characteristics that differentiated them from their host society and therefore merited study. It was at that moment – and in conjunction with the mounting pressure to delineate national borders more firmly by closing them – that a scholarship of immigrant settlement took shape. The transnational social fields of migrants and their engagement in internationalism and other forms of non-state-based social movements increasingly were seen as problematic and finally disappeared from view. The study of migration was divided between demographers and geographers, who studied movement between nation-states, and sociologists, who studied settlement and assimilation.

As a result of that moment, several complementary but differentiated logics were deployed: (1) the sociology of migration was situated exclusively within national territories; (2) the notion of national origin was racialized through the popularization of the concept of national stocks; (3) assimilationist theory was developed within the hegemonic narrative of race and nation; and (4) national stocks came to be seen as differentiated by culture and were designated either as 'nationalities' or as 'national minorities' who resided within a state of settlement. Current scholarship on migrant incorporation and transnational connection continues to be shaped not only by these past approaches but also by the current historical conjuncture in which the leaders of migrant-receiving states are emotively legitimating national discourses and narratives.

Today, the 'ethnic group' continues to serve as the primary unit of analysis with which to study and interpret migration settlement, transnational migration and diaspora. Often termed 'communities', the ethnic group has become the bedrock of studies of migrant settlement. This remains true despite a voluminous historical and ethnographic literature that (1) identifies the constructed nature of ethnic identities and ethnic group boundaries; (2) includes detailed ethnographies of institutional processes through which ethnic categories and identities are constructed and naturalized by local and transnational actors; and (3) provides copious accounts of divisions based on class, religion, region of origin and politics among the members of the supposedly 'same' group (Barth 1969; Brubaker, 2004; Çağlar, 1990, 1997; Glick Schiller, 1977, 1999; Glick Schiller et al., 1987; Gonzalez, 1988; Kastoryano, 2002; Sollors, 1989). The use of ethnic groups as units of analysis is a logical but unacceptable consequence of the methodological nationalism of mainstream migration studies.

The problematic framing of migration research in terms of ethnic groups within nation-states obscures the effects of the global restructuring of capital on the population, both migrant and non-migrant, in a specific locality. Even studies of migrants' transnational connections that seemed to offer an analytical perspective beyond the nation-state have tended to examine specific ethnic trajectories and have said little about the ways in which the restructuring of economic, political and social capital affects specific forms of migrant settlement and transnational connections. Few researchers have noted the significance of locality in shaping migrants' transnational social and economic fields.

In short, the methodological nationalism of many migration scholars, reflecting the entanglements of disciplinary histories with nation-state building projects, precludes them from accurately describing the transnational social fields of unequal power that are integral to the migrant experience. Because their scholarship is built on units of analysis that developed within nation-state building projects, few migration scholars situate national terrains and discourses within an analysis of the restructuring of the global economy, the rescaling of cities, and the rationalization of a resurgent imperialist agenda.

Addressing the neo-liberal restructuring of localities of migrant settlement and ongoing connection

Working within a Marxist framework, David Harvey (2003, 2005) and a number of geographers have emphasized that while one can talk about the intensification of global processes of capital flow and flexible accumulation, capital reproduction always comes to ground somewhere. Since capital is ultimately a social relationship, when it is reconstituted in a specific place, the process destroys previously emplaced social relationships and the infrastructures and environments in which they were situated and constructs others. Although differentiated in terms of the path-dependent trajectories of a specific place, the effects of the restructuring of capital are not confined to only one place; rather, the transformation of one place affects many others. The reconstitution of capital disrupts previous arrangements of power and structures new relationships of production, reproduction of labour, distribution and consumption that extend into other localities.

The process of the creation and destruction of capital – as it represents the concentration of relationships of production within time and space – is an ongoing feature of capitalism. Beginning in the 1970s, however, this general process was reconfigured on a global scale through the uneven and disparate implementation of a series of initiatives widely known as the 'neo-liberal agenda'. Neo-liberalism can be defined as a series of projects of capital accumulation that have reconstituted social relations of production in ways that dramatically curtail state investment in public activities, resulting in the reduction of state services and benefits and the diversion of public monies and resources to develop private service-oriented industries from health care to housing (sometimes in arrangements termed 'public-private partnerships'). At the same time, the neo-liberal project also relentlessly pushes toward global production through the elimination of state intervention in a host of economic issues – from tariffs to workers' rights – including the organization of labour, space, state institutions, military power, governance, membership and sovereignty (Harvey, 2005; Jessop, 2003). Neo-liberalism has allowed for the creation of wealth by destroying and replacing previous relations of production, consumption, and distribution and by generating new forms of desire. These transformations have affected the quality of life of migrants and natives alike.

Neo-liberal projects take the form of specific sets of ideas and policies that may or may not be successfully implemented. These ideas are held, shaped, defended and contested by a range of actors, including social scientists, whether or not they are directly linked to policy. The broader projects involve not just the domain of economics but also politics, cultural practices, ideas about self and society, and the production and dissemination of images and narratives. Neo-liberal plans are implemented on the ground and differentially, depending not just on different national policies but also on specific local histories, including that of migration.

The work of geographers on the neo-liberal restructuring of capital and space highlights the various mechanisms that require all places to compete for investments in new economies (Brenner, 2004; N. Smith, 1995). All of the resources that cities have, including their human resources, which encompass the migrants and their skills and qualities, acquire a new value and become assets in this competition. Migrants are not only part of the new, just-in-time sweatshop industries that accompany the restructuring of some cities. They also provide highly skilled labour that contributes to the human capital profile of various cities. The 'cultural diversity' of migrants is an important factor in the competitive struggle between cities. Beyond the marketing of ethnic culture, migrants contribute to the cultural industries of the cities in which they are settling, from media to cuisine, fashion and graphic design (Çağlar, 2005, 2007; Scott, 2004; Zukin, 1995). The place and role of migrants in this competition might differ, depending on the scalar positioning of these cities.

The implementation of neo-liberal agendas disrupted fixed notions of nested, territorially bounded units of city, region, state and globe. The scholarship on neo-liberalism documents the ways in which all localities have become global in that none are delimited only by the regulatory regime and economic processes of the state in which they are territorially based. The state itself is rescaled to play new roles by channelling flows of relatively unregulated capital and participating in the constitution of global regulatory regimes enforced by the World

Trade Organization (WTO) and international financial institutions. To emphasize the processual, competitive and political aspects of the spatial restructuring of capital, some geographers speak of 'rescaling'. They note that when localities change the parameters of their global, national and/or regional connectedness and lines of power that serve to govern territory, they in effect 'jump scale' (Swyngedouw, 1997). Rather than understanding the local and global scale as either discrete levels of social activities or hierarchical analytical abstractions, as in previous geographies of space, 'the global and the local (as well as the national) are [understood to be] mutually constitutive' (Brenner, 2001, pp. 134–135). Localities do, however, differ in their positioning in terms of globe-spanning hierarchies of economic and political power. I am using the term locality to encompass the analysis of both rural and urban places within the analytic perspective I am constructing. However, I build on a theoretical framework on the rescaling of locality that focuses on the contemporary competition among cities. I extend this framework later in the chapter to the effects of migrants' transnational fields and state actions on the growth of inequality between rural areas.

The scalar positioning of a locality – its success in competing for investments in local development and services, and in the case of cities in attracting highly skilled new economy workers – shapes the incorporation, if differentially, of all residents of that locality. Hence, the research framework I am suggesting – what I call a 'locality analysis' of a global power paradigm – places migrants and natives in the same conceptual framework. Locality analysis turns our attention to the relationships that develop between the residents of a place and institutions that are situated locally, regionally, nationally and globally, without making prior assumptions about how these relationships are shaped by ethnicity, nationality or national territory. All of these factors and others that affect opportunity structures remain a matter for investigation.

Although scale theorists have said almost nothing about migrant incorporation, it is evident that a locality analysis built on that scholarship provides important theoretical openings with which to approach the significance of locality in migrant incorporation. The relative positioning of a place within hierarchical fields of power may well lay the ground for the life chances and incorporation opportunities of migrants and those who are native to the place. In order to understand the different modes and dynamics of both migrant and transnational incorporation, we need to address the broader rescaling processes affecting the cities in which migrants are settling. A scalar perspective can bring into this discussion the missing spatial aspects of socio-economic power, which is exercised differently in various localities. The concept of scalar positioning also introduces socio-spatial parameters to the analysis of locality in migration scholarship (Glick Schiller and Çağlar, 2009, 2010).

For students of migration, this perspective reminds us that migrants, as part of the processes of capital reproduction, are agents of the reshaping of localities. Migrants become part of the restructuring of the social fabric of the several localities to which they may be connected through their transnational networks and become actors within new forms of governing territory. Of course, migrants' roles in each place are themselves shaped in the context of rescaling processes. At the same time, pathways of migrant settlement are shaped by the opportunity structures and restrictions of particular places, including the type of labour needed and the way that labour is recruited and organized within those places.

It is through making this type of locality analysis that we can assess the variety of ways that migrants contribute to the opportunity structures of various locations and the degree to which they become one of several factors in the restructuring of a place. This places the migrants as actors within larger global forces and moves our discussion beyond the limitations of a model of migration, development and remittances. Some of the roles that migrants play as agents of global restructuring are described in the transnational migration literature but are not sufficiently analysed within broader processes of capital development and destruction. Other migrant contributions are rarely acknowledged because they are not clearly visible through an ethnic lens. My list of forms in which migrants serve as agents of restructuring and rescaling includes their role in contributing to the rise of property values, gentrifying neighbourhoods, creating new industries or businesses, developing new trade connections and patterns of marketing and distribution, and changing patterns of consumption.

Contingent on the positioning of a place globally, migrants make different kinds of contributions, which, depending on the stance of the observer, may be judged good or bad. Take, for example, the role of migrants as gentrifiers both in their place of settlement and in localities to which they are transnationally connected. In cities of settlement, which are in the process of successful restructuring, migrants may contribute to the reinvention of urban neighbourhoods previously considered undesirable by buying property in particular localities where property values have been low (Goode, 2010; Salzbrunn, 2010). Migrants may be well placed to buy property because they are able to draw on family credit or pooled resources to invest in and improve the housing stock or local neighbourhood businesses (Glick Schiller et al., 2006). Thus, migrants may stabilize, restore or gentrify neighbourhoods and may even contribute to the global marketing of a city. Migrant investments in housing and property may transform neighbourhoods within their transnational social field in ways that increase economic opportunities or economic disparities between localities.

The global cities literature (Friedmann, 1986; King, 1991; Sassen, 1991) offered a scholarship that could address the dynamic relationship between global flows of capital and the restructuring of spatialized relationships. Looking at a small handful of cities, urban scholars have noted that their prominence has been linked to their dependence on the migration of highly skilled professionals and on migrants who staff the related service sector of the new economy. Global cities, however, often were described as exceptions, as if all other cities and migration flows reflect only the dynamics of national terrains and policies. Consequently the utility of this scholarship for the theorization of locality, rescaling and migration generally has not entered into either migration theory or discussions about migration and development. To note that migrant departure, settlement, and transnational connections are shaped by the positioning of localities and regions within globally structured hierarchies of economic and political power would disrupt the homogenization of the national terrain that is imposed by migration theory and echoed in development discourses.

Placing remittance flows within transnational social fields of uneven power

A transnational social field is a complex of networks that connects people across the borders of nation-states and to specific localities (Glick Schiller, 2003, 2006). Here I use the term 'social field' to refer not to a metaphoric space but to a set of social relations, unequal in terms of the power of the various actors, through which people live their lives. Transnational social fields are networks of networks that link individuals directly or indirectly to institutions located in more than one nation-state. These linkages are part of the power dynamics through which institutionalized social relations delineate social spaces (Basch et al., 1994; Glick Schiller, 2003, 2004, 2005). The term 'field' refers to the linkages between individual migrants within territorially situated social relationships: taxation, employment, education, policing, property ownership, law and public policy, for example. The concept of transnational social fields that I am advocating does resonate with

Bourdieu's notion of fields of power but does not distinguish discrete cultural, social and political domains of power. Instead, building on classic social anthropology and geographers' recent interest in networks, I focus on social relations that intersect and transform discrete territorially based and historically specific social spaces of local community, village, city or state (Epstein, 1969; Mitchell, 1969; Leitner et al., 2007; M. Smith, 2001). Geographers have theorized the social construction of space in relationship to transnational networks but their work has not been adequately utilized by migration scholars despite the popularity of spatial metaphors in transnational studies. Migrants who send remittances may reconfigure social relations as part and parcel of the transnational processes that reconstitute localities. These localities may be hometowns, but migrants may also choose to invest in property and businesses in capital or key cities that were not their places of origin. Migrants' labour, cultural and social capital, and agency contribute to the positioning of localities within unequal transnational relationships of power. The transnational social fields of migrants can contribute to, be shaped by or contest the local or transnational reach of various states' military, economic and cultural power.

Migration processes cannot be seen as a sui generis activity with an internal dynamic that can be studied in its own right, without reference to the global-local interface of the reconstitution of capital. This is not to deny that one can track the development of an internal logic within a migration stream, as Douglas Massey (Massey et al., 1998) has done so well in his research on Mexican migration. As migration takes on its own logic with transnational networks, a specific migration trajectory and the networks that connect places become part and parcel of the restructuring of those places. And each place has its own particular history, as Jennifer Robinson (2006) has argued in calling for an appreciation of each city as 'ordinary'. In order to make sense of migration processes and their variations, however, we need to theorize not only the agency of migrants, whose networks restructure a specific locality, but also the global flows of capital of various kinds, which contribute to stark differences between the competitive positioning of different localities with consequences for all the inhabitants of each city and town involved.

A global power perspective that addresses migration and its relationship to the neo-liberal restructuring of locality leads us to a more nuanced view of the impact of remittances than is currently available in the migration and development field. This global perspective highlights the dual role played by migrant remittances in relation to the impact of neo-liberal restructuring. On the one hand, the impact of the privatization of public services is somewhat deflected as migrant remittances pay for vital needs, such as health care, education and infrastructure. On the other hand, remittance flows within a neo-liberal context highlight locational disparities that are no longer addressed by state policies that would aim to even out regional disparities. On the contrary, as the flow of wealth becomes concentrated in specific localities, and as these towns and cities reposition themselves within local and even global economies through this restructuring, states may further these disparities. For instance, they may facilitate air travel and other infrastructural developments and industries such as tourism in areas developed through migrant remittances, while other places become backwaters whose residents are severely disadvantaged. Yet studies of development and migration tend to ignore both the specificities of localities that migrants connect through their networks of social relations and the insertion of these locations within broader structural disparities of wealth and power. It is important to assess how we frame our questions and analyses and to identify which migrants and which localities are winners or losers because of the role played by migrants in restructuring processes.

The implications of this perspective are many for the study of processes termed 'development' in sending countries and 'urban restructuring' in settlement countries. Migrants are seen as remittance senders without sufficient discussion of how migrants are positioned in a new locality in terms of class and occupation, why migrants should want to send remittances, and to whom and where their transnational relations extend. Migrants' cultural values offer an insufficient explanation as to why migrants send large amounts of remittances and frequently support family members living elsewhere. Such explanations cannot address the fact that migrants from around the world – with different concepts of family and moral obligation – engage in very similar behaviour when confronted by similar migration contexts.

The contexts that facilitate migrants sending remittances and investing in localities within their transnational field seem to be related to the conditions faced by migrants in their place and country of settlement, as well as those that confront relatives and other members of their social network who have been 'left behind' or who are living elsewhere. Because discussions of migration and development have increasingly taken the sending of remittances for granted, we have insufficient research on this subject. Nevertheless, existing ethnographies and surveys about the remittance-sending contexts have indicated that remittances are sent under one or more of the following conditions: (1) when children, spouses, or parents are left behind; (2) when migrants face insecure conditions in a place of settlement because of racism, anti-immigrant sentiment or other forms of political, social or economic discrimination; (3) when migrants secure a steady income in their place of settlement, whatever its size or source; (4) when migrants suffer great status loss through the migration process and a remittance-receiving economy provides them with opportunities to maintain or improve their status and class position; and (5) when a possible remittance-receiving locality – whether a hometown or elsewhere – provides alternative economic possibilities, allowing the migrants to 'hedge their bets'. These factors taken together help explain whether or not a migrant establishes and maintains a transnational social field.

By linking migrants' remittance-sending patterns and motivations to the conditions that they experience in specific localities, we can better account for why some people remain committed to sending remittances or making investments transnationally, while others disengage. The restructuring of localities through neo-liberal processes described above has had variable impacts, in some cases facilitating and in others diminishing the ability of migrants to send remittances. For example, neo-liberal policies have lead to the increased hiring of part-time workers and the inability of migrants to find steady employment. The privatization of public services may, however, mean that there is more demand for low-wage migrant labour and more possibilities for migrants to send money regularly to their hometown or homeland. In the home locality, structural adjustment policies may lead to the reduction of transportation services and less public security. The reduction of services and growing insecurity may curb investments in businesses or new housing. But privatization may also provide opportunities for investment in areas such as transportation or private security services.

The countervailing hegemonic processes encapsulated in state migration policies and development discourses

Culture remains an important variable in a global power analysis of migration, but cultural differences between natives and migrants within a nation-state are not assumed to be the central topic of concern. Instead, a global power analysis queries not only points of contention in which migrants are constructed as culturally different but also the domains of commonality, social relations, openness and conviviality between migrants and natives. Migration scholars often fail to address daily social activities that unite migrants and natives within workplaces, neighbourhoods and leisure activities. They also disregard the forces that construct differences, such as the intersections of the global-political economy and local forms of differentiating power, including those that racialize, feminize and subordinate regions, populations and localities. As a means of addressing these concerns, Ramón Grosfoguel (2008) argues for an analytical framework that he calls the 'colonial power matrix'. He is developing a scholarship that analyses the role of repressive force and discursive power with regard to the North/South divide. Building on the work of Anibal Quijano (2000), Grosfoguel (2008, p. 2) speaks of the coloniality of power as 'an entanglement or... intersectionality... of multiple and heterogeneous global hierarchies ("heterarchies") of sexual, political, epistemic, economic, spiritual, linguistic and racial forms of domination and exploitation... [T]he racial/ethnic hierarchy of the European/non-European divide transversally reconfigures all the other global power structures.'

Grosfoguel emphasizes that the concepts of racial and gender differences and the hierarchies that they substantiate are central to the legitimization of the location and dominance of finance capital in Northern states and institutions. The coloniality of the power framework addresses the disparities of wealth and power that link together the lack of development in the global South, the root causes of migration flows, and the interests of migrants and financial institutions in investments and remittance flows. This framework brings together in a single analytical structure the processes of capital accumulation, nation-state building, the restructuring of place and the categorization of labour by race and gender.

When applied to migration scholarship, the coloniality of power approach allows us to better understand the current contradictory forces that denigrate migrants while celebrating migrant remittances. We can assess how constructions of migrants are used to dehumanize certain sectors of the workforce in order to legitimate more readily their insertion in neo-liberal labour demands. The national discourses of exclusion – which portray migrants as unskilled, threatening and disruptive invaders and which seem rampant in states around the world, from Singapore to Italy – contribute to the current neo-liberal labour regime. Dehumanized through rhetorics of national difference, migrant labour, which is increasingly contractual, meets the needs of localized neo-liberal restructuring more efficiently than the previous, and still current, situation of family reunion, asylum and the use of undocumented workers as a form of flexible and politically silenced labour.

Over the last few decades, growing international competition led to the development of global assembly lines, with de-industrialized centres of capital in North America and Europe and the movement of factories to far-flung regions, where labour is cheap and unregulated. Tariff barriers were demolished, and untaxed export-processing zones were established throughout the world. Today, agricultural and industrial corporations based in Europe and North America increasingly face a contradiction in their production processes – the balance between near and far production. This contradiction is heightened by the huge rise in the price of oil and hence transport, which means it is more profitable to locate production processes closer to areas of high consumer demand. One increasingly popular solution is to use a workforce that is cheap and controllable. As many observers in Europe have pointed out, these contradictions will be heightened by the low birth rate and aging composition of European and North American populations (Castles, 2006).

For several decades, undocumented migrants – first in the United States and increasingly in Europe – made up the quiescent, hyper-exploited and flexible workforces needed within urban restructuring processes. They furnished labour not only for agriculture but also for 'just-in-time' production close to centres of capital and for the various domestic and service industries needed in restructured cities geared toward consumer industries and tourism. In some countries in Europe, such as the United Kingdom, asylum-seekers and refugees have provided this form of labour, legally and illegally. The denigration and criminalization of asylum-seekers and the growing capacity of bio-surveillance measures to limit mobility are essential features of a transition to a form of labour more fitted to the production needs of neo-liberal economies.

It seems likely that we are witnessing a movement toward an EU labour regime made up of circulating labour from within the European Union and new and very controlled forms of contract labour from elsewhere. As Steven Vertovec (2007, p. 2) has pointed out: 'Circular migration is . . . being advocated as a potential solution (at least in part) to a number of challenges surrounding contemporary migration.' The expansion of the EU labour market by the inclusion of accession states with labour policies that emphasize the merits of circulation are part of this larger policy shift. Contract workers and labour circulation are now hailed as arrangements that benefit all parties, and short-term labour contracts are increasingly part of the production process for agricultural and factory work in places as disparate as Canada and Albania.

Migration researchers are contributing to the legitimization of new forms of exploitation by emphasizing the benefits of transnational remittances while neglecting to address the severe and permanent restriction of rights that accompanies short-term contract work and the decreasing access of migrants to naturalization. Some migration scholars have continued to sing the praises of circular short-term migration with regard to development. For example, Alejandro Portes (2007, p. 272) has asserted: 'Cyclical migrations work best for both sending and receiving societies. Returnees are much more likely to save and make productive investments at home; they leave families behind to which sizable remittances are sent. More important, temporary migrants do not compromise the future of the next generation by placing their children in danger of downward assimilation abroad.'

This kind of rosy picture reinforces the desirability of the new migration regime of contract labour, which makes migrant settlement increasingly difficult. New migration laws leave migrants with only short-term options. Absent from this scenario of the benefits of circular migration are the increasing difficulties of sustaining any form of viable existence in many sending areas. Also absent are the dehumanizing aspects of short-term labour contracts with their dramatic restrictions on, or denial of, rights and privileges to the individuals who are producing wealth, paying taxes and sustaining infrastructures and services to which they have no entitlement. The mantras about migrants as major agents of development are also part of this new global labour regime. International financial institutions have made migrant remittances a growing industry just at the moment when migrants may be less interested in transnational strategies and yet less able to choose to settle permanently in a new land.

Transnational migration has in part reflected a strategy on the part of migrants to avoid committing themselves since they were unsure of the long-term welcome they might receive in the states in which they were settling, even if citizenship rights were available and utilized. However, migrants sending remittances did make certain assumptions about the viability of local economies in the sending states. They assumed that there would be enough security of persons and enough of an opportunity structure for those with capital to support their own investment in a home and family. Increasingly, these assumptions no longer hold in many regions of the world due to environmental degradation, destabilization because of structural adjustment policies, and the hollowing out of national economies through trade agreements such as NAFTA and through WTO restrictions. The result is continuing waves of migration as well as a possible growing lack of interest among migrants in investing in their homelands. This may be linked to an increased desire to reunite families in the country of settlement and to unilateral rather than simultaneous incorporation. Transnational migration and connection are not inherent features of migration but rather reflect conditions in both localities.

By examining the relations between the neo-liberal restructuring of capital and the need for an ever more controllable and flexible workforce, the connections between the various and seemingly disparate trends in migration policy and discourse begin to emerge. Nationalist rhetoric and exclusionary policies pave the way for production regimes that rely on the capacity to control labour. The faceless migrating workforce is portrayed as potentially lawless border invaders who require restriction, regulation and contractual constraints that limit their rights to change employers or challenge working conditions. The depersonalization of labour as contractual services allows for labour policy statements in which the separation of workers from home and family, without rights of settlement and family reunion, becomes good economic policy. The depersonalization of the process allows such workers to be categorized as unskilled, despite the fact that many of them have relatively high degrees of education and may be nurses, doctors, teachers or university professors. Their willingness to migrate is integrally related to the structural adjustment and privatization policies in their home localities that reduced wages and ended state-funded public services that had provided employment for professionals.

At first glance, the 'global war for talent', in which multinational corporations compete for highly educated workers, would seem to stand outside the emerging labour regime that I am describing. However, short-term contracts with restructured rights of settlement are increasingly part of this labour market as well, although in many countries highly skilled professionals are still being allowed to settle. Such short-term contracts often regulate high-tech workers to ensure that the current workforce gives way to the next wave of newly educated and eager bodies and brains. Moreover, the very prominence and desirability of the sought-after few highlight the disposability of the faceless many, despite the fact that both labour streams are needed to sustain many contemporary cities.

The dehumanization of migrants allows for them to be manipulated and controlled as various forms of unfree contracted labour. Meanwhile, migrant professionals can be welcomed in specific places as contributors to the neo-liberal restructuring and rescaling of various cities. Also, migrant remittances can be relied on to transmit foreign currency to families, localities and regimes left behind, enabling their inclusion, however unequally, in global patterns of consumption and desire. In short, these seemingly discrepant narratives are part of the globally structured and locally situated mutual reconstitution of social relationships and values that a global power perspective allows us to analyse. Such a perspective also facilitates advocacy of alternative policies and agendas that would allow for environmental protection, public services, increased economic and social opportunities, and an equitable redistribution of profits including social security systems that provide benefits to those who produce the wealth.

It is insufficient, however, to reduce the flood of anti-immigrant sentiments to a justification for exploitative labour. Returning to the coloniality of power framework and using it as part of our global perspective on migration can yield further insights into the current moment of anti-immigrant attacks and contradictory discourses. At the same time, this perspective highlights how US and European imperialist projects are simultaneously justified and obscured through a politics of fear that portrays migrants as the chief threat to national security.

I have noted that states are still important within the globe-spanning economic processes that mark our contemporary world, but of course not all states are equal. Unequal globalization rests on a framework of imperial states that serve as base areas for institutions that control capital, the productions of arms and military power. These powerful states claim and obtain rights and privileges in states around the world and define the institutional limits of less powerful states. The core imperial states also are the key players in institutions that claim to be global, including the World Bank, the WTO and the United Nations Security Council. Increasingly, theorists on the right and the left have recently returned to the concept of imperialism to understand the unequal relationships between states. They stress the significance of warfare, but often ignore the relationship between neo-liberal restructuring, migration and the construction of images of the foreigner as enemy and terrorist (Cooper, 2003; Ferguson, 2004; Harvey, 2003; Ikenberry, 2002; Mann, 2003; Reyna, 2005).

In the face of intense global economic, political, social and cultural interconnections and of growing inequality due to racialized and gendered hierarchies, the popularization of the notion of the migrant as the outsider rehabilitates earlier myths that nation-states contain homogeneous cultures shared by native populations. Once again, the migrant is constructed to reinforce and validate the nationalism that continues to socialize individuals to identify with their nation-state. Once again, a discourse that presents the world as divided into autonomous nation-states is becoming hegemonic.

Increasingly, as states are hollowed out in terms of infrastructure and discrete realms of economic production and are ever more integrally linked to production and consumption processes elsewhere, state narratives stress national identities and cultural difference. In short, nation-states are increasingly identity containers that maintain and disseminate images of the nation as a society that have little to do with the contemporary, transnational institutional structures within which social life and relations of power are produced. The fewer services and rights that states provide for their citizens and the more that they produce citizens who have been educated to identify as customers enmeshed in cultures of consumption rather than forms of civic and social engagement, the more these states promote discourses of social cohesion and national community. The inside is increasingly constructed in relation to framing foreigners as the source of disruption – as being responsible for the decline of social services and of community. The more that ordinary citizens in states around the world find their futures circumscribed by poverty or lack of social mobility, the more they are told by political leaders that the problems are caused by persons from elsewhere. Anti-immigrant discourse remains a nation-state building process, a ritual of renewal that engages its participants in defining their loyalty to a country by differentiating them from stigmatized and racialized others.

Conclusions

Migration studies too rarely address the global system that is reducing the opportunity for social and economic equality and justice around the world and the human costs of new short-term labour contracts. While potent critiques have been made of each strand of the contemporary and apparently contradictory narratives that address migration and development, the critiques remain encapsulated within different literatures. This has made it too easy to keep debates about migration separate from discussions of neo-liberal restructuring and the human toll that this agenda exacts around the world. Short-term labour contracts resurrect older forms of indenture, with limited rights and mobility. Families separated by migration regulations that allow no family reunion means the reproduction of social life at great personal sacrifice, with parents separated from children and spouses from each other, and elderly parents left to survive without the assistance of children. Developing a global power perspective on migration that directs attention to the contemporary neo-liberal moment allows us both to establish a research agenda that calls attention to the human costs of neo-liberal restructuring and to trace its various trajectories and the resistance it engenders.

A global perspective on migration can provide an analytical lens that would allow scholars of migration and development to think beyond the reimposition of nationalist interests yet not endorse unequal globalization. Migration studies are at a crucial juncture. We can follow the pattern of the past, let our research be shaped by the public mood and the political moment, and revive old binaries, fears and categories. Or we can engage in research that clarifies this moment by developing new frameworks for analysis. In short, we need a new scholarship that can build on our understanding of global processes and highlight them, so that we can actually document how migrants live their lives as constitutive actors in multiple social settings. This scholarship will reconstitute migration theory so that it explains current observations and facilitates new ones. To do this, we need to discard methodological nationalism so that our units of analysis do not obscure either the mutual dialectic constitution of the global, national and local or the presence of imperial globe-spanning power and its internal contradictions, its inability to provide consistent development, and its dependence on migrant labour.

The new scholarship should popularize the concept that migration and development processes are part of global forces experienced by people who move and those who do not move. This means that migration scholars must enter into the public debate about social cohesion by putting aside methodological nationalism and identifying the forces of globalization that are restructuring the lives of migrants and non-migrants alike and by speaking to the common struggle of most people of the world for social and economic justice and equality. When delimited by their methodological nationalism, migration theorists confine their units of analysis to the nation-state and the migrant. They are thus unable to track structures and processes of unequal capital flow that influence the experience of people who reside in particular localities. Migration scholars often fail to look at the relationships between migrants and natives that are not framed by concepts of cultural or ancestral difference. Furthermore, they ignore the way in which local institutions that incorporate residents of states in a variety of ways are configured by power hierarchies that interpenetrate in states and regions.

Development discussions that laud migrant remittances yet do not address transnational fields of unequal power serve to obfuscate rather than promote analysis. Many states dominated by imperial power and its new regulatory architecture are struggling because a sizable proportion of their gross national product is channelled into debt service, leaving migrants to sustain the national economy through their contributions. Meanwhile, remittances and the flow of migrant capital across borders contribute to the profitability of banks and other financial institutions (Guarnizo, 2003).

A global perspective on imperial power can also facilitate our ability as socially engaged scholars to theorize the contradictions of imperial dilemmas and find ways in which they can contribute to progressive social transformation. But we can do this only if we set aside born-again assimilationism and other forms of integrationist theory that posit migrants as disruptors of national communities. It is necessary for migrants and natives of countries around the world who find their lives diminished by unequal globalization to understand what the problem is and what it is not. It is not putative hordes of illegal aliens or migrants' transnational connections that are threatening the majority of people in the imperial core countries. Rather, we need to draw attention to the ways in which anti-immigrant rage and subjective feelings of despair, the precariousness of life, and life's unmet aspirations reflect and speak to the global fragility and exploitive character of contemporary capitalism, its restructuring of economies, labour regimes and states, and its dependence on war and plunder.

Note

*This article appeared originally in *Social Analysis*, 53 (3), Winter 2009, pp. 14–37. It has been slightly revised thanks to suggestions from Thomas Faist and Gudrun Lachenmann.

Portions of this article are based on a paper co-authored with Ayse Cağlar entitled 'Migrant Incorporation and City Scale: Theory in the Balance', which was delivered at the conference 'MPI Workshop: Migration and City Scale', in Halle/Salle, Germany, in May 2005. Earlier versions of this article were delivered at the Second International Colloquium on Migration and Development, 'Migration, Transnationalism, and Social Transformation', Cocoyoc, Mexico, 26–28 October 2006; the Volkswagen Foundation Conference on Migration and Education, Hamburg, Germany, 22–23 February 2007; the RDI Conference on New Essentialisms, Paris, France, 22–25 May 2007; and the ZiF Conference on Transnational Migration and Development, Bielefeld, Germany, 30 May–1 June 2007. I wish to express my thanks to the conference organizers and participants, who are not responsible for the perspective of this article. Special thanks are extended to the James H. Hayes and Claire Short Hayes Professorship of the Humanities, which I held; to Burt Feintuch, at the Center for the Humanities, University of New Hampshire, for summer support; to Günther Schlee, at the

Max Planck Institute for Social Anthropology, for broader conceptualizations of integration and conflict; to Hartwig Schuck, for formatting and website posting; and to Darien Rozentals, for editorial assistance.

References

Alba, R. and Nee, V. (2003) *Remaking the American Mainstream: Assimilation and Contemporary Immigration* (Cambridge, MA: Harvard University Press).

Barth, F. (1969) *Ethnic Groups and Boundaries: The Social Organization of Culture Difference* (Boston: Little, Brown).

Basch, L., Glick Schiller, N. and Szanton Blanc, C. (1994) *Nations Unbound: Transnational Projects, Postcolonial Predicaments, and Deterritorrialized Nation-States* (New York: Gordon and Breach).

Beck, U. (2000) 'The Cosmopolitan Perspective: Sociology of the Second Age of Modernity', *British Journal of Sociology*, 51 (1), 79–105.

Bodnar, J. (1985) *The Transplanted: A History of Immigrants in Urban America* (Bloomington: Indiana University Press).

Bommes, M. (2005) 'Transnationalism or Assimilation?', *Journal of Social Science Education*, 1, 1–13.

Bommes, M. and Geddes, A. (2000) 'Introduction: Immigration and the Welfare State', in M. Bommes and A. Geddes (eds), *Immigration and Welfare: Challenging the Borders of the Welfare State* (London: Routledge).

Brenner, N. (2001) 'World City Theory, Globalization and the Comparative-Historical Method: Reflections on Janet Abu-Lughod's Interpretation of Contemporary Urban Restructuring', *Urban Affairs Review*, 36 (6), 124–147.

——— (2004) *New State Spaces: Urban Governance and the Rescaling of Statehood* (New York: Oxford University Press).

Brubaker, R. (2004) *Ethnicity without Groups* (Cambridge, MA: Harvard University Press).

Çağlar, A. (1990) 'Das Kultur-Konzept als Zwangsjacke: Studien zur Arbeitsmigration', *Zeitschrift für Türkei-Studien*, 1, 93–105.

——— (1997) 'Hyphenated Identities and the Limits of "Culture"', in T. Modood and P. Werbner (eds), *The Politics of Multiculturalism in the New Europe: Racism, Identity and Community* (London: Zed Books).

——— (2005) 'Mediascapes, Advertisement Industries: Turkish Immigrants in Europe and the European Union,' *New German Critique*, 92, 39–62.

——— (2007) 'Rescaling Cities, Cultural Diversity and Transnationalism: Migrants of Mardin and Essen', *Ethnic and Racial Studies*, 30 (6), 1070–1095.

Castells, M. (1996) *The Rise of Network Society* (Cambridge, MA: Blackwell).

Castles, S. (2006) 'Back to the Future? Can Europe Meet Its Labour Needs through Temporary Migration?', International Migration Institute, Oxford University, Working Paper No. 1.

Cooper, F. (2003) 'Modernizing Colonialism and the Limits of Empire', *Items and Issues*, 4 (4), 1–9.

De Haas, H. (2007) 'Migration and Development: A Theoretical Perspective', *COMCAD Working Paper*, 29 (Bielefeld: Center on Migration, Citizenship and Development).

Epstein, A. L. (1969) 'The Network of Urban Social Organization', in J. Clyde Mitchell (ed.), *Social Networks in Urban Situations: Analyses of Personal Relationships in Central African Towns* (Manchester: Manchester University Press).

Esser, H. (2003) 'Ist das Konzept der Assimilation überholt?', *Geographische Revue*, 5 (Summer), 5–22.

——— (2006) 'Migration, Language and Integration', *AKI Research Review*, 4 (Berlin: Wissenschaftszentrum Berlin [WZB]).

Faist, T. (2008) 'Migrants as Transnational Development Agents: An Inquiry into the Newest Round of the Migration-Development Nexus', *Population, Space and Place*, 14 (1), 21–42.

Fajnzylber, P., and Humberto López, J. (eds) (2008) *Remittances and Development: Lessons from Latin America* (Washington, DC: World Bank).

Fauser, Margit (2007) 'The Local Politics of Transnational Cooperation on Development(s) and Migration in Spanish Cities', *COMCAD Working Paper*, 24 (Bielefeld: Center on Migration, Citizenship and Development).

Ferguson, N. (2004) *Colossus: The Price of America's Empire* (New York: Penguin).

Friedmann, J. (1986) 'The World City Hypotheses,' *Development and Change*, 17 (1), 69–84.

Gabaccia, D. and Ottanelli, F. M. (2001) *Italian Workers of the World: Labor Migration and the Formation of Multiethnic States* (Urbana: University of Illinois Press).

Gilroy, P. (1992) *The Black Atlantic: Modernity and Double Consciousness* (Cambridge, MA: Harvard University Press).

Glick Schiller, N. (1977) 'Ethnic Groups Are Made Not Born', in G. Hicks and P. Leis (eds), *Ethnic Encounters: Identities and Contexts* (North Scituate: Duxbury Press).

——— (1999) 'Transmigrants and Nation-States: Something Old and Something New in the U.S. Immigrant Experience', in C. Hirshman, P. Kasinitz, and J. DeWind (eds), *The Handbook of International Migration: The American Experience* (New York: Russell Sage Foundation).

——— (2003) 'The Centrality of Ethnography in the Study of Transnational Migration: Seeing the Wetland Instead of the Swamp', in N. Foner (ed.), *American Arrivals: Anthropology Engages the New Immigration* (Santa Fe: School of American Research Press).

——— (2004) 'Transnationality', in D. Nugent and J. Vincent (eds), *A Companion to the Anthropology of Politics* (Malden, MA: Blackwell).

——— (2005) 'Transnational Social Fields and Imperialism: Bringing a Theory of Power to Transnational Studies', *Anthropological Theory*, 5 (4), 439–461

——— (2006) 'Introduction: What Can Transnational Studies Offer the Analysis of Localized Conflict and Protest?', *Focaal*, 47 (Summer), 3–17.

———, Basch, L. and Blanc-Szanton, C. (eds) (1992) *Towards a Transnational Perspective on Migration: Race, Class, Ethnicity, and Nationalism Reconsidered* (New York: New York Academy of Sciences).

——— and Çaglar, A. (2009) 'Towards a Comparative Theory of Locality in Migration Studies: Migrant Incorporation and City Scale', *Journal of Ethnic and Migration Studies*, 35 (2), 177–202.

——— and Çaglar, A. (eds) (2010) *Locating Migration: Rescaling Cities and Migrants* (Ithaca: Cornell University Press).

———, Çaglar, A. and Guldbrandsen, T. (2006) 'Beyond the Ethnic Lens: Locality, Globality, and Born-Again Incorporation,' *American Ethnologist*, 33 (4), 612–633.
———, DeWind, J., Brutus, M. L., Charles, C., Fouron, G. and Thomas, L. (1987) 'All in the Same Boat? Unity and Diversity among Haitian Immigrants,' in C. R. Sutton and E. M. Chaney (eds), *Caribbean Life in New York City* (Staten Island: Center for Migration Studies).
Gonzalez, N. (1988) *Sojourners of the Caribbean: Ethnogenesis and Ethnohistory of the Garifuna* (Urbana: University of Illinois Press).
Goode, J. (2010) 'The Campaign for New Immigrants in Philadelphia: Imagining Possibilities and Confronting Realities,' in Glick Schiller, N. and Çağlar, A. (eds) (2010).
Grosfoguel, R. (2008) 'Transmodernity, Border Thinking, and Global Coloniality: Decolonizing Political Economy and Postcolonial Studies', *eurozine online journal*, at: www.eurozine.com/articles/2008-07-04-grosfoguel-en.html (accessed November 2010).
Guarnizo, L. (2003) 'The Economics of Transnational Living', *International Migration Review*, 37 (3), 666–699.
——— (2007) 'The Migration–Development Nexus and the Post-Cold War World Order', paper presented at 'Transnationalization and Development(s): Towards a North-South Perspective', Zentrum für interdisziplinäre Forschung, Bielefeld University, 31 May–1 June.
Friedmann, J. (1986) 'The World City Hypotheses', *Development and Change*, 17(1), 69–84.
Guarnizo, L., Portes, A. and Haller, W. (2003) 'Assimilation and Transnationalism: Determinants of Transnational Political Action among Contemporary Migrants', *American Journal of Sociology*, 108, 1211–1248.
Hardt, M. and Negri, A. (2000) *Empire* (Cambridge, MA: Harvard University Press).
Harvey, D. (2003) *The New Imperialism* (Oxford: Oxford University Press).
——— (2005) *A Brief History of Neoliberalism* (New York: Oxford University Press).
Heckmann, F. (2003) 'From Ethnic Nation to Universalistic Immigrant Integration: Germany', in F. Heckmann and D. Schnapper (eds), *The Integration of Immigrants in European Societies: National Differences and Trends of Convergence* (Stuttgart: Lucius und Lucius).
Ikenberry, J. (2002) 'America's Imperial Ambition', *Foreign Affairs*, 81 (5), 44–62.
Jessop, B. (2003) 'The Crisis of the National Spatio-Temporal Fix and the Ecological Dominance of Globalizing Capitalism', *International Journal of Urban and Regional Research*, 24 (2), 323–360
Joppke, C., and Morawska, E. (2002) *Toward Assimilation and Citizenship: Immigrants in Liberal Nations* (Basingstoke: Palgrave).
Kastoryano, R. (2002) *Negotiating Identities: States and Immigrants in France and Germany* (Princeton: Princeton University Press).
King, A. (ed.) (1991) *Global Cities: Post-Imperialism and the Internationalization of London* (London: Routledge).
Lapper, R. (2007a) 'Building Futures,' *Financial Times*, 29 August.
——— (2007b) 'The Tale of Globalisation's Exiles,' *Financial Times*, 27 August.
Leitner, H., Sheppard, E. S., Sziarto, K. M. and Maringanti, A. (2007) 'Contesting Urban Futures. Decentering Neoliberalism', in H. Leitner, J. Peck and

E. Sheppard (eds), *Contesting Neoliberalism: Urban Frontiers* (New York: Guilford Press).

Mann, M. (2003) *Incoherent Empire* (London: Verso).

Martins, H. (1974) 'Time and Theory in Sociology', in J. Rex (ed.), *Approaches to Sociology: An Introduction to Major Trends in British Sociology* (London: Routledge and Kegan Paul).

Massey, D. S., Arango, J., Hugo, G., Kouaouci, A., Pellegrino, A. and Taylor, J. E. (1998) *Worlds in Motion: Understanding International Migration at the End of the Millennium* (Oxford: Clarendon Press).

Mitchell, J. C. (ed.) (1969) *Social Networks in Urban Situations, Analyses of Personal Relationships in Central African Towns* (Manchester: Manchester University Press).

Mittleman, J. (ed.) (1996) *Globalization: Critical Reflections* (London: Lynne Reinner).

Morawska, E. (2003) 'Immigrant Transnationalism and Assimilation: A Variety of Combinations and the Analytic Strategy It Suggests', in C. Joppke and E. Morawska (eds), *Towards Assimilation and Citizenship: Immigrants in Liberal Nation-States* (London: Palgrave Macmillan).

Nye, J. S. Jr. (1976) 'Independence and Interdependence.' *Foreign Policy*, 22 (Spring), 130–161.

Østergaard-Nielsen, E. (2007) 'Perceptions and Practices of Co-development in Catalunya', paper presented at 'Transnationalization and Development(s): Towards a North-South Perspective', Zentrum für interdisziplinäre Forschung, Bielefeld University, 31 May–1 June.

Park, R. E. (1950) *Race and Culture* (Glencoe: Free Press).

Portes, A. (2007) 'Migration, Development, and Segmented Assimilation: A Conceptual Review of the Evidence', *Annals of the American Academy of Political and Social Sciences Quick Read Synopsis*, 610, 270–272, at: http://ann.sagepub.com/cgi/reprint/610/1/266.pdf.

Potts, L. (1990) *The World Labour Market: A History of Migration* (London: Zed Books).

Quijano, A. (2000) 'Coloniality of Power and Eurocentrism in Latin America', *International Sociology*, 15 (2), 215–232.

Raghuram, Parvati (2007) 'Which Migration, What Development: Unsettling the Edifice of Nigration and Development', *COMCAD Working Papers*, 28 (Bielefeld: Center on Migration, Citizenship and Development).

Ratzel, F. (1882) *Anthropogeographie* (Stuttgart: J. Engelhorn).

Reyna, S. (2005) 'American Imperialism? The Current Runs Swiftly', *Focaal*, 45 (Summer), 129–151.

Robinson, J. (2006) *Ordinary Cities: Between Modernity and Development* (New York: Routledge).

Salzbrunn, M. (2010) 'Rescaling Processes in Two Cities: How Migrants are Incorporated in Urban Settings through Political and Cultural Events', in Glick Schiller, N. and Cağlar, A. (eds) (2010).

Sassen, S. (1991) *The Global City: New York, London, Tokyo* (Princeton: Princeton University Press).

Scott, A. (2004) 'Cultural-Products Industries and Urban Economic Development', *Urban Affairs Review*, 39 (4), 460–490.

Smith, A. (1983) 'Nationalism and Social Theory', *British Journal of Sociology*, 34, 19–38.

Smith, M. P. (2001) *Transnational Urbanism: Locating Globalization* (Malden: Blackwell).

Smith, N. (1995) 'Remaking Scale: Competition and Cooperation in Pre-National and Post-National Europe', in H. Eskelinen and F. Snickars (eds), *Competitive European Peripheries* (Berlin: Springer Verlag).

Smith, R. C. (2006) 'Black Mexicans, Nerds and Cosmopolitans: Key Cases for Assimilation Theory', paper presented at the Second International Colloquium on Migration and Development, 'Migration, Transnationalism, and Social Transformation', Cocoyoc, Mexico, 26–28 October.

Sollors, W. (ed.) (1989) *The Invention of Ethnicity* (New York: Oxford University Press).

Swyngedouw, E. (1997) 'Neither Global nor Local: "Glocalization" and the Politics of Scale', in K. R. Cox (ed.), *Spaces of Globalization* (New York: Guilford Press).

Torpey, J. (2000) *The Invention of the Passport: Surveillance, Citizenship and the State* (Cambridge: Cambridge University Press).

Urry, J. (2000) 'The Global Media and Cosmopolitanism', paper presented at the Transnational America Conference, Bavarian American Academy, Munich, June.

van Holthoon, F., and van der Linden, M. (1988) *Internationalism in the Labour Movement, 1830–1940* (Leiden: E.J. Brill).

Vertovec, S. (2007) 'Circular Migration: The Way Forward in Global Policy?', Working Papers No. 4 (Oxford: International Migration Institute Oxford University).

Waldinger, R., and Fitzgerald, D. (2004) 'Transnationalism in Question', *American Journal of Sociology*, 109 (5), 1177–1195.

Wimmer, A., and Glick Schiller, N. (2002a) 'Methodological Nationalism and Beyond: Nation-State Building, Migration and the Social Sciences', *Global Networks*, 2 (4), 301–334.

——— (2002b) 'Methodological Nationalism and the Study of Migration', *Archives of European Sociology*, 43 (2), 217–240.

Wolf, E. R. (1982) *Europe and the People without History* (Berkeley: University of California Press).

World Bank (2006) 'Global Economic Prospects: Economic Implications of Remittances and Migration' (Washington, DC: World Bank).

Zukin, S. (1995) *The Cultures of Cities* (Oxford: Blackwell).

3

The Dialectic between Uneven Development and Forced Migration: Toward a Political Economy Framework

Raúl Delgado Wise and Humberto Márquez Covarrubias

The purpose of this chapter is to provide a new analytical overview of the nexus between migration and development in the context of the global capitalist restructuring that has been taking place during the past three and a half decades. We base our approach on a political economy theoretical framework and place the concepts of uneven development and forced migration at the centre of an alternative interpretation of the asymmetrical global relationships between North and South, thus addressing the concomitant role of international migrations. From this point of view, migration appears as an expression of uneven development and a structural pillar of imperialist[1] strategies intended to weaken and cheapen the labour force on a global level. Instead of unilaterally approaching migration as a vehicle of development in places of origin, we address its role as a direct contributor to the accumulation processes of developed nations. Migration also involves the transference of human resources, which is linked to other types of surplus and natural resource transferences that intensify underdevelopment in countries of origin. In this context, migration functions as an important cog in the machinery of the so-called neo-liberal globalization, a source of growing social inequalities and asymmetries among countries that result in a sort of vicious circle leading to the current systemic capitalist crisis.

After the end of the so-called Golden Age of Capitalism, the crisis of accumulation and the resulting fall in profitability experienced by the world capitalist system throughout the 1970s led the core or developed countries, with the United States at the forefront, to implement a strategy for capitalist restructuring at a world scale centred on five supplementary mechanisms:

Mundialization: Internationalization of production, finances and commerce housed under 'free trade', which actually protects the interests of the large multinational corporations and private international banking. The latter in turn export capital and find alternative outlets to repay and expand their profit margins.

Neo-liberalization: Imposition of structural adjustment policies (privatization, deregulation and liberalization), allowing the reintroduction of strategic and profitable economic segments of underdeveloped or peripheral countries into the process of world capitalism restructuring.

Financiation: Predominance of financial capital and speculation as artificial mechanisms to increase profit margins, under the permanent risk of crises triggered by the explosion of speculative bubbles.

Militarization: Unilateral resource of military forces as a mechanism for world-scale imperial domination.

Devalorization of labour: Implementation of extreme modes of workforce exploitation in underdeveloped and developed countries by intensifying and extending the working day, restraining salaries with an actual salary decrease, implementing precariousness and labour flexibilization policies, dismantling the welfare state or its equivalent, and disassembling workers' organizations in a veiled or concealed way. Labour migration plays a crucial role in this process.

In peripheral or underdeveloped countries, the implementation of this combined strategy has resulted in three revealing movements: (1) the dismantling of the national accumulation pattern and outward reorientation, leading to the reduction and re-articulation of the productive apparatus, the contraction of its internal market, the destruction of subsistence and social security systems, and the expansion of social inequality; and (2) the generation of a surplus-population due to the liberalization of large contingents of their means of production and subsistence, which trigger unemployment and underemployment streaks and an increase in poverty and misery, in addition to demonstrations of protest, resistance and rebellion. This situation of social instability leads to state repression, violence, illicit activities and social insecurity; and

(3) the emergence of forced migration. With the destruction of production and subsistence means, millions of workers and their families are driven to abandon their places of origin to emigrate elsewhere within their country or to developed countries demanding cheap labour.

In this context, led by the World Bank (WB) and the Inter-American Development Bank (IADB), most international organizations and governments have been pursuing a political agenda in the area of migration and development. They posit that remittances sent home by migrants can promote local, regional and national development in their countries of origin. By extension, remittances are seen as an indispensable source of foreign exchange that provides macroeconomic stability and alleviates the ravages caused by insidious problems such as poverty. This notion, based on the precepts of neoclassical economics, portrays the orthodox view on the nexus between migration and development.

This view is supported by the growing importance of remittances as a source of foreign exchange and subsistence income for many households in underdeveloped countries. The United Nations Development Programme (UNDP) has estimated that 500 million people (8 per cent of the world's population) receive remittances (IFAD, 2008). According to World Bank figures, remittances sent home by emigrants from underdeveloped countries rose from US$85 billion in 2000 to US$199 billion in 2006. If unrecorded flows through informal channels are considered, this figure may increase recorded flows by 50 per cent or more (World Bank, 2006). Taking unrecorded flows into account, the overall amount of remittances has surpassed foreign direct investment flows and more than doubled official aid received by Third World countries. In many cases remittances have become the largest and least volatile source of foreign exchange earnings.

Although, in a recent document, the World Bank's position vis-à-vis the relationship between remittances and migration has been more cautious (Lapper, 2006), it should be pointed out that the impact of the implementation of structural adjustment programmes as a key element of the neo-liberal policy promoted by the World Bank and the International Monetary Fund is at the root of the upsurge in South–North migration and remittance flows. Moreover, far from contributing to the development of migrant-sending countries, structural adjustment programmes have reinforced the dynamics of underdevelopment and transformed many countries into 'people-exporting' countries.

The great paradox of the migration–development agenda is that it leaves the principles that underpin neo-liberal globalization – referring to the current phase of US imperialism – intact and does not affect the specific way in which neo-liberal policies are applied in migrant-sending countries (Delgado Wise and Márquez Covarrubias, 2007; Castles and Delgado Wise, 2007).

In 2008, a crisis erupted at the very core of world capitalism, the United States, ascribed by the majority of analysts to the detonation of a speculative bubble in the mortgage sector and the predominance of financial or fictitious capital, which had distanced itself from what has been termed the real economy. This crisis, however, is manifestly more important – it has several causes and its effects have spread throughout all the productive, financial and commercial circuits unreleased by the process of capitalist restructuring. Among the multiple causes behind this crisis, in addition to overflowing financial speculation, we may point to the increase in overproduction and, concomitantly, the weakness of massive consumption and the overexploitation of the workforce and of natural resources. In other words, the premature depletion of the restructuring strategy followed since the 1970s has placed the system in an unstable state. This posits the option, on one hand, of mitigating the effects of the crisis by increasingly unloading the burden of costs on the working class, including migrants, and, on the other hand, of opening the possibility of changing the prevailing model of development. The scope of this transformation attempt depends on the organization and projection capacity of social and political movements.

This chapter outlines an alternative methodological and theoretical approach based on a critique of the dominant perspectives regarding the migration–development nexus: *the political economy of migration*. From this perspective special attention is placed on: (1) the relationship between uneven development and forced migration; (2) the role of migrant exploitation in the dynamics of capital accumulation in the core-developed countries; and (3) the role of remittances sent to peripheral-underdeveloped countries of origin, which are chiefly assessed as a wage component embedded in a complex set of transnational social relations and used for the subsistence of a surplus population that is forced to enter cross-border job markets under conditions of labour precariousness and social exclusion.

Most of the studies that address the relationship between migration and development tend to view the relationship from a unidirectional and decontextualized perspective, as if migration were an independent variable and development possibilities were subject to and depended exclusively on the resources and initiatives of migrants. Nevertheless, given the analytical complexity of this relationship, it is necessary to come up with an alternative approach that does not centre on the phenomenon of migration but focuses on the processes of underdevelopment/development (uneven development) in the context of contemporary capitalism.

Departing from the above considerations, this chapter is divided into two main sections and includes a brief section of concluding remarks. The first section offers our analytical framework for understanding the relationship between migration and development rooted in a political economy approach. The second shows the interpretive capabilities of the proposed approach when applied to the analysis of the uneven development process between Mexico and the United States.

The political economy of development and migration: toward an alternative analytical perspective

In theoretical, conceptual and methodological terms, the initial challenge when analysing the relationship between migration and development lies in the fact that the problem has not been properly theorized. Without disregarding the contributions of a wide constellation of studies, authors and topics of debate, we consider that there is a need for a critical reconstruction of the field of migration and development studies. This critical reconstruction implies overcoming the partial and dominant view of migrant-importing countries, which is based on principles such as migration management – favouring temporary worker programmes, a security agenda, co-development and immigrant criminalization. It is essential to advance toward a comprehensive alternative approach which integrates the perspective of underdeveloped migrant-exporting countries, based on an understanding of the context within which contemporary capitalism propels the deepening and expansion of uneven development among and within nations. Worthy of mention is that efforts to theorize from the perspective of underdeveloped countries, implying a thorough view of the phenomenon, are not new. From the 1940s and 1950s to the 1970s, theories of structuralism and dependence – the latter, with some variations, under the umbrella of Marxist political economy – contributed a solid foundation in this sense. These notions went beyond methodological nationalism long before the emergence of the transnational approach which claimed such a premise as its foundational act. In general terms, the oversight of the contributions to the field by theoreticians from Latin America and other underdeveloped countries has been to a certain extent symptomatic.

Methodological principles

An offshoot of political economy and Latin American structuralist and dependency theories, the political economy approach to migration provides an unparalleled set of analytical tools by taking into account the following factors:

1) The wide range of interactions in the North–South (or development–underdevelopment) dynamic without losing sight of the differences intrinsic to each region;
2) The interaction between different spatial levels (local, national, regional and global) and social dimensions (economic, political, cultural and environmental);
3) Ways of creating an interdisciplinary, critical model that aids in the reconstruction of reality as well as theoretical reflection, challenging the preponderant 'economistic' and 'structuralist' views;
4) A notion of development that surpasses the limitations of normative and decontextualized concepts that takes into account the necessary role of social transformation (that is, structural, strategic and institutional changes) in the improvement of living conditions among the general population. This process of transformation must involve a range of actors, movements, agents and social institutions operating on a variety of levels and planes.

Following the above considerations, an approach based on a political economy critique of the orthodox-dominant views regarding the migration–development nexus would posit that international migration is an element of the current imperialist project led by the United States and that the migration phenomenon has to be examined in this context in order to reveal its root causes and effects. In order to approach migration's cause-and-effect relationships with development and examine specific moments in the dialectic interaction between development and migration, the following issues must be addressed:[2]

Strategic practices. These refer to the confrontation between different projects that espouse diverging class interests, which in turn underlie the structures of contemporary capitalism and its inherent development problems. There are currently two major projects. The hegemonic one is promoted by the large transnational corporations (TNC), the governments of developed countries led by US imperialism, and allied elites in underdeveloped nations, all under the umbrella of international organizations commanded by the US government, such as the International Monetary Fund (IMF) and the World Bank. The project's loss of legitimacy under the aegis of neo-liberal globalization means that, nowadays, rather than writing about hegemony we can use the term 'domination'. The implementation of this imperialist project is not the result of consensus but rather military force and the financial imposition of macroeconomic 'structural reform' along the lines of the 'Washington' or 'Post-Washington Consensus'. The second alternative project consists of the socio-political actions of a range of social classes and movements as well as collective subjects and agents, including migrant associations that endorse a political project designed to transform the structural dynamics and political and institutional environments which bar the implementation of alternative development strategies on the global, regional, national and local levels.

Structural dynamics. These refer to the uneven development processes driven by the dynamics of US imperialism on several planes and levels. This includes the financial, commercial, productive and labour market spheres, as well as technological innovation (a strategic form of control) and the use and allotment of natural resources and environmental impacts. These factors condition the ways in which (a) developed, (b) developed and underdeveloped (including 'people-importing' and 'people-exporting' nations), and (c) underdeveloped, peripheral or postcolonial countries relate to each other. They also determine the fields in which interactions between sectors, groups, movements and social classes take place, within and across national borders. All of this entails different – albeit interrelated – dynamics at the global, regional, national and local levels.

Theoretical principles: concepts and postulates

Without attempting to establish theoretical principles of universal validity, there are, however, two concepts that are essential to unravelling the nature of the nexus between development and migration in the context of contemporary capitalism in its neo-liberal phase: uneven development and forced migration.

Uneven development is the historical process of economic, social and political polarization among regions, countries and classes derived from the dynamics of capitalist accumulation, labour division, geopolitics and class struggle in different spatial spheres and hierarchical levels. The most evident result is the expansion of social inequality, expressed by the concentration of capital, power and wealth in the hands of a small capitalist elite vis-à-vis an abundant process of plundering, exploitation and poverty gradually limiting the life and working conditions of the majority of the population. At the level of the world capitalist system there is a symptomatic differentiation among core, imperialist or developed nations and peripheral, underdeveloped or dependent ones. It is not our intention, however, to characterize the development of capitalism as a dichotomy or manicheism but rather to express the complexity of differentiating regions, countries and their domestic situations, thus enabling the identification of hierarchical levels among, for instance, core nations, where the United States is at the forefront. The heart of the system seizes the economic surplus and natural and human resources from the peripheral regions. Relations of domination, exploitation and uneven interchange have developed between the core and the periphery with varying degrees of intensity depending on the historical periods of colonization, post-colonization and imperialism. In the context of neo-liberal capitalism, uneven development has resorted to desperate strategies to expand valorization by adopting modes of labour super-exploitation which put human life at risk, while the pillaging of natural resources is endangering biodiversity and life itself.

Instead of considering migration as a population movement derived from individual or family decisions or a phenomenon with its own dynamics, basically integrated by social networks and transnational relations, it is important to take into account that the massive processes characterizing migration under contemporary capitalism, and which link together domestic and international flows, are fundamentally determined by the contradictory dynamics originating in uneven development. Migration thus adopts the particular mode of *forced migration*, with the following two main characteristics: first, there are expulsion processes resulting from a spiral of social degradation, triggered by the deprivation of means of production and subsistence, and pillaging, violence and catastrophes, jeopardizing the subsistence of large segments of the population in their places of origin. This is not simply an accumulative or gradual process, but an actual breakdown of the social order brought about by structural adjustment policies as well as domination and wealth concentration strategies at extreme levels, forcing massive contingents of the population to sell their labour both nationally and internationally to guarantee their family's subsistence.

Second, there are restrictions on the mobility of the migrant workforce, which depreciate it and subject it to conditions of high vulnerability, precariousness and extreme exploitation. If the process of expulsion is a reprisal of the original accumulation modes characteristic of the first historical stages of capitalism, the liberalization of the workforce today will face obstacles in the labour market, particularly internationally. The state apparatus of the migrant-receiving nation regulates the entry of migrants with punitive and coercive instruments that fulfill a labour-devalorization purpose, in addition to damaging human rights and criminalizing migrants. Conditions for labour exploitation, social exclusion and the diverse risks assumed throughout the different stages of transit and settling endanger the life of migrants. Under the current capitalist restructuring process and within the framework of new modes of exchange and uneven development, forced migration represents a form of human resources transference whose formation and reproduction costs are not paid by the countries of destination.

As might be evident, this notion of forced migration is based on the propositions of political economy posited by Marx in his writings on the Irish question and has been used by other present-day authors. Therefore, beyond the predominantly legal definition employed by international organizations when referring to cases of refugees, asylum and displacement, it should be pointed out that the problem of uneven development also triggers imperial wars and socio-political conflicts with escalations of state, interethnic and religious violence, among others. This leads in turn to massive population displacements under vulnerable and highly risky circumstances.

According to the orthodox view of migration and development, remittances play a central role in the analysis of the phenomenon and the design of public policies. From a political economy perspective it is crucial to reveal the underlying meaning of remittances beyond their monetary manifestation. In other words, remittances emerge as the expression of the social relations of production in a context of super-exploitation, social exclusion and, consequently, the accelerated worsening of workers' lives. The generation of remittances involves transferences of invisibilized social resources and costs: (1) transference of human resources in a productive age including their reproduction and training costs; and (2) social costs evidenced by a loss of population, abandonment of productive activities and breakup of families, among others. More than an instrument of development, remittances constitute a fraction of the salary destined to cover the subsistence of the economic dependents that live in their places of origin. In addition, the emphasis and oversizing of remittances conceals the contribution of migrants to the socio-economic dynamics of the receiving nations.

Within the proposed political economy framework, the relationship between international migration and development involves a dialectical interaction that goes beyond the preponderant unidirectional view of the migration–development nexus. In the specific case of South–North (or underdeveloped–developed) migration, there are several theoretical postulates to take into account:

Current capital restructuring – as a manifestation of the dominant imperialist project – operates as a catalyst for forced migration from peripheral to developed countries. In this context, core-developed countries led by the United States and the European Union employ a geopolitical-imperialist strategy of economic restructuring that internationalizes productive, commercial and financial capital while allowing the major developed countries and their elites to appropriate the natural resources, economic surplus and cheap workforces of underdeveloped nations. The relationships maintained between 'people-importing' countries and peripheral and postcolonial nations exacerbate the latter's conditions of underdevelopment (Petras and Veltmeyer, 2000). Underdeveloped countries find themselves with massive population reserves (and, therefore, vast amounts of surplus population, well beyond the conventional formulation of the *reserve army of the unemployed*), who are unable to find decent working conditions in their countries of origin for ensuring personal and family reproduction. This is the direct result of reduced accumulation processes derived from their uneven relationships with developed nations (an unequal exchange that translates into diverse forms of surplus transference). Petras (2007, p. 41) refers to this impact in the following terms: 'The *de-structuring* of labor (delinking the development of industry and infrastructure from the local population) and the relocation of profits to the receiving country creates a mass permanent surplus labor population in the dominated country.' The above conditions are not socially sustainable and lead to forced migration, which can result in substantial population loss for countries of origin, sometimes even leading to relative or absolute depopulation. The loss of a qualified and unqualified workforce is also associated with the abandonment of productive activities and the loss of potential wealth.

Exploitation of migrant labour contributes to socioeconomic dynamism and to the concentration and centralization of capital in core-developed countries. Developed nations demand large quantities of unqualified and qualified workforce; in most cases, this human merchandise is rendered increasingly vulnerable and is additionally devalued by the regulation of migration criminalization policies imposed by the 'people-importing' countries. First, this ongoing demand results from the developed nations' increased accumulation capacity, which is derived from the transference of resources and surpluses from underdeveloped countries. Second, it is the consequence of processes of demographic transition and an ageing population. Immigrants contribute to an overall cheapening of the workforce since they tend to be employed in work-intensive areas of production where they substitute a national workforce that tends to earn higher salaries and benefits. Although the qualified immigrant workforce belongs to an elite segment, it is still comparatively cheap, as an immigrant's salary is lower than that of a national citizen employed in the same position. In the case of both qualified and unqualified migrants the receiving country reaps substantial benefits, having invested nothing in the formation of the human capital it now enjoys. Not only do immigrants provide static comparative advantages derived from a reduction in production costs: they also bring comparative dynamic ones through their participation in accelerated innovation processes. Overall, working immigrants and their families internally strengthen the receiving country's market through consumption. Even the so-called 'nostalgia market' entails the creation of consumer demand, which fortifies internal economic activity. Additionally, immigrants' taxable contributions enrich the country's fiscal fund but do not translate into the kinds of social benefits enjoyed by the national population, which denotes a criterion of social exclusion. Immigrant workers also help pay for the current crisis faced by pension systems due to the massive retirement of the Baby Boomer generation. Although these contributions counteract some of the effects brought about by the dismantling of the welfare state, they obviously do not constitute a long-term solution.

Migrants help maintain precarious socioeconomic stability in their countries of origin. Migrants' salary-based remittances contribute to the subsistence of family members in their country of origin.[3] To a lesser extent, remittances also help finance small businesses in the subsistence economy. The participative remittances collected by migrant organizations finance public works and social projects in the places of origin. In some cases this practice has become institutionalized: Mexico's *Tres por Uno* (Three for One) programme has been replicated in other countries. Migrants with savings or entrepreneurial plans use their money to finance micro-projects in their places of origin. The most important type of remittance is, however, the salary-based one employed for family subsistence, which means that the resources sent by migrants are rarely destined for processes of development and social transformation. In a macroeconomic context, remittances serve neo-liberal regimes which, without bothering to come up with actual development alternatives, use them as a source of foreign exchange income that sustains the country's fragile macroeconomic stability. In some cases, remittances have even been used as a guarantee when incurring foreign debt. Along similar lines, migrants are portrayed as the 'heroes of development', an utterly cynical move that renders them responsible for the promotion of said development, while the state, opting for the conservative stance of minimal participation, is no longer held accountable. The strategy of market regulation postulated by fundamentalist neo-liberals lacks any sort of development plan that involves migrants as well as other social sectors and promotes processes of social transformation. In truth, underdeveloped 'people-exporting' countries fulfill a particular role as a workforce reserve and their potential development is obstructed by increasingly reduced national elites, which are subordinated to the interests of governing circles in developed countries and, to a great extent, the interests of the imperial powers.

The promotion of development as social transformation could curtail forced migration. Globalization depicts migration as inevitable; we must endorse, both in theory and practice, the viability of alternative processes of development and do so on different levels. We must first redefine the asymmetrical terms that developed countries, aided by principles that have by now turned into fetishes (such as democracy, liberty and free trade), have used for imperialist domination. This involves an exposé of imperialist practices, which have created oceans of inequality and condemned vast regions of the world to marginalization, poverty, social exclusion and unfettered migration. Foreign investment (FI) has been a fundamental driving force in this regard. A genuine process of social transformation involving the migrant and non-migrant segments of society would not only seek to contain the overwhelming flow of forced migration but also reverse the ongoing processes of social degradation that characterize underdevelopment and even pose a threat to human existence (Harvey, 2007; Bello, 2006). As an alternative to the current phase of imperialist domination, Petras (2007, Chapter 15) argues in favour of a social transformation strategy based on six main principles: tax revenues versus tax evasions; profit remittances and privileged salaries versus social investment; high reinvestment ratios versus capital flight; long-term investment in research and development versus speculative investment; social welfare versus capitalist privileges; and fixed capital/mobile labour versus mobile capital/fixed labour.

The dialectic between development and migration: the case of the Mexico–United States asymmetric and subordinated regional integration scheme

The Mexico–United States case is based on an asymmetric integration process that clearly illustrates three major elements in the relationship between uneven development and forced migration: (1) the United States is the main leader in the capitalist restructuring process and requires the largest immigrant workforce; (2) the mode of regional integration posed by the North American Free Trade Agreement (NAFTA) follows the prototypical articulations between central and peripheral nations, with the resultant methods of surplus transference; and (3) Mexico is now a workforce-producing country under a forced migration scheme.

Since the late 1970s, the United States has promoted the implementation of neo-liberal structural adjustment policies in Latin America, which have been carried out by several international organizations in tandem with Latin American elites and national governments. In accordance with new models of regional integration, these policies have focused on exports.

The export-led Mexican economic model and the particular mode of regional integration determined by NAFTA are the result of strategic policies implemented by agents of large transnational corporations and the US government under the umbrella of the international organizations at their service: the World Bank and the IMF. In fact – and as has been amply documented – NAFTA itself was created and implemented by a sector of the US political class allied to the large transnational corporations and their counterparts in Canada and Mexico (Cypher, 1993; Faux, 2006). In the case of the latter, the government and a sector of the Mexican business elite led by the *Consejo Coordinador Empresarial* (Enterpreneurial Council), which is linked to the *Comisión de Organismos Empresariales de Comercio Exterior* (Commission of Entrepreneurial External Commerce Organizations) participated actively in this process (Puga, 2004; Cypher and Delgado Wise, 2007).

Mexico soon became Latin America's major exporter and the world's thirteenth largest. This 'achievement' was irresponsibly and superficially attributed to the successful implementation of the neo-liberal economic reforms (that is the structural adjustment programs). At first glance, 90 per cent of its export platform comprised manufactured products, 39.4 per cent of which was classified as 'technical progress-diffusing goods' (CEPAL, 2002). This stance can create an illusion, and an examination of the subject becomes necessary: what is it that the country really exports?

The basis for Mexico's cheap labour export-led model

The way in which Mexico entered the orbit of US capitalism under neo-liberalism, and particularly in the context of NAFTA, plays a fundamental role in the understanding of the model of 'development' adopted in the country. As has been documented elsewhere and contrary to what Mexico's progress along the secondary-exporting path would indicate (that is, the establishment of a successful model of manufactured exports), the country's export-led model is based on cheap labour (Delgado Wise and Márquez Covarrubias, 2005; Delgado Wise and Cypher, 2005). This model, which, as a component of its renovated imperialist architecture, is crucial to the US productive restructuring process, comprises three interrelated mechanisms that, taken together, indicate the asymmetrical and subordinated integration of the country's economy with that of the United States:

1) *The maquiladora industry*, made up of assembly plants and involving a strategy of productive relocation led by large US corporations in order to take advantage of low labour costs in Mexico. The result is that the nation experiences a very low level of integration with the domestic economy and, in addition, is subject to a further dismantling of its productive apparatus.
2) *Disguised maquila*, or manufacturing plants with productive processes that are more complex than *maquila* assembly operations but operate under the same temporary import regime as *maquiladoras* (such as the automobile and electronics sectors). It should be noted here that *maquila* and disguised *maquila* share two characteristics: first, they are practically devoid of productive upstream and downstream links to the rest of the national production apparatus; and second, they are subject to intense processes of labour precariousness. *Maquilas* issue wages that are around one-tenth of those in the United States, while the difference in disguised *maquila* is one to seven. Due to their high levels of imported components (between 80 and 90 per cent of the total export value), their contribution to the Mexican economy is basically restricted to wage earnings; in other words, the value of the labour incorporated into the exports. This means that the country is engaging in the *indirect exportation of labour*, or a transfer of the workforce that does not require workers to leave the country

(Tello, 1996). This is a crucial conceptual element that demystifies the purported success of Mexican manufacturing exports and reveals retrograde movement in the export platform.

3) *Labour migration*, which involves the mass exodus of Mexicans to the United States as a result of the constrained size and precariousness of the Mexican formal labour market and the process of neo-liberal regional integration.

If we add indirect labour exports to the *direct exportation of the work force* through labour migration, the true makeup of Mexico's exports is revealed. This is why we characterize the current model of export growth as *the cheap labour export-led model*.

The new migration dynamics

Even though Mexico has a long migration history, it is important to point out that the mechanics of the current capitalist restructuring under NAFTA have led to new migration dynamics, both quantitatively and qualitatively.[4] Under the labour export-led model, migration from Mexico to the United States has experienced an exponential growth during the past two and a half decades. This growth was accentuated by the implementation of NAFTA, which turned Mexico into the world's major migrant sender to the United States. The sheer dimensions of the migration phenomenon speak for themselves: in 2007, the US population of Mexican origin – including Mexican-born documented and undocumented migrants (12 million) as well as US citizens of Mexican ascendancy – was estimated at 30 million people. It is the world's largest diaspora to be established in a single country. According to United Nations (2006) estimates, during the 1990–1995 period Mexico was the country with the largest annual number of emigrants (a total of 400,000 people compared to 390,000 from China and 280,000 from India). Between 2000 and 2005, the Mexican annual exodus rose to 560,000. The country has consequently experienced an exponential growth in remittances and, along with India, is the world's major recipient (IFAD, 2007). In 2007, the amount of remittances received by Mexico amounted to US$26 billion (Banco de México, 2009).

Practically all of Mexico's territory shows incidence of international migration. In 2000, 96.2 per cent of all municipalities experienced some type of migration-related activity. This territorial expansion has resulted in the emergence of new migration circuits with particular dynamics and problems (Zúñiga and Leite, 2004). At the same time, even though the Mexican immigrant population in the United States is still concentrated in a handful of states, in the last two decades it has expanded throughout most of the national territory. Migration circuits have also expanded to the eastern and central-northern areas (Zúñiga and Hernández-León, 2005), where some of the most dynamic centres of industrial restructuring are located (Champlin and Hake, 2006).

In 2005, 39 per cent of the population aged 15 years and older born in Mexico and residing in the United States had a level of education higher than a basic high-school diploma (Giorguli et al., 2007). In contrast, the average figure for Mexico is 33.2 per cent, which means that – in general terms and in contrast to what is commonly believed – more qualified workers are leaving than remaining in the country; in other words, there is a clear selective trend, in line with the underlying rationale behind international migration. It should also be noted, however, that in comparison to other immigrant groups in the United States, the Mexican contingent is the one with the lowest average levels of schooling. That situation does not attenuate the problem; on the contrary, it highlights the serious educational shortcomings that still exist in the country and that have been heightened with the adoption of neo-liberal policies (OECD, 2005).

One high-profile form of labour migration that does not fall within the stereotype involves Mexican residents in the United States who have university degrees or postgraduate qualifications. This figure totals slightly more than 590,000 individuals (CONAPO, 2008), indicating that the 'brain drain' has become a significant problem. Thus, under Mexico's prevailing *maquiladora*-based model, there is very limited demand for qualified workers and practically no demand for scientific and technological knowledge, which leads to a hemorrhaging of highly qualified human resources.

These changes have been accompanied by transformations in migration patterns, which have moved from circular to established migration and show increased participation on the part of women and complete families (Delgado Wise et al., 2004). Even though the evolution of migration flows often leads to established migration, in this case the tendency has been accompanied by a unilateral closing of the border that, in contravention of its goals, has not contained the exodus. Rather, given the return risks and difficulties, it has encouraged new migrants to prolong their stay indefinitely. These changes, along with Mexico's decreasing birth rate, have resulted in a worrisome and growing tendency toward depopulation: between 2000 and 2005, one in every two municipalities in Mexico had a negative growth rate (CONAPO, 2008).

Given the hemispheric extension of the economic political integration promoted by the US government, Mexico has also become a transit country and must address the concomitant problems. In 2004, nearly 400,000 people moved through the Mexican southern border. Most of them were Central American undocumented migrants (INM, 2005).

The implications and paradoxes of regional integration under NAFTA

It is evident that the promises made by the promoters of regional integration under NAFTA benefited only a small segment of the Mexican and US elites, particularly the latter. This reveals the policy's true purpose and explains why its supporters continue to brag about the success of the restructuring strategy and the regional integration scheme.

The following is a brief summary of the effects this process has had on the Mexican economy and society, which have been the most affected. We distinguish four major effects.

First, we observe the generation of disaccumulation processes in the Mexican economy. The indirect export of labour force via the *maquila* and *disguised maquila* industries implies a *transfer of net profits* to the US economy. This constitutes a new mode of unequal exchange or surplus transference from the peripheral to the core-developed nations that is even more acute than those examined in the structuralist and dependency theories previously endorsed by the Economic Commission for Latin America and the Caribbean (ECLAC). This surplus transference is closely linked to the drastic reduction of employment in Mexico and the overflowing Mexican workforce's availability in the international labour market, particularly the United States.

Second, there is the loss of labour force whose formation costs fall on the Mexican economy. Mexican labour migration represents a drain of valuable human resources which, in turn, leads to the neglect of productive activities, constitutes a waste of resources spent on the formation of the emigrating labour force, and, to an extent, the displacement of relatively qualified labour. The following data clearly illustrate this phenomenon and highlight the contributions of Mexican immigrants to the US economy – contributions that orthodox approaches to the migration and development nexus tend to ignore:

a) Mexican migrants' economic contribution to the US Gross Domestic Product (GDP) has doubled over the past 14 years, reaching a total of

US$485 billion in 2006, that is, 3.7 per cent of US GDP compared to 57.7 per cent of Mexican GDP.[5]

b) In 2006, Mexican migrants received US$165 billion, which amounts to only 2.2 per cent of the US total labour income even though they represent 4.7 per cent of the workforce in the United States. Remittances sent to Mexico amounted to 14.4 per cent of this income.[6]
c) As consumers, Mexican migrants injected US$268 billion into the US internal market during 2006. This amounted to 47 per cent of consumption expenditure in Mexico.[7]
d) In 2006, Mexican migrants contributed US$22 billion to the US Treasury via job-related direct taxation. This equals the amount of remittances sent to Mexico during that same period.[8]
e) In 2006, Mexico transferred US$99 billion into the US economy in the form of public educational funds spent on its emigrant population; the United States saved US$723 billion, since it did not have to train this workforce using funds from its own educational budget.[9]
f) In 2006 and aside from educational expenses, Mexico transferred US$257 billion into the US economy in the form of reproduction costs spent on its emigrant workers. The United States saved US$1.261 trillion.[10]
g) Mexico transferred US$356 billion (41.6 per cent of Mexican GDP) into the US economy in the form of labour reproduction costs and educational investment,[11] while the United States saved US$1.984 trillion (15.2 per cent of its GDP) in the same areas by importing Mexican labour.[12]

Third, there is the dismantling of a substantial part of the Mexican productive apparatus. Economic regional integration and the implementation of the current export model have contributed to the progressive dismantling of the internally focused production apparatus, which plays an irrelevant role in the neo-liberal agenda. There is evidence that at least 40 production chains in the small- and medium-sized business segment have been destroyed following the reorientation of the economy toward the external market (Cadena, 2005).

Finally, we observe the reduction in and precariousness of formal employment. Neo-liberal policies have failed to create high-quality formal employment; rather, they have destroyed employment sources and increased precariousness and flexibilization in the current formal job market. In the absence of benefits such as unemployment insurance, the informal sector is a source of precarious subsistence for large sectors of the population which have been excluded from the formal job market. The informal employment sector comprises a large population (60 per cent of the employed workforce in Mexico, OECD, 2008) – living at a subsistence level and serving not only as a labour reserve but also as a flexible component of the neo-liberal productive system – that further lower labour costs both in Mexico and the United States.

As a corollary, the asymmetries between Mexico and the United States have not only failed to decrease but have actually grown. Table 3.1 and Figure 3.1, which show the changes in the hourly wage and GDP per capita in both countries, illustrate this.

Table 3.1 Labour compensation per hour (US$)

	Mexico	United States	Differential
1994	6.3	15.4	16.0
2007	22.3	37.8	22.4

Source: OECD Statistics, various years.

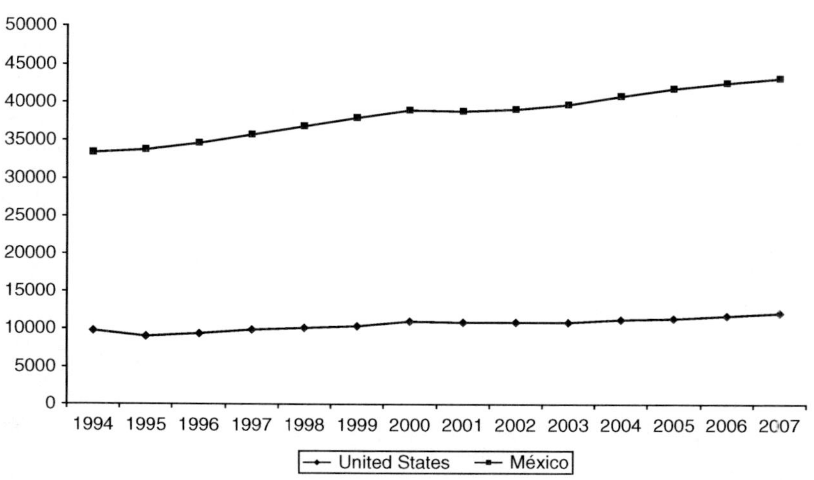

Figure 3.1 GDP per capita (constant 2005, international $)
Source: World Bank, World Development Indicators, 2008.

Social resistance

The profound need for change in the structural dynamics and strategic practices at work in the current schemes of regional integration and neo-liberal national development have given way to two types of social agents, which can be separated into two groups: those 'from above' and those 'from below'. The current economic project has clearly been implemented 'from above' by the agents of US imperialism in tandem with Mexican allies. They work within a political coalition that seeks to maintain the privileges of neo-liberal integration and push them to its very limits. In short, this is an actual class project that promotes economic asymmetries, social inequalities and phenomena such as poverty, unemployment, labour precariousness and migration.

In contrast, those 'below' – particularly in Mexico – are mostly unhappy and disenchanted, although they sometimes engage in open acts of opposition, resistance and rebellion. It is true that there is currently no collective agent that can articulate a project that counters the one being implemented by neo-liberal elites. We should point out, however, that a number of dispersed social alternative movements have willfully, even optimistically, sprung up.

The Mexican agricultural sector, one of the quarters that has been hardest hit by the implementation of NAFTA and which is suffering in the productive, commercial, demographic and environmental areas, has given rise to movements like *El Barzón* ('The Plough'), *El Campo No Aguanta Más* (The Countryside Can't Take Any More; Bartra, 2003) and the campaign *Sin Maíz no hay País* (No Corn, No Country). Other denouncers of the neo-liberal system include the *Ejército Zapatista de Liberación Nacional* (Zapatista Army of National Liberation, EZLN) and its *Otra Campaña* (Other Campaign), as well as some sectors of the social and electoral left which have converged into the *Coalición por el Bien de Todos* (Coalition for the Good of All) and the *Convención Nacional Democrática* (National Democratic Convention). There are also other more or less important national socio-political movements, but what is worth noting is that the widespread popular discontent (which could even extend to the majority of Mexicans) is not expressed in an organized manner and has not yet produced an alternative development project.

On a binational level, the actions of opposition forces have been even more scattered. Initially, the *Red Mexicana de Acción frente al Libre Comercio* (Mexican Action Network in Opposition to Free Trade) communicated with like-minded organizations in the United States and Canada that opposed the signing of NAFTA but since then its actions (which involve agreements between unions and social organizations on both sides of the border) have been few and far between (Brooks and Fox, 2004).

The idea that migrants are agents of development has been promoted for over a decade. This proposal, which is in no way sustainable when applied to large-scale social processes, suggests that migrants should be held responsible for promoting development in their countries of origin. And yet, as Fox (2005) has pointed out, migrant society has produced social actors who operate on three levels: (1) integration into US society (such as unions, the media and religious organizations); (2) networking and promotion of development in places of origin (that is, native organizations); and (3) binational relationships that combine the previous two (that is, pan-ethnic organizations). For example, Mexican migrant organizations fund public works and social projects in their communities of origin with the aid of the programme *Tres por Uno*. During the spring of 2006, US-resident immigrants participated in massive marches demanding their working, political, social and civil rights.

Generally speaking, migrants and their organizations affect the political, social, economic and cultural aspects of sending and receiving countries to varying degrees. However, it would be a theoretical mistake to present migrants themselves as a collective agent of transformation. If we intend to portray them as agents of development, then we had better examine the strategic projects and structural dynamics present on different planes and levels, as well as the interests that prompt participation 'from above' and 'from below'. This will allow us to understand the role played by migrants. Stating that they cannot be considered agents of development does not entail a pessimistic message advocating immobility. Quite the opposite: this can help us unravel possible forms of articulation between migrant organizations and social sectors that seek a new type of development agenda, one that can be applied at the global, regional, national and local levels. Only then will we be able to discuss the configuration of an agent of social transformation that includes migrant participation.

Final remarks

The theoretical framework outlined in this paper for understanding the dialectic relationship between development and migration has four critical components:

First, we need to take a critical approach to the analysis of contemporary capitalism. Contrary to the discourse regarding the inevitability of the current imperialist strategy of economic restructuring, we posit that the current phase of imperialist domination is unsustainable. In this regard, it is fundamental to note that '[t]he principal factor generating international migration is not globalization but imperialism, which pillages nations and creates conditions for the exploitation of labor in the imperial center' (Petras, 2007, pp. 51–52). It is likewise fundamental to: (a) bear in mind the cyclical nature of capitalist development; (b) understand the historical, strategic and structural dimension of the restructuring process/crisis underway; and (c) unravel the multidimensionality and distinctiveness of the processes involved.

Second, a critical reconstruction of the field of development studies is needed. The favouring of a singular mode of analysis based on the belief that free markets work as powerful regulatory mechanisms, efficiently assigning resources and providing patterns of economic convergence among countries and their populations, has clearly resulted in failure. New theoretical and practical alternatives are needed, and we propose a revaluation of development as a process of social transformation through a multi-dimensional, multi-spatial and properly contextualized approach. This integral approach requires the consideration of the strategic and structural aspects of the dynamic of uneven contemporary capitalist development, which should be examined at the global, regional, national and local levels. For this purpose it is crucial to understand, *inter alia*, the central role played by foreign investment in the process of neo-liberal restructuring of peripheral economies, and the new modalities of surplus transference characterizing contemporary capitalism.

Third, we have to engage in the construction of an agent of change. The globalization project led by the United States has ceased to be consensual: it has benefited only capitalist elites and excluded and damaged an overwhelming number of people throughout the world. Economic, political, social, cultural and environmental changes are all needed but a transformation of this magnitude is not viable unless diverse movements, classes and agents can establish common goals. The construction of an agent of change requires not only an alternative theory of development but also collective action and horizontal collaboration: the sharing of experiences, the conciliation of interests and visions, and the construction of alliances inside the framework of South–South and South–North relations.

Fourth, a reassessment of migration and development studies is called for. The current explosion of forced migration is part of the intricate machinery of contemporary capitalism as an expression of the dominant imperialist project. In order to understand this process we need to redefine the boundaries of studies that address migration and development: expand our field of research and invert the terms of the unidirectional orthodox vision of the migration–development nexus in order to situate the complex issues of uneven development and imperialist domination at the centre of an alternative dialectical framework. This entails a new way of understanding the migration phenomenon.

Notes

1. The classic concept of imperialism coined by Lenin refers to the monopolistic stage of capitalism. During the 1960s and 1970s approaches to imperialism focused on the role of unequal exchange as a central factor in uneven development affecting the strengthening of monopolistic capital and imperial states. In the past few years, discussions of imperialism have become particularly relevant outside of Marxist circles as researchers attempt to map the essential features of the restructuring process and the current capitalist crisis (Harvey, 2003; Petras and Veltmeyer, 2000).
2. For our analytical purposes we adopt Petras and Veltmeyer's (2000) approach for understanding the nature of contemporary capitalism and 'unmasking' the notion of globalization by considering, following Marx's method, two critical and interrelated analytical dimensions: the strategic and the structural.
3. For the different types of remittance see Márquez Covarrubias (2006).
4. Elsewhere (Delgados Wise and Márquez Covarrubias, 2008) we provide a historical view of Mexican migration to the United States and show how each phase of accumulation and regional integration corresponds to a different type of migration. This reinforces our view that migration is not an independent variable or a self-sustaining process; rather, it is intrinsically tied to the dynamics of uneven development.
5. Estimate based on the labour average productivity at an industrial level and the volume of Mexican migrant workers participating in this activity. Based on data collected by the US Bureau of Economic Analysis and the Current Population Survey, 2006 (see www.census.gov/cps).
6. Estimate based on data from the Current Population Survey, 2006.
7. For this estimate, remittances sent to Mexico were subtracted from the salary and income multiplier factor for the United States: 1.9 (Dumas, 2003).
8. Estimate based on data from the Current Population Survey, 2006, and the tax scheme applied under the US Tax Law, 2006.
9. Estimate based on expenditures per educational level as reported in the 2007 Mexican Educational Panorama issued by the Mexican Ministry of Public Education and data from the Current Population Survey, 2006.
10. Estimate based on expenditures per educational level recorded by the National Center for Education Statistics, US Department of Education, 2006, and data from the Current Population Survey, 2006.

11. Estimate based on the Current Population Survey 2006 and the reproduction costs of labour force in Mexico; the 'patrimonial' goods and services cost estimates follow the monetary values established by INDESOL for 2006.
12. Estimate based on data from the Current Population Survey and the cost of labour force production in the United States using the monetary value fixed by the Poverty Threshold, US Department of Health and Human Services, 2006.

References

Banco de México (2009) 'Remesas familiares', at: www.banxico.org.mx (accessed March, 2009).

Bartra, A. (2003) *Cosecha de ira: economía política de la contrarreforma agrarian* (Mexico: Itaca).

Bello, W. (2006) 'The Capitalist Conjuncture: Over-accumulation, Financial Crisis and the Threat from Globalisation', *Third Word Quarterly*, 27 (8), 1345–1367.

Brooks, D. and Fox, J. (2004) 'Ten Years of Cross-Border Dialogues', Americas Program, Interhemispheric Resource Center, at: www.irc-online.org (accessed August, 2007).

Cadena, G. (2005) 'Manufactura, en la ruta de la 'desindustrialización', *El Financiero*, 16 August.

Castles, S. and Delgado Wise, R. (2007) *Migración y Desarrollo: Perspectivas desde el Sur* (Mexico DF: Miguel Ángel Porrúa).

CEPAL (2002) *Globalización y desarrollo* (Santiago: CEPAL/ILPES/ONU).

Champlin, D. and Hake, E. (2006) 'Immigration as Industrial Strategy in American Meatpacking', *Review of Political Economy*, 18 (1), 49–70.

CONAPO (2008) *Migración internacional*, at: www.conapo.gob.mx (accessed January, 2009).

Cypher, J. (1993) 'The Ideology of Economic Science in the Selling of NAFTA: The Political Economy of Elite Decision-Making', *Review of Radical Political Economics*, 25 (4), 146–163.

——— and Delgado Wise, R. (2007) 'Restructuring Mexico, Realigning Dependency: Harnessing Mexican Labor Power in the NAFTA Era', working paper, Doctorate in Development Studies, Universidad Autónoma de Zacatecas.

Delgado Wise, R. and Márquez Covarrubias, H. (2005) 'Migración, políticas públicas y desarrollo. Reflexiones en torno al caso de México', presented at the Seminario Problemas y Desafíos de la Migración y el Desarrollo en América, Red Internacional de Migración y Desarrollo, 7–9 April, Cuernavaca.

——— and Márquez Covarrubias, H. (2007) 'The Reshaping of Mexican Labor Exports under NAFTA: Paradoxes and Challenges', *International Migration Review*, 41 (3), 656–679.

——— and Marquez Covarrubias, H. (2008) 'The Mexico-United Status Migratory System: Dilemmas of Regional Integration, Development and Migration', in C. Stephen and R. Delgado Wise (eds), *Migration and Development: Perspectives from the South* (Geneva: IOM).

——— and Cypher, J. (2005) 'The Strategic Role of Labor in Mexico's Subordinated Integration into the US Production System under NAFTA', working document 12/11/2005, Doctorado en Estudios del Desarrollo, Universidad Autónoma de Zacatecas.

———, Márquez Covarrubias, H. M. and Rodríguez, H. (2004) 'Organizaciones transnacionales de migrantes y desarrollo regional en Zacatecas', *Migraciones internacionales*, 2 (4), 159–181.

Dumas, L. J. (2003) 'Economic Multipliers and the Economic Impact of DOE Spending in New Mexico', University of Texas at Dallas, March 2003, at: www.nukewatch.org/facts/nwd/DumasReport033103.pdf (accessed, March, 2009).

Faux, J. (2006) *The Global Class War* (Hoboken: John Wiley & Sons).

Fox, J. (2005) 'Repensar lo rural ante la globalización. La sociedad civil migrante', *Migración y desarrollo*, 5, 35–58.

Giorguli, S., Gaspar, S. and Leite, P. (2007) *La migración mexicana y el mercado de trabajo estadounidense* (Mexico: CONAPO).

Harvey, D. (2003) *The New Imperialism* (New York: Oxford University Press).

——— (2007) 'Neoliberalism as Creative Destruction', *The Annals of the American Academy of Political and Social Sciences*, 610, 21–44.

IFAD (2007) *Sending Money Home. Worldwide Remittance Flows to Developing Countries* (Rome: International Fund for Agricultural Development).

IFAD (2008) *International Migration, Remittances and Rural Development* (Rome: International Fund for Agricultural Development).

INEGI (2006) *Conteo de población y vivienda* (Mexico: INEGI).

INM (2005) *Propuesta de política migratoria integral en la frontera sur de México* (Mexico: Instituto Nacional de Migración).

Lapper, R. (2007) 'Cashing In on Homeward Flows', *Financial Times*, 28 August.

Márquez Covarrubias, H. (2006) 'El desarrollo participativo transnacional basado en las organizaciones de migrantes', *Problemas del desarrollo*, 37 (144), 121–144.

OECD (2005) 'La emigración de mexicanos a Estados Unidos', *Comercio exterior*, 55 (2), 148–165.

——— (2008) 'Panorama del Empleo 2008 (Paris: Organization for Economic Development and Cooperation [OECD]).

Petras, J. (2007) *Rules and Ruled in the US Empire. Bankers, Zionists, Militants* (Atlanta: Clarity Press).

Petras, J. and Veltmeyer, H. (2000) 'Globalization or Imperialism?', *Cambridge Review of International Affairs*, 14 (1), 41–82.

Puga, C. (2004) *Los empresarios organizados y el Tratado de Libre Comercio de América del Norte* (Mexico DF: Miguel Ángel Porrúa).

Tello, C. (1996) 'La economía mexicana: hacia el tercer milenio', *Nexos*, no. 223, pp. 47–55.

UN (2006) 'Seguimiento de la población mundial, con especial referencia a la migración internacional y el desarrollo', Informe del Secretario General, E/CN.9/2006/3, 25 January.

World Bank (2006) 'Global Economic Prospects 2006: Economic Implications of Remittances and Migration' (Washington, DC: World Bank).

Zúñiga, E. and Leite, P. (2004) 'Los procesos contemporáneos de la migración México–Estados Unidos: una perspectiva regional y municipal', paper presented at the Seminar: Migración México-Estados Unidos: Implicaciones y retos para ambos países, México: CONAPO.

Zúñiga, V. and Hernández-León, R. (eds) (2005) *New Destinations: Mexican Immigration in the United States* (New York: Russell Sage Foundation).

Part II

Organizations, Networks and States

4

Diasporas, Recovery and Development in Conflict-ridden Societies*

Nicholas Van Hear

Marked out by the collapse of the communist bloc in 1989–91 and the unravelling of capitalism's neo-liberal variant in 2008–9, the two decades between 1989 and 2009 have featured a welter of conflicts that have involved mass displacement and refugee flight. Major new diasporas have formed from or been augmented by these conflict-induced population movements over the last two decades. As this chapter will show, these new or resurgent transnational social formations have consolidated, are enduring, have undertaken new or extended existing forms of transnational activity, and are becoming integrated into the global order, particularly in respect of relations between affluent countries and conflict-ridden societies.

During the same period, and particularly over the last ten years, the attitude toward both conflict and diaspora in the development community has shifted. From being seen as an aberration from development or even irrelevant to it, addressing violent conflict has come to be seen as a key project in the development business. Further, in recent years, societies in conflict and emerging from it (referred to generically in this chapter as 'conflict settings') have come to be seen as holding opportunities for development and transformation. At the same time, diasporas have moved from being cast negatively as fomenters of conflict and proponents of 'long distance nationalism' (Anderson, 1998) to a more positive role of holding the potential to assist with recovery in conflict settings and development in more stable environments. The resurgent interest in conflict and diasporas has increasingly found its way into the policy arena, with agencies such as the World Bank, USAID, the European Commission, the UK's Department for International Development (DfID), Germany's Gesellschaft für Technische Zusammenarbeit

(GTZ) and Scandinavian development bodies exploring the possibilities for diaspora engagement in recovery and development in conflict settings.

However, the question *what kinds of recovery and development* are likely to emerge from diaspora engagement in the context of conflict is rarely asked. This chapter attempts to address this question by examining forms of diaspora engagement in conflict settings and suggests that such engagement may be driven by concerns somewhat different from the view of recovery and development led by the state and international agencies.

The chapter unfolds as follows. The next section explores some reasons for the rise in interest in conflict and diaspora among humanitarian and development agencies. Then, to gain a deeper understanding of their potential engagement in conflict settings, the following section outlines common patterns of diaspora formation involving migration from conflict-ridden societies, drawing on my research on the Sri Lankan, Somali and Afghan cases over the past 15 years.[1] The chapter then turns to the propensity and capacity of diaspora to engage in conflict settings – in part determined by the formation and character of a given diaspora. Some of the forms and features of diaspora engagement are then outlined, informed again by the Sri Lankan, Somali and Afghan cases in particular. Finally, the chapter reflects on the shape of diaspora engagement in conflict contexts and the forms of recovery and development that might emerge from it.

Strands of thinking on diaspora, conflict, recovery and development[2]

The new interest in the role of diasporas in conflict-ridden societies stems in part from development agencies' wider interest in conflict as the antithesis of development. After a long period of viewing conflict as an aberration or irrelevant, development agencies have come to acknowledge the importance of violent conflict in the development context. In the light of the prevalence and persistence of conflict across large swathes of the developing world, violent upheaval has come to be viewed as something that needs to be addressed by development agencies (World Bank, 1997; DfID, 2006).

Not long after this shift in perspective, a further change occurred in development thinking and policy. As well as destroying assets and livelihoods, dislocating and disrupting local and national economies, undermining trust and social capital, and displacing large numbers of people, conflict came to be seen as an opportunity for socio-economic development. By sweeping away social and economic structures that were held inimical to 'development', conflict could open the way for progressive market-led reform and innovation, it was thought. While conflict was previously seen as regressive, it was now presented as an opportunity for social, political and economic transformation. In some ways this echoed the notion of 'creative destruction' developed earlier in different guises by social theorists and economists as diverse as Marx, Schumpeter and Friedman.

As an overview of the debate prepared for GTZ put it, 'Post-conflict situations often provide special opportunities for political, legal, economic and administrative reforms to change past systems and structures which may have contributed to economic and social inequities and conflict' (Mehler and Ribaux, 2000, p. 37). Further, 'The collapse of states in crisis need not be prevented, since a "better state" cannot emerge until that collapse has taken place' (Mehler and Ribaux, 2000, p. 107). Such a perspective struck a chord with a number of development agencies, which since the mid-1990s have taken roles in conflict and post-conflict management and reconstruction (Doornbos, 2002; Moore, 2000).

This perspective developed in tandem with growing concern about security challenges posed by what came to be known as 'fragile' and 'failing' states and the so-called 'LICUS' grouping of territories: 'low income countries under stress' (World Bank, 2002). In 2008, World Bank president Robert B. Zoellick suggested that fragile states and conflict-affected countries – home to about one billion people – posed 'the toughest development challenge of our era'. He went on to note apocalyptically: 'The diseases, outflows of desperate people, criminality, and terrorism that can spawn in the vacuum of fragile states can quickly become global threats' (World Bank, 2008).

Somalia was a case in point of such state collapse and conflict and the threats and opportunities that this posed. The United Nations Development Programme's (UNDP) percipient *Human Development Report* of 2001 for Somalia remarked: 'The prolonged absence of a central Somali government means that Somali society is more directly exposed to both the beneficial and the harmful effects of globalization. [...] The civil war achieved what the structural adjustment programmes of the 1980s did not, that is, economic deregulation that has enabled the expansion of the private sector' (UNDP, 2001, pp. 40–41).

The realization of the 'creative' potential of conflict has been manifested in policy shifts within the World Bank concerning conflict and post-conflict societies. The Bank set up a Post-Conflict Unit in 1997, and established a Post-Conflict Fund which aimed at supporting countries in transition from conflict to sustainable peace and economic development. The PCU transmuted subsequently into the Conflict Prevention and Reconstruction Unit, reflecting an expanding remit (World Bank, 1997, 1998). The new emphasis meant that the Bank now embraced use of conflict settings to promote economic adjustment and recovery. The Bank cooperated with other agencies engaged in post-conflict activities in which forced migration issues were prominent, notably through the 'Brookings Process', a partnership between the Bank, the UN Refugee Agency UNHCR and UNDP initiated in 1999. This was later revived in 2002 as the '4Rs' initiative – Repatriation, Reintegration, Rehabilitation, and Reconstruction – as an integrated inter-agency 'relief to development' approach for countries in transition from conflict (Lippman, 2004).

Critics were wary of this new approach to conflict by the World Bank and other powerful donors. For the critics, such agencies saw 'the terrain of post conflict situations as ripe for implementation of their kind of state, economy and society' (Moore, 2000, p. 14). 'The wake of war leaves the "level playing field" so beloved by... neo-liberal discourses' (Moore, 2000, p. 13). In this perspective, social and economic structures governing property, labour and other economic factors which existed before conflict may well have been impediments to the development of markets; if these structures were destroyed or fatally undermined by conflict, the foundations could be laid for market-friendly 'good governance' (Moore, 2000, p. 11). The dispensers of humanitarian relief could be enlisted to join with those implementing reconstruction and development for these market-friendly purposes. Money was on offer to humanitarian agencies through an array of transition budgets and reconstruction funds, which were increasingly attractive as other sources of humanitarian funds were on the wane.[3]

While the critique has substance, the degree of 'neo-liberalism' attributed to the World Bank and other donors in such critiques was arguably overstated. The new interest of the World Bank and other agencies in conflict-ridden societies coincided with the move from the 'Washington Consensus', promoting structural adjustment and other measures of neo-liberalism up to the 1990s, to the 'Post-Washington Consensus' from the later 1990s (Stiglitz, 1998; Maxwell, 2005), associated with Poverty Reduction Strategies, the Millennium Development Goals, bringing back the developmental state, emphasizing 'good governance', and nurturing civil society: it was a shift from 'getting the prices right' – that is, un-hobbling markets from the constraints of the so-called dead hand of the state – to 'getting the institutions right' – that is, bringing back in the state and other institutions that underpin the economy. The 'Post-Washington Consensus' was certainly still market-friendly, but acknowledged the need for means to counter the harm done by the market and by 'market imperfections': it was the promotion of *liberal* capitalism rather than *neo-liberal* capitalism. The increasing popularity of the notion of social capital, much touted by the World Bank (Fine, 2001), and of strengthening civil society, were in part recognition that relations and dimensions outside the market matter – although admittedly for the World Bank the point was that they mattered for successful functioning of the market. For those critical of this perspective, social capital, a robust civil society, and relations outside the market also mattered for different reasons, not least as means of welfare or social security for the poor and conflict-affected. It was thus the nature, scale, and control of such social security mechanisms and social capital, and more widely the nature of 'development', that were the real terrain of argument, rather than the desirability of the market itself. As one critic put it, 'the debate is not really about "relief" or "development", but *what kind* of development in war-torn societies and indeed in the rest of the periphery' (Moore, 2000, p. 17). This remains a salient question for the societies and communities embroiled in or emerging from conflict and related forced-migration consequences.

Concurrently with the growth in interest in conflict and its potential as terrain for development, interest also revived in the development role of migration in general and remittances in particular (Maimbo and Ratha, 2005). This later found expression in the role diasporas might play in development, building on the growth of interest in diaspora and transnationalism as growing fields of enquiry (Van Hear and Nyberg-Sørensen, 2003; Kapur, 2005; Faist, 2008; Gamlen, 2008). Most of the attention was on migration, diaspora and transnational engagement in relatively stable settings. To the extent that diasporas were considered in the context of conflict, it was largely as a negative force, fomenting or sustaining violence and insurgency. In the last decade there has been a general shift in perception from ascribing diasporas a negative role in fomenting and supporting conflict as 'war mongers' or 'peace-wreckers' (Collier and Hoeffler, 2004; Kapur, 2007) to a more nuanced view that diasporas can assist with relief, peace-building and post-conflict recovery as 'peace-makers' or 'peace-builders', or that their influence is ambivalent – sometimes negative and sometimes positive (Van Hear, 2002, 2003, 2006a, 2006b; Orjuela, 2003; Smith and Stares, 2007). Crucially, it was realized that while conflict undermined development by destroying assets and resources and by killing and displacing people, displacement itself contributed to the formation of diasporas which could themselves constitute a resource for conflict-ridden societies. Diaspora formation can thus be seen as another manifestation of the 'creative destruction' dynamic of conflict. When coupled with the notion of the development potential of conflict settings, the reasoning went that diasporas could play a significant part in this transformation and even be a vehicle for it, especially if they were steeped in liberal values after having lived in the west.

One of the principal resources that refugee diasporas could be seen to contribute to relief during conflict and recovery afterwards were remittances and other transfers, as in more stable settings. It was increasingly recognized that remittances often become key components of livelihood strategies in conflict settings – maybe not for all, but at least for some people (Van Hear 2002, 2006a; Horst, 2006; Lindley, 2007). This and other research suggests at least three settings in which diaspora transfers could influence the living conditions of displaced and conflict-affected people. First, during the course of conflicts such transfers could provide a survival lifeline for those who could not get out of conflict zones, or alternatively means of flight for those who could move out of such areas. Second, in neighbouring countries of first asylum remittances might supplement other means of refugee survival and coping, such as humanitarian aid. Last, perhaps the greatest potential was in post-conflict settings where diaspora remittances and other transfers could enable households to get beyond survival to coping, and even lay the basis for accumulation. There was also potential here for diaspora contributions to broader economic and social reconstruction, beyond the immediate concerns of their kin in conflict areas.

These kinds of interventions in conflict settings are considered further below. To sum up the unfolding of thinking on diaspora and conflict over the last decade or so, from the point of view of the 'global North', conflict-ridden societies were seen as a source of unwanted people, forces and trends: refugees, fundamentalists, criminals, terrorists and the export of insecurity generally. But at the same time the development arms of the global North have increasingly come to recognize that such conditions may present opportunities for remoulding society. The emergence of this perspective was accompanied by a rise of interest in the development potential of diasporas, and later of their potential for assisting with recovery in conflict settings. This perhaps at least partly accounts for the interest of the World Bank and other agencies in conflict and in diasporas' possible influence on it. The notion of enlisting conflict-induced diaspora to transform conflict societies into stable, sustainable communities has become a project of relief and development agencies. To understand better the ways in which diaspora might engage, the following sections look more closely at how diasporas are formed, how this may influence their capacity and motivation to engage, the kinds of engagement they pursue, and the kinds of recovery and development they may foster in conflict settings.

The formation of diasporas in the context of conflict

When people flee conflict, a common pattern is for most to seek safety in other parts of their country, for a substantial number to look for refuge in neighbouring countries, and for a smaller number to seek asylum in countries farther afield, perhaps on other continents. Some of those in neighbouring countries of first asylum may later be resettled farther afield, or migrate to new destinations as part of onward movements, joining those who have gone there directly. If exile persists and people consolidate themselves in their territories of refuge, complex transnational relations will develop among these different locations: that is, among those at home, those in neighbouring territories (what might be called the *near diaspora*), and those spread further away (what might be called the *wider diaspora*) (Van Hear, 2003, 2006a).

As the international migration regime has become more stringent, the main factors which determine the ability to reach these locations have increasingly become cost, connections and chance. At least the first two of these are shaped by socio-economic standing and associated formation of networks. It follows that access to more prosperous and desirable destinations will be limited to better resourced refugees and migrants. Put simply, there tends to be a hierarchy of destinations that can be reached by migrants and asylum-seekers, according to the resources – financial and network-based – that they can call upon (Van Hear, 2006a).

To give this schema some empirical basis, the following outlines processes of diaspora formation induced by conflict among three prominent cases – Sri Lankan Tamils, Somalis and Afghans – which each feature these dynamics:

Tamils from Sri Lanka have been driven to flee by civil war since 1983, intensifying in the 1990s, and resuming after an uneasy cease fire agreed in 2002 broke down in 2005 (Fuglerud, 1999; Van Hear, 2002, 2006a). Those displaced include: poorer people and households moving to safety within Sri Lanka – between half a million and a million at any one time, according to the intensity of the conflict; those with some resources fleeing by boat to south India – around 100,000 at peak, declining to about 50,000–60,000, and then increasing again with the resumption of intense conflict in 2008–9; some who went as labour migrants to the Middle East, both as a livelihood strategy and to escape the conflict; and others, with substantial resources to pay smugglers, and often helped by earlier migrants, who were able to make it as asylum-seekers to affluent countries – notably the UK, Scandinavia, Switzerland, Canada, and Australia – contributing to the 800,000 Sri Lankan Tamils in wider diaspora. In addition to these movements, there has been movement back, between and among these various locations, varying over time with the conditions of conflict and with possibilities for migration.

Somalis have experienced state collapse and civil conflict since the late 1980s (Van Hear, 2006a; Lindley, 2007). Forms of displacement and dispersal include: internal displacement for poorer households within what are known as the 'Somali regions', which include southern Somalia, Somaliland and Puntland in the north; migration to neighbouring countries Ethiopia, Kenya, Djibouti and Yemen by those who have some resources to move; some migration to the Gulf as labour migrants and to set up small businesses, both in pursuit of livelihoods and to escape the conflict and its consequences; and movement to Western or other affluent countries, usually by those well-endowed with resources and network connections, including 'secondary migration' of Somali refugees from Kenya to Europe. Here again there has been some 'regrouping' recently, with substantial onward movement from continental Europe to the UK, of erstwhile asylum-seekers who have successfully secured EU citizenship.

Afghans have likewise experienced war and displacement since the late 1970s (Van Hear, 2003; Monsutti, 2005). Patterns of forced migration and dispersal include: internal displacement within Afghanistan – around two million, depending on the state, phase and nature of the conflict; large numbers of refugees moving to Pakistan and Iran – three million and two million respectively at the peak of outflows; return at various points, when conflict has abated, sometimes substantial, as in 1992 and 2002; labour migration to Iran, as refugee pathways have transformed into labour or betterment migration routes; and substantial numbers of asylum-seekers in Europe, North America and other affluent countries of the 'global North', these being usually better off than refugees in Pakistan and Iran.

From the perspective of receiving countries such as the US, the UK or Germany, the locations of wider diasporas, a typical pattern is a number of waves of migration from conflict-ridden countries such as Sri Lanka, Somalia and Afghanistan. Commonly the following categories of arrival feature in varying combinations: elite and professional migrants who wish to pursue professional qualifications in law, medicine or engineering and/or who anticipate trouble and upheaval in their homelands are typically among the earliest waves: political exiles may well be among them; alternatively, there may have been earlier labour migration pathways (seafarers in the case of Somalis) that pave the way for later refugee arrivals; students may also arrive as tensions rise before conflict breaks out, especially if their educational opportunities are blocked at home, as in the case of Tamils in post-independence Sri Lanka. As conflict escalates and violence erupts, refugees and asylum-seekers arrive, often again in waves depending on the intensity of fighting, numbers escalated particularly in the 1990s. Associated with each of these waves or cohorts of 'primary' arrivals are those migrating for family reunion and/or formation, and these arrivals may continue long after the conflict ends. Last, as diasporas become established and people find or gain the right to move from their new locations, onward or secondary migration may increase, as families split by forced migration are able to re-group: this has been the case among Somalis, Tamils, Afghans and others who have finally gained EU citizenship after many years in the asylum determination process, many of whom have moved to the UK from continental Europe.

As can be seen from these examples, the people who move from conflict-ridden countries are not all refugees, but include people who move for a variety of reasons, involving varying degrees of force and choice. In the analysis of migration, a basic distinction is often made between those who choose to move and those who are forced to – that is, between so-called 'voluntary' and so-called 'forced' migrants (Van Hear, 1998). This distinction is maintained in the policy world, where the governance of international migration is shaped by the conceptual distinction between 'voluntary' and 'forced' migration as mutually exclusive categories. In reality of course the distinction is far from clear-cut. For those who are classed as 'voluntary', especially toward the lower levels of the socio-economic scale – such as labour migrants from lower-income backgrounds – only limited choices may be available. Conversely, those classed as refugees or asylum-seekers – that is, 'forced migrants' – may have more choice than is immediately apparent, for example, looking to expand their life opportunities, especially once they have reached a place of relative safety; in a way they may transmute from refugees to economic or betterment migrants. The coexistence of poverty, lack of income opportunities, inequality and conflict-induced displacement mean that much of the migration in many parts of the world is 'mixed' in nature, both in terms of motivations and the character of the flows: those who flee a country where violence, persecution, discrimination and human rights abuse are rife, for example, may also be trying to escape dire economic circumstances – which themselves feed into such violence, persecution, discrimination and human rights abuse. 'Mixed migration' has therefore been salient in recent diaspora formation (Van Hear, 2009).

In summary, there is commonly a *spread* of people who move within and from conflict-ridden countries: some, typically the less endowed, are dispersed within their own countries as internally displaced people; some find their way to neighbouring countries; and still others, with the resources to do so, are able to move to countries farther afield. The migrants include not just refugees, but people who move for a variety of reasons, and with varying degrees of force and choice. With their dispersal comes the establishment of transnational relations and networks among the dispersed groups and it is through these networks and relationships that diasporas can exert influence on their countries of origin.

Diaspora engagement in conflict-ridden homelands

Such diasporas can be seen as new social formations formed by conflict-induced migration. Diasporas formed in this way are of course shaped both by the society from which they have come and the new society in which they find themselves, as well as by their experience of conflict and flight: they carry with them the values of their homeland, while absorbing to a greater or lesser degree the values of their host society. These values, together with the socio-economic character of the diaspora – which of course is differentiated on class, ethnic, generational and gender dimensions – will help shape their disposition, capacity and inclination to influence the homeland, and in turn determine the shape of that society, if and when a semblance of stability emerges.

It is perhaps useful to distinguish between the *capacity* and the *desire* to engage (Al-Ali et al., 2001). *Capacity* to engage will be shaped by, among other things, security of status, having an income above subsistence level, having the freedom to speak out, and developing social competence and political literacy – knowing how to lobby, campaign, speak in public, write leaflets, draw up funding proposals and so on. The *desire* to engage may be shaped by personal or private motivations, such as the imperative to protect one's family, kin or friends; by wider humanitarian concerns for the community, society or nation; and/or by harder political motivation, driven by political engagement or perhaps by ethno-nationalist sentiments.

The hope of relief and development actors is that, by virtue of gradual incorporation into Western societies, diasporas – or at least some of their members – will be drawn into nurturing 'liberal peace' in conflict-ridden societies (Duffield, 2001). As will be shown below, however, diaspora engagement in conflict settings (as in more stable environments: Mohan, 2008) tends to be privately oriented to family and community rather than concerned with broad societal renewal.

Transnational engagement in conflict settings can include a range of activities – economic, political, social and cultural. The focus here is on forms of transnational transfer that are largely economic, rather than other forms of activity such as lobbying, participation in elections, and cultural events that have a transnational dimension. However, such transfers are not simply bald economic transactions: like other transnational activity they are embedded in social relations – all the more significant in conflict settings since the repair and enlargement of such social relations is very much part of the recovery of conflict-ridden societies.

Here, the generic term *transnational transfers* is used to embrace a range of transactions, including remittances, gifts in kind, donations, some kinds of investment and other transfers. Somewhat misleadingly, these tend to be conflated under the rubric of 'remittances', even though they are, or may be, rather different phenomena.

The most common and most significant form of transfer is the private one of money or goods between individuals, or between individuals and households. I prefer to reserve the term *remittance* for this transaction, which is usually between a migrant in a host country and an individual or household in the country of origin. As several analysts have commented in relation to such transfers in relatively stable settings (Guarnizo, 2003), remittances to family and friends are private, rather intimate transactions. Nevertheless in the aggregate they have substantial public consequences: 'the volume and stability of monetary remittances worldwide have transformed this intimate transaction in one of the most important transactions in the global economy' (Guarnizo, 2003, pp. 671–672). These observations hold in conflict settings, but the trajectories of transfer in such conditions may be more complex: they may be between a host country and a country of first asylum, between a country of first asylum and the country of origin, or among all three sites of the diaspora (Van Hear, 2002, 2006a).

The uses of these remittances by individuals and households are somewhat similar to those in more stable conditions – to cover basic daily needs, to help with construction or reconstruction of housing, to help with education or health care, or (rather infrequently) to invest in a business. But other uses, such as the payment of debt incurred to pay for refugee flight, or to meet the costs of migration of relatives to get them out of conflict zones – are of greater significance in conflict settings than in more stable contexts (Van Hear, 2002).[4]

In addition to these private, individual transfers between individuals or households, there are transfers to wider collectivities: the individual who makes a donation in a temple, church or mosque for relief in the home country, for an orphanage or a clinic; the home town association or old school association that collects funds to rebuild a school, equip a hospital, or refurbish a library; collections by welfare organizations to provide relief for the victims of conflict; or, more darkly, the collections by supporters of insurgent groups for funds to buy weapons or otherwise support insurgency. These transfers, for more public or collective purposes, are somewhat different in nature from the private remittances described above. In the aggregate they are also probably smaller in scale than the private remittances. In conflict settings, however, the significance of such collective transfers goes beyond their immediate economic and material effects, since they can help repair the social fabric frayed by years of conflict, not least by helping to re-establish social linkages ruptured during war and re-building trust and confidence.

Turning to the consequences of transfers, both individuals and communities, recent work on livelihoods in general and livelihoods in conflict specifically is instructive (Deshingkar and Start, 2003; Le Billon, 2000; Collinson, 2003; Bhatia et al., 2003). Some of this work prompts us to think about how individuals, households, families and communities survive, cope and perhaps even prosper under conflict conditions, and the place of transnational transfers in such livelihood strategies. Looking at seasonal and circular migration in rural India, Deshingkar and Start (2003, p. vi) distinguish between migration for coping and migration for accumulation: 'migration is not just by the very poor during times of crisis for survival and coping but has increasingly become an accumulative option for the poor and non-poor alike.' This kind of analysis is applicable in conflict and post-conflict settings. Looking at conflict and other settings of severe strain, and taking Afghanistan as a case study, Bhatia et al. (2003, p. 74) suggest that, in the course of conflict, '[b]roadly, households can be divided into those who profit (add to their asset base), those who cope or get along (non-erosion of assets) and those who survive (erosion of assets)',

Diaspora transfers can usefully be disaggregated along these lines. So we find:

Transfers for survival. During acute crisis, including intense violence, bombing and shelling, money may be sent to get people out of the area of immediate danger. Such transfers may also be necessary for poorer households simply to sustain life during times outside acute crisis when assets, resources and means of livelihood are destroyed, looted or have to be sold off.

Transfers for coping. Acute crises are the exception rather than the rule. During the more usual condition of chronic instability and sporadic violence that characterizes such societies, funds from relatives and friends abroad are sent to meet daily needs, so as to avoid disposal of assets to meet such needs. Money may again also be sent to assist people to leave and get them out of danger.

Transfers for accumulation. During windows of opportunity such as ceasefires and while peace processes are under way, as well as after conflict abates, money sent may be used to reconstruct houses and perhaps to (re)develop livelihoods or even businesses. Informal and formal systems of transfer may be used at this stage, since money and other markets may have been re-established. Some – among them conflict entrepreneurs who may profit from violence – may be able to accumulate not only during ceasefires and semi-peaceful interludes, but also during low level and acute periods of conflict.

These outcomes and possibilities shift over time with the conditions and course of conflict in the homeland – outright war, acute and low-level violence, ceasefire, fragile or uneasy peace, reconstruction and recovery – and vary with the shape, composition and position of the household in the conflict-ridden society. The three types of transfer often co-exist within a given conflict setting, since individuals, families and communities will be affected differently by different conditions. Those conditions are also seldom clear cut. As Le Billon (2000, p. 4) has put it: 'The transition between states of war and peace has become increasingly blurred. There is neither total war nor total peace, but a state of high uncertainty and vulnerability associated with the prevalence of violence.' Outcomes will also vary with the capacity and inclination of diaspora members abroad to make transfers, as outlined above. Again, as well as transfers to individuals and families, collective transfers may also be made for the same purposes – to enable a community to survive, cope, or rebuild and accumulate.

In conflict settings the 'transfers for accumulation' possibility is seldom realized since conditions are often inimical to investment and helping kin survive and cope takes precedence. Most transfers – individual and collective – fall within the 'survival' and 'coping' rubric: together they form part of a safety net or a form of social security for people in conflict settings, a safety net that may also draw on humanitarian assistance and whatever other resources can be called upon to construct what has been called a 'livelihood portfolio' (Collinson, 2003, p. 12).

People, families and communities in conflict areas need to balance different transnational and local resources in their livelihood portfolios. Class and identity politics are involved in gaining access to these different resources: as I have argued elsewhere with respect to migration itself, drawing on Bourdieu's notion of class and forms of capital, access to these resources requires the mobilization of social capital (Van Hear, 2006a) to generate an adequate portfolio of resources. The possibilities for such mobilization help to determine whether households are enabled just to survive (by combining such receipts with selling off assets), to cope (combining such receipts to maintain themselves, and avoiding disposing of assets), or to accumulate or prosper (to cope, and beyond that to profit and accumulate further assets) (Bhatia et al., 2003).

Meanwhile, as has been shown elsewhere (Van Hear, 2006a, 2007; Lindley, 2007), refugee households abroad in the diaspora have to balance the demands of their own livelihoods and futures (most importantly perhaps the education of their children), those in other destination and transit countries, and those left at home, or in neighbouring countries of first refuge. There is thus a countervailing 'portfolio of obligations' among those in the diaspora, as well as a portfolio of livelihood resources for those trying to manage in conflict settings. That portfolio of obligations may become unsustainable and debilitating: for example, to meet the needs of those suffering in conflict conditions at home, tertiary education of children in host countries may have to be forgone. Differences of wealth, resources, social capital and class shape the capacity and level of support than can be offered and thus the circulation of resources among these different sites. This brings us back to the capacity and inclination – the disposition – of the diaspora to engage in conflict settings, which is in turn linked to the kind of recovery development that might emerge as a result of diaspora engagement.

Conclusion: diaspora engagement in conflict settings

Over the past two decades or more, conflict has created much displacement, an unambiguously negative outcome. At the same time, that displacement has played a major part in the formation of new or resurgent diasporas over the last two decades or more – diasporas that are becoming increasingly influential on the global stage. The diaspora created by forced dispersal, conflict and displacement thus generates the means or potential for interventions in conflict settings – in a way another manifestation of 'creative destruction'. Such diaspora interventions may help to alleviate conflict, help resolve it, support reconstruction and aid recovery; equally, as the diaspora sceptics have it, such engagement may foster the continuation or escalation of conflict.

As the first section of this chapter showed, the rise in significance of diasporas in conflict settings has coincided with a number of shifts in thinking and policy concepts on recovery and development, shifts which are themselves located within the wider and growing appreciation of the significance of the 'migration–development nexus' that is the subject of this volume. Notably, there has been a shift in the development agencies' view of conflict and displacement from being unalloyed negative phenomena to episodes that open up opportunities for transformation: this in part harks back to older notions of progress through 'creative destruction'. This shift has more or less coincided with the emergence of the 'Post Washington Consensus' and its more balanced approach to the state–market–civil society triumvirate than obtained during the more nakedly neo-liberal period when the market was all: robust institutions, trust and civil society are among the dimensions that are now given greater value than before. Both of these shifts in perspective have coincided with the rise of diasporas as players in both stable and conflict settings: partly in response to scholarship and analysis that has highlighted their importance, diasporas have increasingly come to be seen as agents of development in stable contexts, and as possible agents of recovery in conflict settings. To some degree, diasporas and their organizations have also come to be seen as an element of civil society – or transnational variants of civil society – and therefore of interest to development agencies in this regard, as well as in terms of the economic transfers and exchanges they make. Whether or not diasporas will be willing or able to meet the expectations being placed upon them by development agencies is a moot point. Their orientation toward recovery and development – implicit and rarely articulated – is largely private, toward fostering the survival and coping of kin and community, rather than geared to notions of recovery and development led by the state, which they may well distrust (Van Hear, 2002, 2007; Mohan, 2008) .

As the foregoing discussion has shown, at least two levels of engagement that make a difference in conflict settings can be distinguished. At the micro-level, the level of the individual or family, are largely private transfers within and among transnational families, involving individuals or small groupings of kin and friends. This is the most common and principal focus of most efforts of members of diaspora groups. In conflict settings these transfers are largely palliative, enabling those back home in conflict zones to survive or cope: they essentially sustain individuals, families and communities during and after conflict and displacement rather than transforming their conditions of life. These transfers usually comprise modest movements of resources individually, but in the aggregate they amount to a substantial shift of resources from diaspora members in affluent countries to poorer, conflict-ridden parts of the world. At the meso-level are more public and collective transfers, sometimes supporting insurgents and sometimes supporting more philanthropic community-level interventions such as rebuilding or re-equipping schools, hospitals and clinics through home town associations, old school organizations, and churches, mosques or temples. Each transfer of this kind is likely to be larger than typical private remittances to individuals and households, but in aggregate terms they are much smaller than remittances are collectively. While sometimes such interventions do make a difference to local communities trying to recover, their impact is likely to be more symbolic than substantive. Nevertheless, taking remittances and collective transfers together, diasporas can be seen as providing elements of social security or a safety net that, prior to the neo-liberal turn, might have been seen as falling to the state to provide (Mohan, 2008): in this way diasporas have arguably become significant both as part of transnational civil society and as providers of transnational social security for kin and community back home.

Diasporas formed as a result of conflicts have then arguably emerged and consolidated themselves as integral to the current world order in the sometimes contradictory ways in which they engage in their conflict-ridden homeland societies. While at times they support insurgents and contribute to the prolongation of conflict, they often also help to ameliorate the effects of conflict, and arguably the vagaries of globalization, through their part in the provision of transnational social security – the remittances and collective transfers they make to individuals, households, families and communities in conflict-ridden territories. If, as we may expect, conflict becomes more common as a result of the current economic crisis, and as the resources for and effectiveness of humanitarian aid shrink, diasporas may find themselves called upon increasingly to help their co-nationals in distress in conflict-ridden societies. The shape of recovery and development that results from diaspora engagement will continue to be a matter of contestation.

Notes

*The author is grateful for comments on earlier versions of this chapter by Thomas Faist and the Transnationalization and Development Cooperation Group at Bielefeld University, as well as for critical comments by participants in 2008–9 at conferences in Trondheim, Groningen, Penang, Oxford and Columbia University in New York.

1. This work encompasses fieldwork by the author in Sri Lanka and Tamil diaspora locations since 1998, in Somaliland and Somali diaspora locations since 2002, and largely secondary research on the Afghan case since 2000.
2. This section draws on Van Hear (2006c).
3. This critique has recently been trenchantly restated by Klein (2007) in her exposition of what she calls 'the shock doctrine' and 'disaster capitalism'.
4. This can involve transfers made for marriage and associated migration. See Fuglerud (1999) on the complex transnational transformation of dowry circulation between the Tamil diaspora and those left at home.

References

Al-Ali, N., Black, R. and Koser, K. (2001) 'Refugees and Transnationalism: the Experience of Bosnians and Eritreans in Europe', *Journal of Ethnic and Migration Studies*, 27 (4), 615–634.

Anderson, B. (1998) 'Long Distance Nationalism,' in B. Anderson (ed.), *The Spectre of Comparisons: Nationalism, Southeast Asia and the World* (London: Verso), 58–74.

Bhatia, M. and Goodhand, J., with Atmar, H., Pain, A. and Suleman, M. (2003) 'Profits and Poverty: Aid Livelihoods and Conflict in Afghanistan', in S. Collinson (ed.), *Power, Livelihoods and Conflict: Case Studies in Political Economy Analysis for Humanitarian Action,* HPG Report 13 (London: Humanitarian Policy Group, Overseas Development Institute [ODI]).

Collier, P. and Hoeffler, A. (2004) 'Greed and Grievance in Civil War', *Oxford Economic Papers*, 56 (4), 563–595.

Collinson, S. (2003) *Power, Livelihoods and Conflict: Case Studies in Political Economy Analysis for Humanitarian Action*, HPG Report 13 (London: Humanitarian Policy Group, Overseas Development Institute [ODI]).

DfID (2006) *Preventing Violent Conflict* (London: Department for International Development [DfID]).

Deshingkar, P. and Start, D. (2003) *Seasonal Migration for Livelihoods In India: Coping, Accumulation and Exclusion,* Overseas Development Institute working paper 220 (London: Overseas Development Institute [ODI]).

Doornbos, M. (2002) 'State Collapse and Fresh Starts: Some Critical Reflections', *Development and Change*, 33 (5), 797–815.

Duffield, M. (2001) *Global Governance and the New Wars: The Merging of Development and Security* (London and New York: Zed Books).

Faist, T. (2008) 'Migrants as Transnational Development Agents: An Inquiry into the Newest Round of the Migration–Development Nexus', *Population, Space and Place*, 14, 21–42.

Fine, B. (2001) *Social Capital versus Social Theory: Political Economy and Social Science at the Turn of the Millennium* (London: Routledge).

Fuglerud, Ø. (1999) *Life on the Outside: The Tamil Diaspora and Long Distance Nationalism* (London: Pluto Press).

Gamlen, A. (2008) 'The Migration State and the Modern Political Imagination', *Political Geography*, 27 (8), 840–856.

Guarnizo, L. (2003) 'The Economics of Transnational Living', *International Migration Review*, 37 (3), 666–699.

Horst, C. (2006) *Transnational Nomads: How Somalis Cope with Refugee Life in the Dadaab Camps of Kenya* (Oxford: Berghahn).

Kapur, D. (2005) 'Remittances: the New Development Mantra?', in S. Maimbo and D. Ratha (eds), *Remittances: Development Impact and Future Prospects* (Washington, DC: World Bank).

Kapur, D. (2007) 'The Janus Face of Diasporas', in B. J. Merz, L. Chen, and P. Geithner (eds), *Diasporas and Development* (Cambridge, MA and London: Harvard University Press).

Klein, N. (2007) *The Shock Doctrine: The Rise of Disaster Capitalism* (London: Penguin).

Le Billon, P. (2000) 'The Political Economy of War: What Relief Agencies Need To Know', Overseas Development Institute Humanitarian Practice Network Paper 33 (London: Overseas Development Institute [ODI]).

Lindley, A. (2007) 'The Early Morning Phone Call: Remittances from a Refugee Diaspora', Centre on Migration, Policy and Society Working Paper No. 47 (Oxford: COMPAS).

Lippman, B. (2004). 'The 4Rs: the Way Ahead?' *Forced Migration Review*, 21 (September), 9–11.

Maimbo, S. and Ratha, D. (eds) (2005) *Remittances: Development Impact and Future Prospects* (Washington, DC: World Bank).

Maxwell, S. (2005) 'The Washington Consensus Is Dead! Long Live the Meta-narrative!', Overseas Development Institute working paper 243 (London: Overseas Development Institute [ODI]).

Mehler, A. and Ribaux, C. (2000) *Crisis Prevention and Conflict Management in Technical Cooperation: An Overview of the National and International Debate* (Eschborn: Deutsche Gesellschaft für Technische Zusammenarbeit [GTZ]).

Mohan, G. (2008) 'Making Neo-liberal States of Development: The Ghanaian Diaspora and the Politics Of Homelands', *Environment and Planning D: Society and Space*, 26 (3), 464–479.

Monsutti, A. (2005) *War and Migration: Social Networks and Economic Strategies of the Hazaras of Afghanistan* (London and New York: Routledge).

Moore, D. (2000) 'Leveling the Playing Fields and Embedding Illusions: "Post-Conflict" Discourse And Neo-Liberal "Development" In War-torn Africa', *Review of African Political Economy*, 83, 11–28.

Orjuela, C. (2003) 'War, Peace and the Sri Lankan Diaspora', in A. Swain (ed.), *Diasporas, Armed Conflicts, and Peacebuilding in Their Homelands* (Uppsala: Uppsala University).

Smith, H. and Stares, P. (eds) (2007) *Diasporas in Conflict: Peace-makers or Peace-wreckers?* (Tokyo: United Nations University Press).

Stiglitz, J. (1998) 'More Instruments and Broader Goals: Moving Towards the Post-Washington Consensus', World Institute for Development Economics Research Annual Lecture, January 1998 (Helsinki: United National University).

UNDP (2001) *Human Development Report 2001 Somalia* (Nairobi: United Nations Development Programme [UNDP] Somalia Country Office).

Van Hear, N. (1998) *New Diasporas: The Mass Exodus, Dispersal and Regrouping of Migrant Communities* (London: Routledge/University College London Press).

——— (2002) 'Sustaining Societies under Strain: Remittances as a Form of Transnational Exchange in Sri Lanka and Ghana', in K. Koser and N. Al-Ali (eds), *New Approaches to Migration: Transnational Communities and the Transformation of Home* (London and New York: Routledge).

——— (2003) *From 'Durable Solutions' to 'Transnational Relations': Home and Exile Among Refugee Diasporas*, UNHCR Evaluation and Policy Analysis Unit, New Issues in Refugee Research, Working Paper 83 (Geneva: UNHCR).

——— (2006a) '"I Went As Far As My Money Would Take Me": Conflict, Forced Migration and Class', in F. Crepeau et al. (eds), *Forced Migration and Global Processes: A View from Forced Migration Studies* (Lanham: Lexington/Rowman & Littlefield).

——— (2006b) 'Refugees in Diaspora: From Durable Solutions to Transnational Relations', *Refuge*, 23 (1), 9–15.

——— (2006c) 'Re-casting Cocieties in Conflict', in N. Van Hear and C. McDowell (eds), *Catching Fire: Containing Forced Migration in a Volatile World* (Lanham: Lexington/Rowman & Littlefield).

——— (2007) 'Pulled Every Which Way: Refugee Responsibilities in Today's Britain', Commentary for the Consultation on Refugee Rights and Responsibilities by the Information Centre about Asylum and Refugees (ICAR), March 2007.

——— (2009) 'The Rise of Refugee Diasporas', *Current History*, 108 (717), 180–185.

——— and Nyberg-Sørensen, N. (eds) (2003) *The Migration–Development Nexus* (Geneva: International Organization for Migration [IOM]).

World Bank (1997) *A Framework for World Bank Involvement in Post-conflict Reconstruction* (Washington, DC: World Bank).

——— (1998) *Post-conflict Reconstruction: The Role of the World Bank* (Washington, DC: World Bank).

——— (2002) *World Bank Group Work In Low Income Countries under Stress: A Task Force Report* (Washington, DC: World Bank).

——— (2008) Fragile States: 'Toughest Development Challenge of Our Era', Press Release, 19 September 2008.

5

Business as Usual? Urban Actors and Transnational Investments in Accra, Ghana*

Lothar Smith

Many businesses around Accra have foreign links. For some their link is immediately clear, visible in their exotic, foreign names, or in the products they sell, such as Italian floor tiles or foreign fashion items, or secondhand cars displaying bumper stickers that indicate the country they came from. Yet other businesses provide services to customers seeking connections to the outside world, such as communication centres. Beyond these kinds of businesses are many others that also have strong transnational connections, albeit more subliminally, as in the case of locally oriented businesses such as bars or restaurants, which were set up with the help of a loan from a migrant.

There is general recognition by migration scholars that of all remittances sent by migrants, a large share is meant for businesses (De Haas, 2003; Hamann, 2000). For instance, Mazzucato et al. (2005) have calculated that 28 per cent of all remittances sent to Ghana by Amsterdam-based Ghanaians were meant for businesses. These investments were mainly located in the major cities of Accra and Kumasi. According to Asiedu (2005) and Diko and Tipple (1992), unskilled Ghanaians in particular go abroad to accumulate savings to invest in houses and businesses in Ghana. For them few opportunities exist to generate such savings by staying in Ghana. Asiedu (2005) goes so far as to conclude that there is a direct relationship between the length of time spent abroad by migrants and their objective to accumulate sufficient capital to realize certain investments in Ghana.

With the notable exception of the slave trade, Ghana has known large-scale emigration of its citizens to destinations outside West Africa only from the 1980s onward. After independence in 1957 Ghana enjoyed an initial period of economic prosperity and political stability which compared well with situations in other newly independent countries of Africa and resulted in immigration of migrants from its neighbour countries. However, in the decades that followed, economic decline set in (Aryeteeh and Fosu, 2008). By the mid-1980s, Ghana had fallen into severe debt, leaving the Rawlings government with little option other than to apply for the Structural Adjustment Program (SAP) of the World Bank and International Monetary Fund.

The SAP, with its primary focus on macro-economic adjustments, gave little attention to changes at the micro level (Herbst, 1991; Kaag et al., 2004; Riddell, 1997; Stiglitz, 2003). Thus, local businesses generally suffered under the liberal policies introduced under the SAP. Clark (1999) argues that economic reforms under the SAP resulted in declining profits for local businesses, due to increased competition from foreign businesses. The situation worsened with large-scale retrenchment of government employees, who turned to the informal, small-scale business sector for alternative employment. Clark (1999) concludes that in general terms the SAP had adverse effects on the urban population and important repercussions on rural–urban relationships, as urban actors diluted their economic relationships with rural actors, struggling to meet own needs (Smith, 2007). The general decline of livelihood opportunities in Ghana during the 1980s led many to leave Ghana for Europe and North America, seeking 'greener pastures'.

The changed economic climate brought about by the SAP did result in a gradual stabilization of the national economy. This stable environment, helped further by trade liberalization policies meant to encourage foreign investment in Ghana, encouraged migrants to invest in Ghana. The liberalization of foreign currency in Ghana, in 1984, further promoted their interest to invest in their country of origin. Namely, the effectuation of this policy allowed Ghanaians to import and possess foreign currency in Ghana. This helped them realize their investments, but also had the effect of making them less vulnerable. On the one hand this related to chances of reduced income loss due to inflation of the Ghanaian currency, and on the other hand to economic or political instability as they would always be able to withdraw investments if necessary (Parker et al., 1995; Yeboah, 2000).[1]

To expand foreign investment in Ghana the national government set up the Ghana Investment Promotion Centre (GIPC) in 1994. Initially the GIPC tried to gain the interest of foreign investors, notably Pan-African movements in the United States. However, following research into cases of other developing countries with nationals abroad, notably India, the GIPC shifted its focus toward Ghanaian migrants, and the role they could play for Ghana's economy. To pursue this change in course the GIPC organized a Homecoming Summit in 2001, with the purpose of providing a platform to discuss the potential role of Ghanaians abroad for Ghana. The event attracted a few thousand Ghanaian migrants from around the world. As a follow-up to this event, the GIPC, Bank of Ghana and the commercial banks took policy measures to encourage Ghanaian migrants to invest their overseas earnings. These went beyond the economic policies already effectuated under the SAP, and included giving political recognition to Ghanaian migrants through voting rights, providing better monitoring of remittance services, and reducing complex import regulations (personal communication, Mr Filson, research director GIPC, 15 January 2003).

The contribution of remittances to local economies through business investments is increasingly recognized and welcomed by national governments, notably when these remittances are 'production' oriented. Therein a strong debate has arisen in Ghana over the extent to which current business incentives of Ghanaian migrants represent desirable contributions to local economic development. At a national level criticism relates particularly to the orientation of migrants toward the urban economy (notably Accra), and within it the trade and service sectors, rather than toward investments in sectors that would add value to Ghana's natural resources.

While certain levels of control over remittances and migrant investments have had the interest of academics and policymakers for various decades (see Penninx and van Renselaar, 1978; Van Velzen, 1977), the conceptualization and implementation of policies to achieve desirable transnational investments for the benefit of society as a whole have largely failed. This relates especially to sustained misconceptions of policymakers, but also academics, about the meaning and role of migrant investments (cf. De Haas, 2005; Skeldon, 2004). In the first place there is a general lack of recognition of what led the majority of migrants to migrate; namely to accumulate savings for their own benefit. Second, too little consideration is given to how migrants achieve investments in their country of origin, notably while they are still abroad. Third, while much attention is given to migrants and their abilities and incentives to realize transnational investments in their country of origin, little attention is given to the actors involved with these investments in the country of origin. While migrants are often the primary financial investors, their investments are seldom realizable without strategic support from those they involve in their country of origin.

In this chapter the second and third misconceptions are addressed by focusing on the roles of urban actors in transnational investments of migrants. Thereby insights are provided in how transnational investments in businesses take place, establish which social processes guide these incentives, and arrive at a conclusion whether these investments imply a continuation or transformation of existing social configurations.

How migrant investments in business activities in Accra are significant for sustaining pre-migration social configurations, or alternatively, for transforming these, is the focus of the next section. Following this the actual involvement of urban actors in transnational entrepreneurial activities with migrants is discussed. This helps to establish a typology with which to differentiate various modes of transnational engagement in business activities. This typology seeks to capture the main modes of engagement, as derived from data collected through research conducted with 38 respondents in Accra with ties to migrants living in the Netherlands and elsewhere abroad concerning a wide range of economic domains, including business. Of all 38 respondents 22 were active in transnational business activities (with a further 11 involved in local business activities). These 22 respondents and their transnational business activities with migrants are the focus of this chapter. Case studies are provided which represent different types of business engagements between urban actors and migrants, helping to grasp how the economic influences of migrants, even within one sector, relate to a wide variety of arrangements, some continuing pre-migration relationships, while others take on hybrid or new formats. In the concomitant discussion the relationship between different types of transnational business activities and sets of characteristics concerning relevant forms of capital and particular socio-cultural configurations are examined. The concluding section of the chapter considers the degree to which transnational business investments represent continuity or mark important new developments in the field of migration and development.

The role of socio-cultural configurations and locality

With regard to the relationship between migration and development, notably where this concerns the influence of migrants on the urban economy, two issues dominate the debate in Ghana. The first is the productivity of migrant savings, raising the concern that migrants misspend their savings on so-called consumptive activities, building urban mansions, buying cars and organizing lavish ceremonies, rather than channelling their savings into 'productive' investments (Black et al., 2003).

The second issue concerns the quality and sustainability of the so-called productive investments that migrants do realize, particularly with respect to their contribution to the Ghanaian economy. The core argument here is that larger businesses would be better suited to strengthening Ghana's economy than small businesses, because they may be geared to higher levels of investment in new niches that are likely to remain economically sustainable, in contrast to small businesses that often copy one another, with rapidly declining profits as soon as the market becomes saturated. Yet the reality is that most businesses in Accra, including those of migrants, are small to medium in size (Private Enterprise Foundation, 2003). The preference for such small to medium enterprises relates to a number of factors. The most often mentioned one is lack of trust between investors to co-invest in a single business. This relates to a general fear that at any time, and especially during times of crisis, one of these owners might succumb to social pressure from outside the firm, notably the family, and deplete the firm of its capital, in order to meet other needs. There is also a disinclination to invest in high-risk activities because of fear that a government might suddenly introduce policies, such as income taxes, that would strongly reduce the returns to investment. Finally, there is strong distrust of governments for use of patronage when allocating contracts for public service investments. For those wanting to establish companies that depend heavily on the state for contracts, the risk of not being able to gain the favour of the government would simply be too high (Collier and Gunning, 1999).

The two issues raised interrelate through a mutual concern for the role of migrant investments in Ghana's economy: alleviating poverty and boosting various sectors of the economy, such as agriculture. In both arguments it is suggested that to attain such objectives current investments of migrants in businesses need to change, as they are insufficiently innovative. The apparent unwillingness of migrants to change the nature of their investments confirms the perception that migrants are entrepreneurs by default rather than by choice. They invest in businesses primarily because they see few alternatives for sustaining their livelihoods upon returning to Ghana (Ammassari, 2004; Black et al., 2003).

The concerns raised insufficiently acknowledge the actual impact of migrant business investments on the urban and national economy, creating countless jobs and producing all kinds of trickle-down effects to other sectors (Asiedu, 2005; Black et al., 2003). The greatly reduced opportunities for state employment, as a result of liberal policies introduced under the SAP, have made migrants and their business investments key actors in the urban economy. More fundamentally, this debate fails to take into account the role of the particularity of the urban economy, in this case Accra, as well as the specific socio-economic configurations associated with transnational business investments.

In this context the concept of social transformation may be of help. It usually refers to fundamental changes in the organization of societal life that can be conceptualized through analyses of changes in social spaces, that is, spatial dimensions in connection with social networks (Faist and Reisenauer, 2009). Such an analysis may help to establish the position of migration as an integral component within larger processes of globalization. This embedded position of migration in globalization not only relates to the way social configurations are shaped due to possibilities for increased mobility within transnational configurations through global technologies (notably in the field of communication); it also relates to neo-liberal policy regimes, which have shifted responsibility of economic and social development from states to individuals. Therein migrants are accorded increasingly important positions in their societies of origin. Both global dimensions, albeit in different ways and at different levels, influence the shape of the migration–development nexus. With regard to the second dimension the role of the neo-liberal agenda in the migration–development nexus has already been discussed. Primary attention in this chapter, however, is paid to the former dimension, that is, to exploring whether, and how, migrant investments in the economy of Accra change the shape of social configurations, notably for urban actors.

With regard to the conceptualization of transnational social spaces or fields, Nina Glick Schiller argues earlier in this book (Chapter 2), for the need: (1) to take the networks encapsulated by transnational fields, rather than ethnicity or nationality, as the conceptual framework with which to study cross-border flows; and (2) to pay attention to the specific role of locality within these transnational social fields. In her view, this helps to understand the position of migrants as part of capital reproduction processes. Through their choices with regard to the destination of remittances they send, they become agents that can reshape localities.

These arguments resonate in this research, as this analysis also seeks to understand changes in social configurations that can be expected to arise out of the choice of migrants to locate certain investments in Accra. This decision not only has implications in terms of the geographical shift of investments, namely in the urban rather than rural economy. It also arises out of the explicit choice about whom to involve in these investments in Accra. Migrants may, for instance, give preference to friends rather than family. This points to an important, possibly fundamental, shift in the relationships which migrants maintain with their countries of origin, notably their (extended) families, kin and others in the hometown. While cultural units such as the extended family have always been contested (Clark, 1999), they did provide default social configurations and mechanisms through which lives and livelihoods could be organized. Following migration to foreign destinations, however, migrants began to find the principles of these social configurations increasingly problematic, mainly due to the dramatic change of their status. With the expectation that migration would produce major economic benefits, families, kin and hometowns readily assigned increased responsibility to migrants, expecting them to provide financial support through remittances. Migrants who succumbed to such social pressure found it increasingly difficult to achieve the personal goals with which they had set out in the first place (Mazzucato, 2008). For the Ashanti migrants in this research, Accra then provided an opportunity to achieve projects in Ghana as Accra was physically distant enough from their region of origin to be also economically detached, notably if investments were realized with urban actors who were sufficiently autonomous themselves from other Ghana-based actors who were also part of the social networks of migrants. At the same time the achievement of these projects did not necessarily imply a neglect or abandonment of ties with their extended families and others in the region of origin, as migrants continued to perceive such ties as important (Mazzucato et al., 2006). However, urban investments could generate means to provide migrants, from abroad or upon return to Ghana, the opportunity to commit themselves to those in their region of origin, on their own terms, without sustained detrimental effects.

Methodology

This chapter draws on research conducted under the auspices of the Ghana TransNet research programme. In this research programme a simultaneous matched methodology was used, whereby research was conducted in three significant geographical locations within social networks of migrants (Mazzucato, 2009). These locations were Amsterdam, an important European destination for Ghanaians; the Ashanti Region, from where many Ghanaian migrants in Amsterdam originated; and

Accra, Ghana's capital and largest urban economy, an important destination for remittances. The transnational networks of migrants provided direct links between the three sub-projects. This chapter provides findings from the Accra project, in which 38 urban actors, who had ties to Amsterdam-based migrants, were studied. Their selection had followed from the selection of migrants in Amsterdam. The 33 migrants selected in Amsterdam provided a representation of the diversity, in terms of their social, migration, and network characteristics, among a larger migrant population.

The simultaneous matched sample methodology used in the research programme enabled a continual and direct comparison of findings between the three sub-projects, enhanced through the application of the same set of quantitative and qualitative research tools. These tools included a network survey, a monthly transaction study, and life-histories with respondents which focused on the changing role of relationships within respondents' networks over the course of time (Mazzucato, 2009). Through these efforts insights into the respective roles and interests of actors in all three locations vis-à-vis one another for a range of social, cultural and economic domains could be compared and contrasted. This approach helped to establish that, in particular, transnational relationships are seldom static or fixed, a conclusion concurring with Faist (2000). Nor do the transnational flows in these relations just 'happen'. Instead they result from often active, complex and often strategic arrangements. The range of tools used, together with a simultaneous matched sample approach, not only helped to establish the scale and nature of transnational flows between migrants and urban and rural actors in Ghana respectively, but also, more fundamentally, how and why these flows took place.

As mentioned earlier, of the 38 respondents studied, 33 were active in business activities. Their business activities differed immensely in their nature, economic scale, geographical scale (notably regarding the role played by transnational ties to migrants) and the role of the respondents themselves. Table 5.1 provides an overview of the roles of respondents in businesses.

While this overview provides an indication of the kinds of involvement urban actors have in businesses, it does not provide insight as to the extent to which these activities concern migrants. Nor can it establish the significance of transnational relationships in these activities. To provide such insights a second typology is set out in the next section that differentiates between transnational business activities on the basis of three main empirical dimensions: (1) duration or extent of

Table 5.1 Business activities of respondents

Position	Number of respondents	Business types
Business owners	22	Wholesale store, retail store, drinking bar, hotel, travel agency, secondhand car business, transport service (taxis, tro-tros [share taxis]), real estate firm, construction company, agricultural export firm, agro-chemical supplies, construction supplies, beauty salon, communication centre, water/ice distributor, hawking
Management	5	Law firm, education institute, beauty salon, taxi service, commercial bank, industrial chemicals supplier, construction company
Other position	6	Handling agent (air freight), clearance agent (harbour), transport services (driver)

Source: Monthly transaction studies, respondent interviews (2003–4).

the transnational engagement; (2) predominant direction of support in this activity (between migrant and urban actor); and (3) the nature of the activity, that is, the mode of transnational involvement. By exploring transnational activities between urban actors and migrants along these three dimensions insight is sought into more fundamental issues such as the consequences of how they are manifested – who is involved, who is not, their socio-cultural meaning, and the role of human and financial capital of urban actors.

Following the discussion of the main types, seven case studies are presented, to help establish how the different types constitute different modes of transnational relationships. By addressing the extent to which these form continuities of pre-migration relationships, or rather develop only after migration, it is also possible to establish whether, and how, these entrepreneurial activities produce societal transformations.

Deconstructing transnational business investments: a typology

As was explained earlier, this chapter seeks to provide insight into the roles and positions of urban actors in migrant investments in businesses in Accra. By taking urban actors and their objectives as the starting point, the range of ways in which migrants and urban actors are involved with each other in business activities can be established, providing insight into the nature of these relations, for instance in terms of reciprocity and agency.

The earlier overview of respondents involved in business activities gave some indication of the involvement of urban actors in businesses. However, it did not reveal how these activities related to migrants. Table 5.2 explicitly examines transnational business activities of urban actors, thereby differentiating between: (1) the extent of the role of the transnational relationship between migrant and urban actor for business activities; (2) the direction of this transnational relationship; and (3) the mode of the transnational activity, that is, the way in which the transnational influence took place. These three dimensions emerged as particularly relevant from in-depth interviews held with respondents during one and a half years of fieldwork (2002–4). On the basis of these three dimensions a typology of transnational engagements can be developed, with which to structure the discussion of the extent to which transnational activities between urban actors and migrants produce social transformations.

In Table 5.2 a clear distinction is made between duration and importance of transnational influences on business activities of respondents. This division does not necessarily equate to the overall involvement of respondents in business. What it does point to is the relative importance of transnational relationships for their economic impact on business activities of respondents. The table also differentiates transnational engagement by longevity of investment, that is, it distinguishes between transnational exchanges limited to a few transactions and forms that are more continuous. As will also be set out in the case studies below, this differentiation is important as it relates to different kinds of economic rationales, and their associated socio-cultural configurations.

With the case studies that follow the meaning of transnational business activities for different urban actors can be established and contrasted. This relates to how transnational business activities take place, but also to why transnational business activities are important for urban actors.

Mark: supporting migrants for the benefit of the nation

While Mark is now a decisive member of Accra's elite – with a mansion in up-market Legon North, along with various businesses – as well as a prominent sponsor and member of the charismatic church he attends, his roots are modest. Coming from a poor family, based in a rural town in the Ashanti Region, Mark worked in various towns in Ghana for many

Table 5.2 Role of transnational ties in respondent business activities[2]

Extent of role	Direction of influence	Mode of transnational involvement	Number of respondens	Case study
Limited or temporary role	Respondent ↓ Migrant	*Temporary support to migrants*: These respondents gave advice to migrants on developments in the Ghanaian market, but also legal and organizational issues. Some were also involved in first stages of businesses migrants were setting up in Ghana, prior to their return.	5	Mark
	Respondent ↑ Migrant	*Temporary support from migrants*: Two respondents received remittances from migrants on a regular basis. These helped sustain their businesses. The motivation for migrants to provide support often related to the role the respondent played in other domains, for example, caring for children or parents of the migrant. Two other respondents depended on migrants to send stock with which they could run their businesses.	4	Angelina
	Respondent ↑↓ Migrant	*Indirect business involvement*: Three respondents were engaged in businesses linking them indirectly to migrants through import and sale of secondhand goods. While they had ties with migrants, these contacts did not provide them a sufficient flow of goods for their businesses. Thus they had to rely on local actors, selling goods received from migrants on their behalf.	3	Douglas

Important or sustained role	Respondent ↓ Migrant	*Sustained support to migrants*: Three respondents managed businesses for migrants. Although, they received salaries for their efforts, their strategic role in managing businesses of migrants classified them as giving support to migrants.	3	Kenneth
	Respondent ↑ Migrant	*Capital injection from migrants*: Three respondents received a sum of money from migrant friends/family to help them start a business. The migrants did not ask for a repayment of the loan provided, nor a share in the profits of the business.	3	Grace
		Anticipation of capital injection from migrants: Two respondents sought sponsorship from migrants for their business activities. One respondent wanted to join the trade in secondhand clothes to get a basic income. The other wanted to become involved with real estate development.	2	Kwasi

Source: Monthly transaction studies, respondent interviews (2003–4).

years, seeking to save enough money to go abroad. Upon doing so he migrated to Canada, where he lived for 10 years, slowly accumulating savings that would enable him to set up businesses in Ghana that would comfortably sustain him and his family. Upon return to Ghana he established himself in Accra, thereby avoiding his extended family and their endless requests for support. Nonetheless, in recognition of the poverty of his extended family, he built a completely new family house for them, in the hometown.

Mark exports medicinal seed to Europe and North America which requires him to meet with his business partners there. During these trips he also looks up Ghanaian migrants, notably members of branches of the charismatic church he attends. Some of these migrants he considers as his most trusted friends. At the same time, Mark adds that, not unlike his business relationships in Ghana, his business relations with Ghanaians abroad are, at times, problematic. In a conversation he related how he discovered at one time that some of his migrant friends had been cheating him out of business. They had pretended to act on his behalf in negotiations with a Belgian company to get a contract to supply seed but, in the course of their negotiations, had indicated that they could provide seed through other contacts, at much lower prices.

In the same vein, it is Mark's conviction that migrants who are interested in setting up businesses in Ghana must be very careful about whom they involve, and will need to find out how dependable and trustworthy their potential business partners are:

> In Ghana it is very difficult to do business. People more often than not are greedy; they think of the short-term profit from cheating their partners and others instead of having honesty and trustworthiness as their values and thinking of the long term. (Interview, 12 May 2004)

Because of his general distrust of Ghanaians as business partners, Mark avoids becoming heavily committed as a partner to migrants in business activities. Yet, at the same time, his migrant friends are always welcome to stay with him when they come to Accra, and he readily provides advice on market developments, stores and arranges the sale of their goods, or checks on the status of businesses they have set up. In his view they involve him in their activities because they can see with their own eyes that he is well off, which makes him less likely to misuse migrant resources for own purposes. Furthermore, the business activities he has set up are generally innovative and profitable, showing his expertise in the market in Ghana. Mark's own reasons to be involved come down to his ambition to make Ghana prosper as a nation:

> I want to make people prosper, I want to contribute to the progress of humanity, help people become comfortable and make progress in life. (Interview, 12 May 2004)

It is Mark's vision that Ghana becomes a 'first class' country whose citizens are regarded with respect rather than pity. This means overcoming the preoccupation with things derived from Western society, especially if these are cast-off, as in the case of secondhand goods. If he can contribute to this, by supporting business initiatives of migrant friends that benefit Ghana's economy in a structural way, this is enough reward in itself. That his support of migrants also generated direct benefits became clear when his brother passed away in 2003. On that occasion his migrant friends provided him with substantial financial support, which he could not get elsewhere, helping him finance his brother's hospital and funeral expenses without him needing to impose on his business activities.

In sum, this case presented a clear case of a transnational cooperation between migrants and urban actors where the latter invested in the transnational relationship mainly for the betterment of the migrant and, in this case, also the nation as a whole.

Angelina: mixing business and social commitments

Angelina runs a 'small plastics' store in the multiple-floor Kaneshi Market. She became involved in this business in 1997, when she was summoned to Accra by a sister, who asked her to take over the plastics store, which belongs to an aunt based in London, as she was about to join her husband in the Netherlands. When her sister was about to leave Ghana, she asked Angelina if she could also take care of her child. Angelina readily agreed to this, not least because it also gave her certain agency to ensure future support from her sister.

While the plastics store gives Angelina a regular income, it has never prospered much and hardly allowed her to accumulate savings. Angelina attributes the limited success of the business wholly to the unwillingness of her aunt in London to invest in the expansion of the business, despite being its owner. Angelina: 'She has always washed her hands of the store.' However, because her aunt is the owner, Angelina has only usufructuary rights and cannot sell the shop to anyone else to begin a business elsewhere.

On various occasions, Angelina has had to call on her migrant sister and husband to support her with the business, advancing money to help her restock it. When asked why this stock had depleted, surely a sign that the business was not profitable, she explained that both daily and less regular needs competed with the store for her financial resources. Each month she needed to deduct money from the business funds to pay for food, clothes, education fees, and donations in church and at funerals. This meant that she sometimes depleted the funds required to run the business. When asked how she was able to secure the financial support of her sister and husband for the business she provided the example of Christmas in 2003. At that time her stock had once again been depleted, and her financial means were insufficient to pay the deposit asked by her supplier. Hence, when her brother-in-law called her from Amsterdam, she told him:

> I know that you must have some money for a particular programme [the school fees for the next term of the two children]. Can you not release this money to me more immediately? (Interview, 5 February 2004)

Her plea was urgent, and she promised that she would repay the amount in increments. She explained to her brother-in-law that she was asking for only a short-term loan, and that it was because of her care and dedication to their child and other family members that she had arrived at the present situation. They were convinced by these arguments and lent her the amount she asked for.

The arguments provided by Angelina intricately interwove the commitment of the migrants to their family, including their own child, in Ghana, with her own needs to keep the business going. She felt that their financial support not only rewarded her commitment to their family, to the extent that this had been undertaken at the expense of her business; she also felt that it was provided to ensure that she was able to sustain her role.

In sum this case presents a transnational business relationship in which migrants returned the support they had received from an urban actor in other domains, such as care, through an investment (in this case in the form of a soft loan) in the business of the urban actor.

Douglas: searching for the right transnational ties

Some respondents ran businesses strongly influenced by migrants but without that influence resulting from direct links with migrants. This was the case for Douglas, who ran a secondhand car dealership for 'home-used' cars imported from Europe by Ghanaian migrants.[3]

When discussing his business situation, Douglas complained that he was not selling enough cars. This was not due so much to a lack of demand, but rather because his 'network was not good'. Douglas felt that he would be able to improve his business substantially if he could associate with Ghanaian migrants in Belgium, Germany or the Netherlands, favourite markets for sourcing secondhand cars, who would be prepared to be on the lookout for models that sold well in Ghana, sending them off to him to sell on their behalf. Yet, despite having an extensive social network of friends and family abroad, none shared his interest, or possessed the necessary capital, to become such a partner in the business.

His quest to link up with migrants who would be interested was also hampered by migrants' distrust of Ghana-based businessmen, echoing the words of Mark in the first case. With insufficient trust being at the heart of the matter, and Douglas too financially constrained to go abroad himself to select, buy and export cars, he had to rely on cars brought to him by local persons, usually cars recently imported by migrants. For such cars he could take only a five per cent commission on their sale, producing much lower profits than cars he could sell through direct links with migrants.

The case of Douglas provides a clear example of urban actors who are in a position in which their business activities are clearly influenced by migrants, yet who have to rely on indirect rather than direct ties to migrants to sustain these activities.

Kenneth: playing out the role of the trusted friend

For a few years Kenneth has been running a taxi on behalf of his friend Darkwa, who lives in Amsterdam. This partnership in the taxi is the outcome of a relationship that has gradually intensified over the course of 10 years. The friendship of Kenneth and Darkwa began in 1994 when they met at a funeral ceremony in a rural town in the Ashanti Region, where Darkwa worked as a schoolteacher. As Darkwa intended to go abroad, to the Netherlands, he regularly travelled to Accra to sort out his paperwork. During these visits he would always visit Kenneth, and thus a friendship developed. This relationship intensified in the final year prior to Darkwa's departure, when Darkwa also came to live in Accra. When Darkwa left in 1998 he asked Kenneth to look after his wife and children, as they could not join him immediately in the Netherlands.

Kenneth earned sufficient income at the time to be able to take on that responsibility, and felt that this responsibility might further cement their relationship, despite the physical distance between them.

When Darkwa had arrived in the Netherlands he began to call Kenneth regularly. This was a clear sign to Kenneth that they were indeed close, and he felt sure that it would only be a matter of time before Darkwa would deliver on the promise he made just before his departure, namely that he would send him a car to run on their behalf as a taxi. By 2002, four years after leaving Ghana, Darkwa sent Kenneth a message that he was shipping a car off to Ghana. This car would not only provide Kenneth with a steady income when put to use as a taxi, but also formed a useful income for Darkwa, supplementing the remittances he sent, to pay for the daily expenditures, education costs and housing rent for his children and their caretaker. Kenneth had anticipated this message, expecting that Darkwa would ultimately reward his investments in their friendship by sending the taxi for him to use, at some point in time. Beyond the taxi he also expected that Darkwa would soon ask him also to supervise the construction of his house in Accra, providing a further opportunity to supplement the income he was earning with the taxi.

A combination of characteristics typifies the transnational engagement between Kenneth and Darkwa. Trust plays a crucial role, achieved after years of commitment toward one another. The case of Kenneth and Darkwa shows how a business partnership could also bring a different result. In their case, it resulted from the combined effects of: (1) longstanding trust; (2) continual reciprocity; (3) an explicit role of Kenneth as friend rather than family member; and (4) his strategic location in Accra.

Grace: reciprocal support with migrants in business

A young woman in her mid-twenties, Grace has been engaged in an assortment of income-generating activities in and around Accra, trying to sustain her livelihood. One of the most important activities was the 'drinking spot' (a local bar) belonging to her mother. In 2002, Grace's mother had bought this business and asked Grace to join her, by 'taking care' of the kasapreko (strong alcohol) section. After thinking it over, she decided that this would be a profitable venture, boosting the income she was earning with the wholesaling of powdered drinks around the streets of Accra. However, this business incentive would require the equivalent of about one hundred euros, with which she would be able to buy a liquor licence and a first stock of liquor.

Given the fact that her mother, nor other local actors, would not lend her this money, she finally brought it up in a phone conversation with Asantewaa, a close friend in Amsterdam. She explained to her that she completely depended on her for joining her mother as co-owner of the bar. In setting out her request Grace was careful not to ask for a particular sum of money, as this would make the request easier to refuse. Instead, she simply asked for her friend's help. Within a month Asantewaa sent her one hundred euros.

Why had Asantewaa honoured Grace's request? On the one hand, Grace explains that this related to the long-term friendship she had with Asantewaa, which had continued unabated after Asantewaa had left Ghana. Over the phone they had continued to confide their personal 'secrets' as a sign of trust in each other. However, Grace was also involved in a continuous range of activities, commercial and socio-cultural in nature, in and around Accra, on behalf of Asantewaa. Thus she was also present at the funeral meeting of a deceased family member to Asantewaa, whom Grace had never met. She attended this occasion to provide Asantewaa with an independent account of the arrangements made.

What emerges from this account of the transnational relationship between Grace and Asantewaa is that the range of their transactions, including the hundred euros remitted to help Grace set up her business, seems quite unstructured; they relate to both business and social activities. In this respect this case seems quite similar to the prior case of the taxi partnership of Kenneth and Darkwa. What is fundamentally different about this relationship, however, is the role of the business for both actors. In contrast to the prior case, Asantewaa had no interest in a joint venture. Instead, Grace explained Asantewaa's support as the reward for her role in supporting Asantewaa's business activities in Accra. Concomitantly she also ensured that Grace would remain available to conduct activities on her behalf.

Kwasi: vesting hope on migrants in order to establish their own businesses

From the first occasion, Kwasi, an elderly male respondent, indicated his interest in entering the real estate business. To this end he had developed a complicated plan whereby he would sell land on the outskirts of Accra, to which he had a partial claim, to his maternal nieces in

Amsterdam. With the profit from the sale of this land, and financial benefits he expected to derive from the consequent supervision of the construction of their houses, Kwasi hoped to save enough money to set up a number of more permanent real estate businesses. The income they would generate was of crucial importance to him, as it would enable him to remain in Accra following his retirement, and not force him to return to his hometown. Without savings, despite having been abroad a number of years, and with a poor reputation among his family, whom he had largely neglected, he vested all hope in his nieces to buy the land to launch this chain of developments. Indirectly, this research, in which his nieces had identified him (amongst others) as a person to contact in Accra, might have strengthened his resolve for this project.

Ultimately his nieces had showed little interest in the land, however. The only reason he could imagine for their lack of interest was that they were not yet 'ready' to make an investment of this magnitude. In a final attempt to persuade his nieces, he had called them and warned them that further delay in their decision would mean that he would need to sell the land to other buyers, and that they were certain to face much higher prices for land at a later moment.

What is particular about this transnational relationship is the level of speculation involved. Both in Accra, but also toward his nieces, Kwasi had very little control over the decisions of others he needed to engage with for the final purpose of establishing his own business. Yet the complexity of the arrangements Kwasi had worked out, with very limited funds, shows the possible intricacy of transnational arrangements, but also the expectations of the benefits attached to these.

Colin: the role of assets and entrepreneurial insights

After completing secondary education in Kumasi, Colin came to Accra to work in his brother's chemical supplies business. Although he was able to rise to a managerial position, he still felt that he should establish a business of his own, once he had passed the age of 30. To achieve this goal, he started developing the idea of setting up a wholesale business in deep-frozen fish. This niche was relatively undeveloped, not least because of the starting capital it required. The business was therefore certain to remain profitable for some time.

Colin possessed neither the required capital to make this investment, nor adequate knowledge of the particularities to fishing industry and so he began to look out for a suitable business partner. After closely examining his social network (to quote his own words) he approached

Peter, an old classmate. Peter had left Ghana a few years ago to work in the United States. As part of his arguments to convince Peter to join him in the business venture, Colin indicated that he had capital of his own to set up the business, to supplement Peter's. Colin strategically made this point to emphasize that he was also willing, and able, to invest his own capital in the business. This would also ensure that Peter would consider him a 'serious business partner', helping to gain his interest but also securing certain negotiating power for an equal share of the profits. Peter agreed to the partnership and did not call on Colin to help pay the costs of the secondhand freezer container he had purchased and shipped off to Ghana. Had Peter demanded a financial contribution, Colin would have turned to his brother for a loan. Had his brother refused, then Colin would have lost his reputation as a trustworthy person within the 'old boys' network of his school, effectively closing off that network to him.

When the freezer arrived, Colin sold it off at a profit and remitted the money, almost US$8,000, back to Peter. This was used to buy another second-hand deep-freeze container. A few months later Colin explained that Peter had managed to acquire this second container, and that this was now on its way to Ghana. Once it arrived Peter would also come over so they could sign a formal business contract and choose a suitable location for the store, buy stock and promote the business. Thereafter Peter would return to the United States, entrusting full responsibility to Colin for the management of their business.

This case provides an example of transnational business activities in which respondents seek to engage with migrants in sustained business activities, without thereby becoming dependents of these migrants, and losing ownership of businesses. Colin, but also other respondents in similar situations, argued that to achieve partnerships, and ensure certain equality in position and benefits, it was crucial to convince migrants of their own entrepreneurial expertise. This included hinting at insights on profitable new sectors of the economy, showing managerial skills and expertise, and showing a preparedness to invest own assets.

Discussion of empirical findings

From the case studies presented in the previous section those dimensions that were key in shaping transnational business activities can be distilled. Although there was a strong relationship between these dimensions, they are treated separately in order to emphasize the importance of each of these factors.

Importance of business to urban actors

In the discussion of migrant investments in their country of origin the role of local actors, and their motivations and interests to get involved in transnational projects, is paid scant attention, despite the strategic importance of these local actors and the roles they play.

From the prior sections it has emerged that business activities constitute a major source of income for urban actors. In Table 5.1 it was made clear that 33 of all 38 respondents involved in the research were involved in business activities. Of these 33 respondents 22 depended on transnational ties for their business activities. Indeed, seven of these 22 respondents had gone abroad themselves with the specific objective of saving money to start a business in Ghana. Going abroad was one of the few opportunities available for urban actors to gain sufficient capital to establish a business, and with which also to improve their livelihoods. Of the seven respondents who went abroad to save, five had successfully set up their own businesses in Accra, two others being less successful. Six other respondents had relied on funds from migrants to establish their businesses. A few other respondents were able to draw from alternative sources of capital within Ghana to set up businesses. These sources included family capital derived from profitable cocoa sales or savings of businesses established by prior generations within families.

Most urban actors in Accra found it difficult to accumulate savings on the basis of low incomes while meeting other needs. Their incomes largely went 'from hand to mouth' – a phrase commonly used in Accra. Only a few respondents had been able to save enough money to establish their own businesses, choosing to live frugally for a number of years. In nearly all cases the businesses developed were small, and had required little capital to establish. This made them vulnerable to competition from other urban actors, reducing their profitability.

Table 5.2 focused on a number of respondents for whom relationships with migrants were crucial to start their business activities. Some of these respondents related to migrants as immediate family or significant members in the extended family, for example, maternal uncles. In their arguments they made clear that their kinship relation to the migrant, but sometimes also support they had given to the migrant in the past, was important in eliciting support. Whether their businesses would be profitable did not seem very important to migrants as they neither demanded nor showed an interest in becoming business partners in these ventures. Instead, the migrants preferred to remit a one-off sum of money to enable the respondent to set up his/her business as this would fulfil their obligations toward this family member and limit any further commitments.

Trust and social embedding

Not all urban actors were deemed equally suitable by migrants as partners for the investments they wanted to initiate in Accra. One factor of importance was the type of relationship through which transnational business activities were established, notably the difference between friendship and family. Thus it emerged that there was an almost even division between family and friends involved in business activities in Accra with migrants (Mazzucato, 2003; Smith, 2007), which is a striking finding in itself, given the fact that in other research on ties between Ghanaian migrants and their country of origin, friends hardly figure at all (Black et al., 2003; Tiemoko, 2003). The more fundamental point is that there are important differences between urban actors who relate to migrants as family and those who relate to migrants as friends, despite the fact that neither category is homogeneous, resulting in very different ways in which transnational business activities are manifested (cf. the cases of Mark and Kenneth, both friends to migrants). The involvement of friends rather than family relates to one major concern of migrants: that engaging family members in Accra in business activities may result in the involvement of the family as a whole, thereby using business assets and capital to meet all kinds of other needs. This is seen to have certain possible repercussions for the profitability of the business.

By contrast, close and trusted friendships, respondents argued, which had developed out of continuous transnational engagements, enabled migrants to establish businesses in Accra without committing themselves to a larger network. Whilst the extended family, as a relatively close-knit network, provided migrants with a mechanism to monitor and sanction the behaviour of those involved in their businesses, it also meant involving their family, leading to claims on the earnings of businesses. On the other hand friendships enabled migrants to conduct business activities on their own terms, as these friendships were often forged in the urban context (Accra or Kumasi), and sometimes abroad. These transactions thus developed relatively separately from those in which migrants maintained ties with kin. Through friendships migrants could define the extent to which they wanted business arrangements with urban actors to be explicit.

Urban actors did emphasize that migrants had to be careful in their selection of a friend to involve. They had to trust this person unreservedly, ensure that this urban actor understood the importance of the investment, and be confident he or she shared an interest to get it established. Furthermore this urban actor would need to be sufficiently experienced and skilled, and discreet about the business investment to others, particularly the family of the migrant (also see Mazzucato, 2003).

Of the respondents selected by migrant friends to supervise businesses, many had also been abroad themselves. Their first-hand experiences meant that they were well positioned to understand their migrant partners' economic and financial position, and the importance of business investments for migrants; namely that these were instrumental for providing them with a source of income, especially upon their return to Ghana.

Urban actors selected by their migrant friends were also seldom 'persons in need' (Mazzucato, 2003). Both migrants and Accra respondents argued that this was important, as it reduced the likelihood that they would appropriate funds for their own purposes. While more well-off family members might also qualify, migrants could more easily terminate friendships once they discovered that their trust in the other had been abused. Nonetheless, as friendships often derived from various social and economic contexts, these also limited opportunities for migrants to monitor the behaviour of their Accra-based friends.

The value of transnational friendships related particularly to the way with which they provided migrants with room to manoeuvre in establishing desired economic activities. In this research various cases were encountered in which respondents explained that in their association with the family of migrants in Ghana they remained highly discreet about their ties to these migrants, notably the economic activities they engaged in. A focus on the urban economy through transnational friendships allowed migrants to withhold certain investments from parts of their social networks, particularly their extended families, who might seek to incorporate migrants and their hard-earned assets for their own interests and needs, or those of the family. In the context of prevailing cultural notions stipulating that financially able members invest in assets of the extended family, notably the family house (Van der Geest, 1998), urban-based friends thus played a crucial role in enabling migrants to secure their own economic future first, before committing themselves to investments benefiting their families as a whole.

Balancing transnational relationships

As stated in the introduction to this chapter, literature on the impact of migration on development focuses mostly on migrants, based on the premise that migrants and their remittances are the principal drivers and agents of change. This would also make their position in transnational relations with actors in their country of origin asymmetrical. In this chapter it is demonstrated that this holds only for some cases of transnational business activities, and certainly not for all. First, in some cases it was the urban actor and not the migrant who had taken the first initiative to develop a certain business activity with a migrant. Second, while in most cases migrants were the principal financiers of business activities, they depended on concurrent investments of the labour, skills and insights of urban actors to realize actual business activities. Third, in situations where there was clear evidence of differences in investments between migrants and urban actors in a particular transnational business activity, their involvement with one another could be explained by reciprocal investments in other domains, such as caring for family members of migrants or representing migrants at important cultural events. Furthermore, in some cases, for instance where support of migrants by urban actors was temporary in nature, and where personal benefits were unclear and/or limited, the preparedness of urban actors to invest in business incentives of migrants was explained as a way to ensure that the support they gave would be reciprocated in the future, for instance when they encountered a major crisis, or when they required a large sum of money perhaps to buy a plot of land on which to build a house (also see Smith and Mazzucato, 2009).

The role of capital

The cases of Angelina, Grace, and Kenneth constitute examples of urban actors who benefited from migrant support for their business activities resulting from a dependency of migrants on them to carry out important activities in Ghana on their behalf. These kinds of transnational engagements show a clear trade-off between the social capital of urban actors and the financial capital of migrants to produce reciprocity in their relationship. However, where in other cases there was a direct (and formal) link to a joint business venture, in the case of Grace reciprocity from migrants took on an a rather intricate form: financial investments of migrants in her business were linked to reversed investments by Grace toward the migrants in the reproductive domain, minding their children and parents.

In other cases respondents sought to establish equal partnerships in businesses with migrants by committing their own financial investments, or showing their preparedness to do so (cf. the case of Colin). While exceptional, other cases are known of urban actors who had invested capital they had derived from their own sources, for example cocoa sales, to become business partners with migrants. As mentioned before, the research sample population also included a number of business owners who were in such economically independent positions that they did not require any financial, or other, forms of support from migrants for their businesses.

Respondents who needed financial or organizational support from migrants tried to convince them to become involved in their business activities by revealing to them some of their ideas and insights on new market developments, arguing that they had the necessary expertise to complement the resources of migrants. With a track record of previous, smaller business dealings, their reputation and skills as business partners could be confirmed. Word of mouth amongst migrants confirming the entrepreneurial skills of urban actors also helped their case for subsequent partnerships with migrants who lacked a suitable and trustworthy business partner in Accra.

Conclusions

This chapter has focused on transnational business activities in Accra. The case studies presented here have given insight in key dimensions of transnational business relationships, how these relationships developed, and what significance they held.

The analyses of the roles of reciprocity, capital, trust and relationships has unravelled important differences in the way transnational relationships are manifested, and the relative positions and interests taken by actors involved. Yet, such an analysis still cannot answer the question whether transnational business investments in the urban economy relate to prior or to new socio-economic affiliations. If the latter is the case then this will have adverse effects on solidarity and welfare redistribution mechanisms manifested through more traditional social configurations, such as extended families, kinship and hometowns. On the other hand, these traditional forms can also persist, perhaps in a hybrid form, as in instances where migrants support their families and hometowns through urban friends. For an answer to the question of whether transnational business investments in Accra produce social transformations three key issues are discussed.

First, note needs to be taken that the urban population, even when narrowed down to those with ties to migrants, is not homogenous. Thus for the latter group it is shown that where some urban actors clearly engaged with migrants on their own terms, others were largely dependent on them for financial support. This last category of dependents was usually dominated by urban actors who related to migrants as family members. Their situation may be considered as comparable to that of rural actors in Ghana with ties to migrants, namely having asymmetric economic relationships with migrants within which they have very little agency (Kabki, 2007). Given that migrants did support business incentives of their urban-based family members, even though these initiatives would generate few direct benefits to them, this points to a continuity of kinship or family-related relationships, albeit in hybrid form: family supported by migrants in their country of origin no longer only resided in the rural region of origin, but could also be based in urban parts of Ghana.

Second, in the debate on the migration–development nexus, migrants are considered as the principal agent of change, notably when they operate as collectives, to achieve development in communities of origin (cf. Mazzucato and Kabki, 2009). While the importance of this particular role is not disputed, this chapter has presented rather different dimensions on the role of migrants in development processes in their countries of origin. In this analysis focus was upon: (1) individual rather than collective efforts of migrants; (2) businesses as transnational projects, rather than more generally recognized development projects (in domains such as health, education); (3) the urban rather than rural economy; and (4) the position of urban actors in these transnational projects, rather than those of migrants.

Using a methodological approach focusing on individual urban actors and their social networks, this research sought to widen the debate on the migration–development nexus. Indeed, this analytical point of departure helps to produce a diverse range of rationales and explanations for transnational activities organized by migrants together with actors in their country of origin. Insights developed through this research showed that the migration–development nexus can take on a significant and productive meaning, albeit in a very different way from more traditional development aid-derived formats.

With this focus an attempt is made to widen the debate on the migration–development nexus by helping to establish the notion that business incentives also represent valuable forms of development. They help to expand the economy, even if the choice for particular sectors may be considered to be somewhat conservative and risk-averse. Furthermore, the income generated with business activities also provides support and generates changes in other domains – improving social security, generating human capital and so on. Some of the case studies gave ample evidence of this. Finally, the focus on the perspective of urban actors showed that migrants are not necessarily the principal agents of (economic) development. Case material indicated instead those situations where urban actors took the first step in engaging with migrants in business activities, combining their own resources with those of migrants.

Third, the preference of migrants for investments in the urban rather than rural economy, and Accra specifically, points to the important role of locality in defining transnational investments. As related earlier, Glick Schiller (Chapter 2 in this book) not only argues for a focus on social networks as the conceptual framework with which to study cross-border flows, but also for more attention to the role played by localities in defining the shape of transnational social fields. From this research on transnational ties between migrants and urban actors the conclusion can be drawn that Accra not only formed a logical location for business investments from a business perspective; it also provided migrants with certain economic room to manoeuvre, helping them to achieve and sustain economic investments while concomitantly managing their level of commitment toward their social networks in Ghana, notably their family and hometown. In this development friendships with urban actors who could initiate and carefully manage these businesses were often particularly important, indicating a certain shift in economic allegiances.

Given the relocation of investments and responsibilities, as expressions of capital reproduction, implied with migrants' investments in businesses in Accra, it would seem that the response to the question whether these urban investments then lead to social transformations is: 'yes'. Yet the achievement of these urban projects seldom resulted in a total neglect or abandonment of ties with the extended families and their region of origin, which most migrants continued to perceive as important and relevant. Indeed, they showed their preparedness to go to great lengths to show this commitment, for instance at times of family crises (Mazzucato et al., 2006).

To answer the question of whether the commitment to, but also the interest in, investing in the country of origin is sustainable – and to what extent this may then be termed as a social transformation given the permanently shifting roles of institutions such as the family, the hometown, but also nationality – requires further, longitudinal research design. Such an approach would re-examine the nature of transnational relationships between migrants and those in their country of origin, notably for migrants who remain abroad and/or are succeeded by second and third generations.

Notes

*This chapter draws on earlier work (Smith, 2007; Smith and Mazzucato, 2004). In its final form, it benefited a great deal from comments provided by fellow contributors to this book at the occasion of the ZiF Workshop held in Bielefeld (19–20 February 2009). Particular thanks go to Boris Nieswand and Gudrun Lachenmann, for the issues and comments they raised in the capacity of referents. Further thanks go to Valentina Mazzucato for her critical comments. Notwithstanding this input, the contents of the chapter remain my sole responsibility.

1. For a counter case see the chapter by Van Hear in this book, in which he discusses the influence of migrants in development of their conflict-ridden societies of origin through collective efforts out of diasporas.
2. As mentioned before, of all 38 respondents involved in the Accra research, five had no association with business activities. Furthermore, of all 22 respondents who were (co-)owners of businesses, 13 neither required nor used ties with migrants for their own business activities. However, three of these respondents had set up businesses with capital saved from when they were abroad. Given the emphasis of this chapter on transnational ties between urban actors and migrants in business activities in Accra, these actors have been left out of the analysis.
3. In Accra these imported secondhand cars from Europe were also referred to as 'Eurocarcas'.

References

Ammassari, S. (2004) 'From Nation-Building to Entrepreneurship: The Impact of Elite Return Migrants in Côte d'Ivoire and Ghana', *Population, Space and Place*, 10, 133–154.

Aryeteeh, E. and Fosu A. K. (2008) 'Economic Growth in Ghana: 1960-2000', in B. J. Ndulu, S. A. O Connell, J. P. Azam, R. H. Bates, A. K. Fosu, J. W. Gunning and D. Njinkeu (eds), *The Political Economic of Growth in Africa 1960–2000: Country Case Studies* (Cambridge: Cambridge University Press).

Asiedu, A. B. (2005) 'Some Benefits of Migrants' Return Visits to Ghana', *Population, Space and Place*, 11, 1–11.

Black, R., King, R. and Tiemoko, R. (2003) 'Migration, Return and Small Enterprise Development in Ghana: A Route out of Poverty?', Sussex Migration Working Paper No. 9 (Brighton: Sussex Centre for Migration Research).

Clark, G. (1999) 'Negotiating Asante Family Survival in Kumasi, Ghana', *Africa*, 69 (1), 66–86.

Collier, P. and Gunning, J. W. (1999) 'Explaining African Performance', *Journal of Economic Literature*, 37, 64–111.

De Haas, H. (2003) *Migration and Development in Southern Morocco: The Disparate Socio-Economic Impacts of Out-Migration on the Todgha Oasis Valley*, unpublished PhD dissertation (Nijmegen: Catholic University of Nijmegen).

——— (2005) 'International Migration, Remittances and Development: Myths and Facts', *Third World Quarterly*, 26 (8), 1269–1284.

Diko, J. and Tipple, A. G. (1992) 'Migrants Build at Home: Long Distance Housing Development by Ghanaians in London', *Cities*, 9 (4), 288–294.

Faist, T. (2000) 'Transnationalization International Migration: Implications for the Study of Citizenship and Culture', *Ethnic and Racial Studies*, 23 (2), 189–222.

——— and Reisenauer, E. (2009) 'Introduction: Migration(s) and Development(s): Transformation of Paradigms, Organizations, and Gender Orders', *Sociologus: Journal of Empirical Social Anthropology*, 59 (1), 1–16.

Hamann, V. (2000) 'Migration and Development: The Investment of Migrants in the High Emigration Area of Zacatecas', Mexico, paper presented at the ISA Conference 'International Migration in Latin America Enters a New Millennium', 2–4 November, Buenos Aires, Argentina.

Herbst, J. (1991) 'Labour in Ghana under Structural Adjustment', in D. Rothchild (ed.), *Ghana: The Political Economy of Reform* (Boulder: Lynne Rienner Publishers).

Kaag, M., van Berkel, R., Brons, J., de Bruijn, M., van Dijk, H., de Haan, L., Nooteboom G. and Zoomers, A. (2004) 'Ways Forward in Livelihood Research', in D. Kalb, W. Pansters, and H. Siebers (eds), *Globalization and Development: Themes and Concepts in Current Research* (Dordrecht: Kluwer Academic Publishers).

Kabki, M. (2007) 'Transnationalism, Local Development and Social Security: The Functioning of Support Networks in Rural Ghana', *African Studies Collection*, 6 (Leiden: African Studies Centre).

Mazzucato, V. (2003) 'Asante Transnational Relations: Historical Renegotiation or Changing Structure of Social Relationships?', paper presented at CERES Summer School, panel 'Poverty in a World of Excess: Contradictions of Transnational Flows', 23–26 June, Amsterdam.

——— (2008) 'The Double Engagement: Transnationalism and Integration – Ghanaian Migrants' Lives between Ghana and the Netherlands', *Journal of Ethnic and Migration Studies*, 34 (2), 199–216.

——— (2009) 'Bridging Boundaries with a Transnational Research Approach: A Simultaneous Matched Sample Methodology', in M. A. Falzon (ed.), *Multi-sited Ethnography: Theory, Praxis and Locality in Contemporary Social Research* (Aldershot: Ashgate).

——— and Kabki, M. (2009) 'Small is Beautiful: The Micro-politics of Transnational Relationships between Ghanaian Hometown Associations and Communities Back Home', *Global Networks*, 9 (2), 227–251.

———, van der Boom, B. and Nsowah-Nuamah, N. N. N. (2005) 'Origin and Destination of Remittances in Ghana', in T. Manuh (ed.), *At Home in the World: International Migration and Development in Contemporary Ghana and West Africa* (Accra: Sub-Saharan Publishers).

———, Kabki, M. and Smith, L. (2006) 'Locating a Ghanaian Funeral: Remittances and Practices in a Transnational Context', *Development and Change*, 37, 1047–1072.

Parker, R. L., Riopelle, R. and Steel, W. F. (1995) 'Small Enterprises Adjusting to Liberalization in Five African Countries', Discussion Paper No. 271, Technical Department, Africa Region (Washington, DC: World Bank).

Penninx, R. and van Renselaar, H. (1978) 'A Fortune in Small Change: A Study of Migrant Workers' Attempts to Invest Savings Productively through Joint Stock

Corporations and Village Development Co-operatives in Turkey (The Hague: REMPLOD/NUFFIC).

Private Enterprise Foundation (2003) *Study in Forming Larger Business Units* (Legon: Private Enterprise Foundation).

Riddell, B. (1997) 'Structural Adjustment Programmes and the City in Tropical Africa', *Urban Studies*, 34, 1297–1307.

Skeldon, R. (2004) 'More than Remittances: Other Aspects of the Relationship between Migration and Development', paper presented to the Third Coordination Meeting on International Migration, Population Division, Department of Economic and Social Affairs, United Nations Secretariat, 27–28 October, New York.

Smith, L. (2007) 'Tied to Migrants: Transnational Influences on the Economy of Accra, Ghana', *African Studies Collection*, 5 (Leiden: African Studies Centre).

——— and Mazzucato, V. (2004) 'Miglioriamo le nostre tradizioni: Gli investimenti dei migranti Ashanti nelle abitazioni e nelle imprese', *Afriche e Orienti*, 6 (1–2), 168–85.

——— and Mazzucato, V. (2009) 'Constructing Houses, Building Relationships: Interdependencies of Ghanaian Migrants and Urban Actors through Transnational Investments in Houses', *Tijdschrift voor economische en sociale geografie*, 100 (5), 662–673, Special issue on transnationalism.

Stiglitz, J. E. (2003) 'Democratizing the International Monetary Fund and the World Bank: Governance and Accountability', *Governance: An International Journal of Policy, Administration, and Institutions*, 16 (1), 111–139.

Tiemoko, R. (2003) 'Migration, Return and Socio-Economic Change in West Africa: The Role of Family', Sussex Migration Working Paper 14 (Brighton: University of Sussex).

Van der Geest, S. (1998) 'Yebisa Wo Fie: Growing Old and Building a House in the Akan Culture of Ghana', *Journal of Cross-Cultural Gerontology*, 13, 333–359.

Van Velzen, L. (1977) 'Peripheral Production in Kayseri, Turkey: A Study for Prospects for Industrialization Arising from Small- and Middle-Scale Enterprises in a Peripheral Growth Pole', A NUFFIC/ IMWOO/ REMPLOD-project (Ankara: Ajans-Türk Press).

Yeboah, I. E. A. (2000) 'Structural Adjustment and Emerging Urban Form in Accra, Ghana', *Africa Today*, 47 (2), 61–89.

6
How Receiving Cities Contribute to Simultaneous Engagements for Incorporation and Development

Margit Fauser

In the year 2007 migrant organizations from Madrid, Barcelona and a number of southern Spanish localities founded the REDCO network. REDCO is the abbreviation for Network of Immigrant and Co-development Associations. It is dedicated to the active involvement of migrant communities and migrant organizations in cross-border development projects, summarized by the now popular term co-development. Most, if not all, of the 16 founding member organizations of this network have previously been engaged in politics and service delivery in the realm of migrants' local reception and incorporation. It includes even a local, Barcelona-based network whose representative in an interview in 2006 still maintained that development cooperation or other cross-border projects in origin countries were not on the agendas of any of their member associations. In the meantime, migrant organizations in Madrid and Barcelona engage simultaneously for reception and incorporation 'here' and development 'there'.

Since the second half of the 1990s sub-national levels of government in Spain have initiated co-development policies which heavily promote such engagements, and today they are joined by other levels and institutions. Although co-development still is a diffuse term (Escrivà and Ribas, 2004; Pacheco Medrano, 2003), these initiatives share a perspective on migration–development linkages involving localities and immigrant communities in transnational cooperation (Giménez Romero et al., 2006).

What these initiatives from local authorities and migrant organizations, and also other non-state actors, reflect is the changing paradigm of the migration–development debate and the related shift concerning the newer role attributed to locality and community (Faist, 2008; Glick

Schiller and Çağlar, 2009). Global restructuring, policy reforms from above, and civil society claims for participation from below have led to greater local autonomy and stronger community and non-state actor participation. This applies to political governance and socio-economic development in the more developed as well as in the less developed world regions. Thus, migrants' transnational involvement takes place in the midst of decentralization strategies in developing countries, their promotion within development aid schemes, and against the background of efforts toward decentralized development cooperation from local levels in industrialized countries. Further, it is part of the re-evaluation of the relationship between migration and development. Whereas earlier perspectives on the relationship – expressed in post-war guest-worker policies, for instance – saw migrants' contribution to development in their return and successful reintegration, this recent positive evaluation of the linkage acknowledges settlement and incorporation of migrants in the receiving society (Faist and Fauser, Chapter 1 in this volume). In this newer perspective, migrants are identified as agents of development. Rather than opposing transnational, cross-border engagement to incorporation, both processes are considered to be mutually reinforcing.

Hence, this chapter argues that, first, even though immigration is very recent in Spanish cities, migrant organizations follow simultaneous agendas for reception and incorporation into the host society and for development in places of their origin. Second, current initiatives in these receiving cities promote and shape these agendas. By combining a focus on new (local) opportunity structures and a transnational perspective on migrant organizations this chapter shows how the new local initiatives emerging against the background of the migration–development debate shape migrant organizations' transnationalism and their simultaneous engagements. Although policy frameworks are not determining in this respect, they are one source of opening new opportunities and resources for transnational activities. So far, the active role of both receiving side institutions and of sub-national levels from the receiving, but also from the sending side, have received scarce attention in the study of migrants' transnationalism. And although transnational migration scholarship has contributed many important insights already, the study of transnational migrant organizations and their potentially simultaneous agendas is only just emerging.

In empirical terms, this chapter explores the activities of local authorities and migrant organizations from two Spanish cities, Madrid and Barcelona. Therefore it draws on material from qualitative research conducted by the author.[1] This material includes print and digital documents as well as interviews, gathered from 13 selected migrant organizations and networks of different nationality backgrounds, but all from non-European and developing countries, in the two cities; from local public authorities and representatives from other levels of government; and from a number of non-governmental organizations and trade unions.

The chapter proceeds as follows. The next section discusses the theoretical approaches in the research on migrant organizations and their determinants. A transnational perspective is advocated which allows observing simultaneous agendas and the intensification of cross-border activities over time. Further, it is argued that receiving-side institutions shape migrants' transnationalism. This is currently promoted in the context of the newer role of locality and community in migration and development policies. An empirical analysis of the two city cases is provided, starting with a focus on the activities of local public authorities and agencies. The focus then shifts to the migrant organizations and it is shown how new opportunities contribute to the emergence of simultaneous agendas. The analysis also reveals how this leads not only to the tackling of development issues, but also to dealing with migration and incorporation transnationally. Against the background of these findings, the conclusion points to the implications of these processes which strengthen the role of migrant organizations and other non-state actors together with local authorities not only in relation to international development but also in the realm of migration management and thus beyond their role for local incorporation.

Debates and concepts in the research on transnational migrant organizations

Migrant organizations, incorporation and development

So far, two perspectives predominate in the research on migrant organizations pointing either to tensions between or to simultaneities of engagements for host incorporation and home(town) development. Classical as well as more pluralist incorporation theories consider migrant organizations either as a bridge and mediator to incorporation or regard them as an indicator of the failure of incorporation, in particular when home-oriented attachments persist. This scholarship has pointed out that migrant organizations' contributions to incorporation are dependent on whether their focus is on the culture and country of origin or on incorporation into the country of settlement. Only in the latter case would migrant organizations be seen as being able to promote migrants' collective and individual incorporation effectively (Schöneberg, 1985). Over time, a natural evolution from ethnic and 'homeland' identities to host attachments has generally been expected (Layton-Henry, 1990; Park and Miller, 1969). Most frequently, though, the research on migrant organizations focuses on their engagement with incorporation, and simply ignores cross-border activities (see, for instance, Schrover and Vermeulen, 2005).

Transnational migration scholarship provides a different lens and reveals partly different empirical realities. It particularly points to the continuity of homeland ties of migrants over longer periods of time, emerging in the context of changing global and national structures at the end of the 20th century (Faist, 2000; Glick Schiller et al., 1992; Pries, 1999). Transnational research has also started to investigate cross-border migrant organizations and shows their growth in the numbers, more intense engagement and growing financial volumes of transnational transfers for many communities in the US (Goldring, 2002; Levitt 2001; Orozco and Lapointe, 2004; Portes et al., 2007; Sassen, 2002; Zabin and Escala, 2002). Less well known are European cases of transnational migrant organizations, although these also exist and have been gaining strength over the last years (Baraulina et al., 2006; Çağlar, 2006; Grillo and Riccio, 2004; Lacroix, 2005; Pries and Sezgin, 2010; Sieveking et al., 2008). Many of these studies saw a close relationship between the sending of collective remittances and support for community development on the one side and return perspectives and mobility of the migrants themselves on the other side. Engagement with incorporation, in turn, often was found limited (Zabin and Escala, 2002) and where it emerged it led to internal tensions within the transnational networks between those abroad and those at home (Levitt, 1997). Thus, from different angles researchers have pointed to tensions between host incorporation and home development.

Still less represented is a second perspective which highlights simultaneity. A number of more recent research findings sustain the existence of simultaneous engagements among migrant organizations for settlement and incorporation into the receiving society and for their hometowns and countries (Cordero-Guzmán, 2005; Portes et al., 2008; Portes et al., 2007; Pries, 2010; Waldrauch and Sohler, 2004). The programmes, official statements and articulations as well as the networks of these organizations reflect the compatibility of this dual engagement and even its mutual reinforcement. One important argument here is that the transfer of experiences, knowledge and resources, and hence social capital acquired through transnational activism, allows for successful engagement with respect to the processes of settlement and incorporation (Portes et al., 2008, 4; Smith, 2007; Vertovec, 2004). In sum, this scholarship stresses simultaneities with transnational engagement being paralleled by efforts for local incorporation in the course of time.

Current dynamics may require a third perspective on possible evolutions. Today it appears that locally established communities and organizations are also becoming more transnational. For instance, among relatively settled communities of Turkish immigrants in Germany, unrelated to new inflows, new hometown associations emerge. These organizations address socio-economic development in Turkey as well as incorporation in Germany (Çağlar, 2006). In the new Southern European immigration settings the situation is even more dynamic. Being of recent formation because of the recent nature of immigration, migrant organizations in Spanish cities are often at first mainly concerned with reception and incorporation. Increasingly, however, these organizations display transnational projects on their agendas. This process is at least partly related to emerging state initiatives originating from or involving local government levels. Such initiatives are now frequently, although not exclusively, based on the concept of co-development.

The role of the state and the local

In their accounts for migrant transnationalism, scholars have put special emphasis on the responses and initiatives of 'sending' states. In fact, many of the major emigration countries have become rather active in promoting close relations with their migrant communities abroad and actively tried to influence their efforts (Goldring, 2002; Østergaard-Nielsen, 2003; for an overview of state measures see Itzigsohn, 2000, p. 1132, Table 1 and Smith, 2003).

The role of receiving countries in relation to migrants' collective transnationalism is most often seen in restrictive migration policies and limited support for immigrants' incorporation, which hinders emerging organizations from linking up with receiving authorities. It is argued that, being unwelcome, organizations and their members cannot develop strong identification with the host society and as a result withdraw from it in favour of deepening origin country attachments. Following this logic, open and positive policy approaches would then lead to political and social commitment to incorporation (Koopmans and Statham, 2003; Layton-Henry, 1990).

In light of newer research results and changing social realities this somewhat dichotomous conceptualization of government policies of countries of origin for (transnational) development and receiving countries for incorporation is being challenged in at least two ways. First, policies contributing to incorporation may also contribute to transnationalization. A number of indications suggest that often the better educated, more established and better off are more likely to be transnationally active (Guarnizo et al., 2003). Accordingly, favourable policies of incorporation may also, although indirectly, contribute to transnational activism. This is even more likely when such policies explicitly recognize ethnic identities, cultural diversity and transnational organizing (Faist, 1998, 2000, p. 214; Glick Schiller and Fouron, 1999; Kivisto, 2005, p. 314ff.). Second, active encouragement of migrants' cross-border activities from receiving-side institutions is emerging in the new round of the development–migration debate. In these initiatives migrants are identified and supported as agents of development of their hometowns (De Haas, 2006; Faist, 2008; Faist and Fauser, Chapter 1 in this volume).

In relation to sending and receiving side initiatives, an additional influence on migrants' involvement in local community development can be detected. While most emphasis in migration, transnationalization and development research still is on national-level institutions, the local is playing new roles and is becoming a new focus of political and academic attention throughout the last two decades. The newer emphasis put on transnational migrant organizations and communities can be seen as entrenched in a number of interconnected dynamics which attribute great importance to locality and community in the project of development.

First, in many developing countries a focus on community development has been gaining strength over the past decades. In many places the state had been absent previously and current global economic restructuring has often led to further withdrawal. Economic and political reforms are, in addition, accompanied by decentralization of authority and competencies, allowing for more local autonomy. Within this space, initiatives from sub-national governments and from migrant communities are taking place. Local authorities from countries as diverse as Mexico, Mali or Turkey and many others actively engage with migrant organizations in Western immigration localities and promote their transnational engagement with the intent to attract financial remittances, infrastructure investment, and political support (Çağlar, 2007; Daum, 1993; Fitzgerald, 2006; Goldring, 2002; Grillo and Riccio, 2004; Lacroix, 2005; Sieveking et al., 2008; Smith, 2003).

Second, parallel to the new local relationships in developing countries, stronger emphasis on locality, local actors and community development is also promoted in development aid policies of more developed countries, resembling the general shift from state-level to smaller units of governance in this field (Faist, 2008). In this respect, great hope is invested in the self-organizing power of sub-national governments and non-state actors in the 'third world'.

Third, decentralized cooperation schemes involving local governments and non-governmental actors in the developed world have become a characteristic of cooperation policies around Europe since the 1980s. Many cities across Europe count on municipal development cooperation today (Grillo and Riccio, 2004; InWEnt, 2007; Lacroix, 2005; Petiteville, 1995). Within these schemes migrant actors are now also incorporated. In this respect some governments and agencies have taken up the originally French concept of *co-développement* (Lacroix, 2005; Naïr, 1997). In this reading, the concept of co-development stresses decentralized cooperation, involvement of local authorities and non-state actors from developing/emigration and developed/immigration sides, and the incorporation of migrant actors in the project of development. Although at the beginning the concept was more closely connected to return perspectives and programmes, in some places at least it has become more independent from migrants' return (Grillo and Riccio, 2004; Lacroix, 2005; Sieveking et al., 2008). In the meantime, politicians and public officials highlight migrants' settlement and incorporation as beneficial for and benefiting from their development engagement. This approach has many repercussions in Spanish cities and localities. This is facilitated by the role of local authorities in responding to international migration and because of the existence of decentralized development cooperation. At the same time, different approaches exist as we will see next in the analysis of the concepts developed in Madrid and Barcelona.

Local contexts, new opportunity structures, and the promotion of transnational (co)development

International migration into Spanish cities and localities is relatively recent and has been growing dynamically for the last 10 to 15 years. The two major Spanish cities, the capital Madrid and the capital of the Autonomous Community of Catalonia, Barcelona, also host the majority of immigrants. In both cities the foreign immigrant population has reached 17 per cent, displaying a sharp rise from less than 2 per cent in the mid-1990s (data from padrón de habitantes, Ayuntamiento de Madrid and Ajuntamiento de Barcelona, various years). In absolute numbers Madrid hosts twice the total number of inhabitants and foreign residents than Barcelona. Madrid has a population of around 3.1 million inhabitants of which over half a million hold foreign passports; Barcelona has a population of 1.5 million which includes 280,000 foreigners.

In general, national responses to increased immigration and ethnic diversity, beyond border control, have been only slowly evolving in Spain. For their part, local levels are not only most directly confronted with these arriving and settling populations, they are also responsible to a great degree for social policy implementation. As a consequence, local levels have played a crucial role with respect to the reception of immigrants. Local authorities have begun to deal with new immigrants within their existing schemes and frameworks, while many bigger cities and smaller villages have also developed new policies and plans for their reception and integration and set up specific measures toward this end (Agrela and Dietz, 2006; Aragón Medina et al., 2009; Fauser, forthcoming; Pájares, 2006; Ramos et al., 1998).

At the same time, development cooperation has a decentralized character in Spain. And at least in the two cities investigated the two tasks of incorporation and development cooperation are also institutionally connected. In this respect, Madrid and Barcelona share a similar history. Throughout the 1980s Spain turned from a recipient into a donor of development aid, with some timely overlap of the two roles (Casas Álvarez, 2000). Already in this period, sub-national levels also enacted some measures to combat poverty and social exclusion in the 'third world'. At the beginning of the 1990s, concerted mobilization and broadly supported solidarity campaigns called for the fulfilment of the 0.7 per cent budget ratio to development cooperation according to international agreements, the repercussions of which were felt significantly in many places (Ruiz Jiménez, 2006). Madrid and Barcelona, but also many smaller localities, started to launch their own international cooperation policies and funds. Today, decentralized development cooperation is an important feature of development policies in Spain. Contrary to national-level development aid which has stagnated since 1993, local and regional expenditures are continuously growing, today making up around 15 per cent of Spanish Overseas Development Aid (ODA). Many localities are striving toward the goal of 0.7 per cent of the municipal budget and beyond (Intermón-Oxfam, 2005; Ruiz Jiménez, 2006). Simultaneously, the impact of migration was becoming more apparent in many Spanish locales just as the institutionalization of development cooperation on the local level was taking place. As a consequence, in both Madrid and Barcelona development cooperation and immigrants' reception were intimately related from the outset with respect to the responsible departments within the municipalities as well as the funding schemes. In both cities, the then newly introduced subsidies for non-state actors' initiatives in development cooperation were open to support projects for the reception of immigrants. At different points in time these two aspects were institutionally separated, already in 1997 in Barcelona and in 2004 in Madrid. Both issues are currently coming together again within the new paradigm of the development–migration nexus and the concept of co-development. In the words of two public officials in Madrid interviewed in the course of this research, the evolution of co-development policies is thus something 'natural' (Interview with representatives from the municipal development department, Madrid, 2006).

In Madrid, the city government already had funded some individual projects of migrant organizations abroad starting in 1995. The concept of co-development itself emerged at the end of the 1990s, when the annual development report referred to it for the first time. Throughout the following years the reports regularly mentioned the funded projects. In the meantime, documents on both municipal development cooperation and immigrants' integration explained the city's approach in detail. In 2004 the city also announced the first explicit call for tender for co-development projects. In Barcelona, neither the departments dealing with incorporation nor those responsible for development cooperation have yet formulated a co-development policy. Nonetheless, the municipal *Barcelona Sòlidaria* programme for development cooperation financed a feasibility study among Moroccan migrant organizations evaluating interest and possibilities in such projects (Ruiz, 2003). In addition, the consortium of Catalan municipalities for Development Cooperation, *Fons Català*, launched co-development projects in the year 1996. These have included some organizations from Barcelona, but also many others from smaller municipalities in Catalonia. Projects subsidized by *Fons Català* so far focus exclusively on Africa.

In relation to the concept of co-development and migration–development linkages three aspects can be distinguished in the municipal approaches. First, in both cities, programmes and documents make reference to source regions of local immigration communities as a geographical priority for municipal development cooperation. Second, the approaches taken in both cities also put emphasis on the involvement of local immigrant communities and organizations, although what this means in terms of projects and recipients of funding is somewhat different. Third, in Madrid co-development is also related to channelling migration flows.

Concerning the first aspect of geographical priority, municipal development cooperation emphasizes regions of high emigration, relevant to the city in question. Accordingly, Madrid has paid special attention on Ecuador, Colombia, Morocco, the Dominican Republic and Peru since the second half of the 1990s. Since 2005 the annual development report also refers to Romania, Bolivia and Senegal, from where more and more migrants have been arriving. It is noteworthy that the share of Senegalese immigrants in Madrid is comparatively small in statistical terms, but has been growing dynamically. More importantly, it receives considerable media coverage not least because of the dangerous and sometimes deadly ways in which African immigrants arrive in Spain. In Barcelona, development cooperation guidelines of the municipality and other agencies also consider migration source regions as geographic priorities, and the 'root causes of migration', namely poverty and under-development, are relevant issues to be addressed even if the term co-development is not referred to. A report of *Fons Català* in the framework of its 'Migration and Local Development' (MIDEL) project maintains that the primary objective of its work – extending this to its other collaborators as well in Catalonia – is to improve the socio-economic conditions in the migrants' communities of origins as a way to reduce the '*exode rural*' (rural exodus) and hence 'indirectly the migration to Europe' (Fons Català, 2006, p. 16).

The second aspect is the involvement of immigrant communities in development. In this respect, local incorporation in the Spanish cities and migrants' transnational engagements with their places of origin are expressed as mutually reinforcing based on the resources, skills, experiences and networks both require. This is thought to enable the transfer of these skills from one type of engagement to the other. The local integration plan for social and intercultural conviviality, the *Plan Madrid* (Ayuntamiento de Madrid, 2005a), for instance, defines the primary objectives of *codesarrollo* (co-development) in the following way: to relate the migrant communities to the social and economic development of their countries of origin, given their incorporation into the local society of Madrid and their contributions to the development of 'our city'. Accordingly, measures include raising awareness and promotion of the role of migrants as agents of development, among the migrants themselves as well as among the local community in Madrid, advocating the positive contribution to development in Madrid and in the countries of origin. In the same vein, *Fons Català* describes similar features and also aims to 'connect the organizations of immigrants with the projects in decentralized international cooperation' (Fons Català, 2007, translation MF).

The ways in which the involvement of migrants is addressed in the two cities differs, however, to some degree. Among the organizations funded by the city of Madrid, both in the lines of development cooperation as well as within the newer scheme on co-development, migrant organizations constitute a minority. Other non-governmental development organizations have received the majority of funds, some of which have been at least collaborating with migrant organizations or with unorganized migrant groups. Public officials also maintain that collaboration with migrant communities or migrant organizations was crucial for successful application for co-development projects (Interview with representatives of the municipal development department, Madrid, 2006). The projects funded by *Fons Català*, in turn, all involve migrant organizations as well as in most cases the municipalities where these migrants reside and other local actors from these places (Fons Català, 2006).

A third aspect, which explicitly relates only to Madrid, concerns migration issues which are tackled in project guidelines and implementation. This is expressed, for instance, in the three types of projects eligible for funding described in the development cooperation report (Ayuntamiento de Madrid, 2005b). Type one projects cover activities in countries of origin designed to strengthen rootedness in the region and the canalization of migratory flows to Spain. This includes initiatives oriented toward the promotion of legal migration through assistance and information as well as projects promoting vocational training, capacity building and job opportunities – intended to prevent irregular migration. Type two projects are economic activities which make use of the development potential of migrants, that is, productive and commercial projects, fair trade and remittances. Type three activities promote return and reintegration. These activities may include support for assisted return and successful re-integration and embrace vocational training and other capacity-building possibilities to be provided to migrants in Madrid before as well as through assistance after returning. These initiatives constitute influential frameworks for migrant organizations. Although *Fons Català* also expresses concerns for out-migration, migration management is not a topic explicitly addressed in its guidelines and projects. The differences are partly reflected in the intensities, characteristics and financial foundation of the activities which migrant organizations undertake.

Simultaneous engagements of migrant organizations

Turning now to the analysis of migrant organizations' engagement, this section will show the similarities and differences which can be encountered among these actors. It becomes obvious that while simultaneity for incorporation and development exists among organizations in both cities, intensity and topics of these engagements partly differ. Before entering into the analysis it seems necessary to describe briefly the situation of migrant organizations in Madrid and Barcelona.

Migrant organizing in Spanish cities is a relatively recent phenomenon, reflecting the recent increase in international migration. Data are difficult to obtain even on formalized associations, but according to a recent survey there are around 200 organizations in both cities (Morales et al., 2004; Morales and Jorba, 2010). Given the different sizes of the immigrant populations (550,000 vs. 280,000), the fact that the total number of migrant organizations in Madrid and Barcelona is roughly the same may be rather surprising These numbers reflect at least in part the fact that migrant organizations in Barcelona tend to be of smaller scope and membership, whereas some of the Madrid organizations can count on a very large number of members and to a greater extent have developed into established service providers of both local and national scope (Fauser, forthcoming). For instance, the Moroccan organization ATIME counts over 15,000 members. Other organizations in Madrid as well claim several thousand members (Morales et al., 2004, p. 10).

As many others, the investigated migrant organizations were formed in Madrid and Barcelona during the late 1980s and the early 2000s when inflows from many countries were rising. One organization had already been functioning as a foreign student organization since the early 1960s. All of them are actively engaged in the support of migrants' reception, settlement, and incorporation. Their activities include information, legal advice, and other kinds of service delivery as well as political participation in collective mobilization and/or consultative bodies on local, regional and national levels.

A dual orientation toward the situation in Spain and the place of origin existed from early on in most of these organizations. Sometimes this is reflected in the founding statutes voicing concern for the improvement of the situations 'here and there' and the will to contribute to the betterment of living conditions in both places. At relatively early stages these migrant organizations also founded counterparts and networks in their country of origin. Many of them opened up a branch or an office abroad only a few years after their formal establishment in the Spanish cities, some even in the same year of their foundation. This form of transnational network is meant to establish contacts with family members and returnees at home as well as – in the meantime – to carry out or coordinate transnational cooperation projects.

When referring to situations here and there, a keen perspective on simultaneous engagement is articulated. The aim is to involve migrants both in local and national politics in Spain as well as in the country of origin. In this respect, migrant organizations advocate the active political and social participation of migrants on both sides simultaneously. Representatives of some migrant organizations clearly specify transnational engagement also as an alternative to return because 'return never occurs' (Interview with a migrant organization representative, Madrid, 2006). Although this may be an exaggerated interpretation of uncertain future developments, it highlights the perspective of longer-term settlement which should go hand in hand with engagement with the places of origin.

In line with the call for participation of migrants, the meaning of development is 'not only about sending things'. It is articulated as a form of dual engagement, a reflection of the solidarity of migrants and non-migrants, partly embedded in current development discourses on community participation. This does not preclude the organizations' active involvement in politics and their advocacy for migrants' voting rights and political participation in Madrid and Barcelona.

> We feel that as immigrants we have to be involved in these projects and we have to cooperate. Even if it is with few resources. If I speak of cooperation, we are not only speaking about help or sending things. But that the people participate, the autochthon population; in the projects, in the implementation and once it is finished, that they participate in taking care [...]. And this somehow, first, can help to stop this immigration, sometimes uncontrolled, and then, also makes the [Nationality] immigrant not forget his origins and the reality. (Interview with a migrant organization representative, Barcelona, 2006)

It is only over time, as the findings show, that more concrete transnational engagement emerges or expands. This takes place when primary needs are satisfied and the organization together with the community in which it is based has become more established. Organizations' representatives describe how inflows from their reference country have dropped in numbers and changed their nature over time. Among certain nationalities, new immigration is based on family reunification; the community is altogether more settled and thus requires less support for initial reception from these organizations. In this situation, cultural activities become more extended, new groups are formed around youth and, depending on the community, women, and relationships and engagements with the country of origin become more institutionalized. This reflects what other studies found which have investigated migrants' (co)development potentials. These explain the thus far limited engagement of many migrant organizations with the country of origin on the basis of the still more urgently felt needs of new arrivals (Fons Català, 2006; Ruiz, 2003). Along the same lines, representatives from development agencies and municipal departments interviewed in the course of this research refer to the very recent growing interest in development cooperation on the part of migrant organizations, attributing this to the increased settlement and security of these populations.

Organizations in both cities which were not yet engaged in more concrete projects still referred to this perspective as a plan for the nearer future in documents and flyers or on their websites. In interviews some persons explained that, now that the organization and its community were more established, they planned to apply for newly available funds and that they already entered into contact with representatives from the respective departments and agencies to this end. Other organizations were already engaged in transnational development cooperation, some for many years. This is also reflected in organizational changes and new internal departments. This is visible, for instance, with the acronym ACULCO which at the beginning stood for 'Cultural Association for Colombia and Latin America'; later it was spelled out to read 'Socio-cultural Association and Development Cooperation for Colombia and Latin America'. The Moroccan organization ATIME, which was founded 1989 in Madrid, created in 1997 the Euro-Mediterranean Network for Development Cooperation (REMCODE) as an independent organization.

Increasingly, the term co-development is employed since 'of course, at first, you don't think in terms of co-development', as one interviewee described the emerging discourse and financial support (Interview with a migrant organization representative, Madrid, 2006). Sometimes, the term is also used to establish a difference between development cooperation (with the country of immigrants' origin) and co-development (involving contributions of immigrants).

Although a perspective on dual orientations and an intention to engage in development cooperation seems widely shared among migrant organizations in the two cities, some important differences also exist. Overall, transnational projects are represented to a greater degree among organizations in Madrid. More organizations from Madrid in the sample carry out projects abroad, and individual organizations also have more than one project. In Barcelona only one organization from the sample was found active in this respect, while others are currently planning to be, and all maintain cross-border contacts and networks to some degree. Interestingly, in both cities, projects were mentioned only in relation to public funding. The encountered local difference is supported by quantitative data. Between 70 and 80 per cent of all migrant organizations in the two cities are actively involved in some kind of transnational activity according to the survey cited at the beginning of this section (Morales and Jorba, 2010). These transnational activities include a great variety of contacts, networks and meetings with representatives from media, politics, administration and civil society from the country of origin. Those actively engaged in cross-border activities in the country of origin represent 20 per cent of the organizations in Madrid and 13 per cent in Barcelona. In addition, organizations in Madrid are not only numerically more engaged in transnational activities, their engagement is also more comprehensive, that is, covering various types of activities.

Another difference is the topics of the projects from organizations in the two cities which partly differ. In both cities classical development aid projects can be found. The issues which are addressed cover micro-credit and savings systems among poor households, malnutrition and undersupply of health care facilities, especially among children and women. There are projects promoting capacity building and labour market insertion, cultivation and commercialization of agro-cultural products, among other things. Other projects are located in the educational sector and support schools or provide computer classes and other skills training for marginalized sectors of society.

In addition, transnational projects involve channelling migration flows, but so far only among Madrid-based organizations. Concerns in relation to unregulated migration can be identified in many documents and conversations with representatives from the public administration and from migrant organizations as illustrated in the citation above. Projects specifically addressing the combat against irregular migration and the support of regular migration predominate in Madrid, though. Various activities are designed to inform potential migrants about the dangers and possibilities of migration to Spain, including advice about the application process within existing bilateral agreements for labour migration. Further initiatives are focused on returnees, in order to support their re-insertion. To this aim, migrant organizations maintain information centres or smaller projects, work with radio and TV programmes, and collaborate with other institutions in the origin country. To give an example, the Colombian newspaper *El Diario* informed its readers in December 2009 about the work of the Colombian branches of the Madrid-based organization AESCO, describing their efforts of the year:

> Throughout the year 2009, the Centre for Information, Assistance and legal support of AESCO in Pereira was visited by 3,700 persons, in Cali 3,000, and in Bogotá 3,100 citizens. In relation to return, it offered services to 136 persons in Pereira, 74 in the city of Cali, and 12 in the capital of the republic, a significant increase over 2008. 'This centre is dedicated to preventing uncontrolled migration and to offering services of assistance and legal support for regulated migration to the citizens who are potential migrants and for those who return from abroad helping with their re-insertion,' emphasized Ruge Mapi [the president of AESCO Colombia]. (*El Diario*, 29 December 2009)

Since at least some of the organizations in the sample are well-established service providers and others are similarly active although more informally and with fewer resources, they have long-standing experience with the legal procedures related to residence and work permits; they know the local labour market; they have their own networks on job opportunities; and they have acquired considerable knowledge in many other respects over the years. This vast fund of knowledge allows the organizations to provide follow-up advice and information when the migrants have arrived in Spain and hence can supplement the work of their branches in the country of origin.

> [The organization] wants to be involved in this process, both with the offices in [the origin country] that we have, and with us in the central office [in Madrid]. Trying to do everything related to adaptation. This is intended, in [the origin country], to inform the people a little, bring the reality in Spain closer to them, politics in Spain,

> what they will be confronted with, what they need to know, and to learn a bit before coming here. At least that they know where to buy a ticket for the metro, how to get their health care card, things which are the most basic, but which are necessary to know. And once they are here, it's all about social services, to support them in the process of adaptation, psychological advice. Everything. (Interview with a migrant organization representative, Madrid, 2006)

What can be encountered in Barcelona as well are indications for more informal collaborations with similar initiatives, but which so far are not carried out by the migrant organizations themselves. Nonetheless, migrant organizations there have been collaborating with similar institutions in the origin country, as for instance the *Casa del Migrante* in Ecuador's capital Quito, which is subsidized by the municipality of Quito and seems to collaborate with Barcelona-based organizations. However, more in-depth research in multiple locations, including the places of origin, would be necessary to determine this type of collaboration in more detail.

Several reasons can be identified which explain these differences between the two cities. First, the greater intensity among Madrid-based actors reflects their great size and strength as well as the early undertakings by the city of Madrid. In general, civil society organizations in the Spanish capital often are of both local and national scope. Networks and resources tend to be concentrated in the capital, allowing for easier access given the politically and geographically privileged location, a situation that also applies to migrant organizations. They have easier access to national funds, and, moreover, migrant organizations formed in Madrid have spread across the country, opening various branches in different regions and cities. This has also contributed to the spread of the concept to other places in Spain (Giménez Romero et al., 2006). This in turn allows for multi-locality organizations' access to various local funds. Most importantly for the issues concerned, the city of Madrid has had an earlier and stronger focus on co-development than other localities, which opened many opportunities to organizations based in the Spanish capital.

Another difference lies in the character of projects. Organizations in Barcelona are predominantly engaged (or plan to be) in more classical development projects and issues. In Madrid, migrant organizations are additionally active in relation to the management of migration. This is also explained by the different approaches in both cities, with the city of

Madrid following a focus on migration management within guidelines and funding schemes of co-development.

The spectrum of engagements is becoming more diverse: many other municipal and regional authorities, the national government through its latest 'Plan for Citizenship and Integration' (MTAS, 2007) as well as through the national agency for development AECID and other state and non-state actors, including those from origin places, join these efforts. Reports from organizations in Barcelona already contain references to information and assistance for future migrants in the origin country, supporting initiatives from other actors there. With the growth of attention on the migration–development nexus and the concept of co-development across Spain, local differences are likely to diminish. In the meantime, country-wide networks like the REDCO mentioned at the beginning of this chapter bring together migrant organizations from different Spanish cities. They contribute to an enhanced focus, and an exchange and elaboration of a shared understanding on migrants' transnational engagements and the concept of co-development. The central government's development agency AECID as well as the latest governmental Plan for Citizenship and Integration have moved the topic to a prominent place on the national level and also provide funding for such projects. These for their part also involve municipalities on both sides. Many other initiatives emerging in the migration–development and co-development debate activate local authorities 'here and there' in an effort to promote development and channel migratory flows (see, for instance, the description of co-development programmes by the Madrid-based Spanish development organizations Cideal in Ecuador and Colombia [Fernández, 2009]).

Efforts made in the localities of reception can thus be considered important opportunities, supplementing, shaping and reinforcing other initiatives. The important role of locality and community in current dynamics strengthens local-to-local or trans-local relationships. The organizations maintain, or aim to maintain, relations with the public authorities at both ends of the migratory process, and try to establish themselves as interlocutors between the sites of origin and reception. The intent is to bring together public officials in order to connect both sides more closely. In their description of the work in the country of origin, a Dominican migrant organization based in Madrid highlights first results on its website:

> Last year we were successful in bringing together the mayors of the Dominican Republic from the localities where the immigrants come

from with the Spanish mayors who receive them to engage around the different problems that emigration brings about. (Vomade, 2006)

Conclusion

The analysis presented in this chapter has addressed the newly emerging patterns of migrant transnationalism in the context of the current migration–development debate. This debate and the subsequent policies arising from it expand an already established emphasis on locality and community in development politics and projects, now also including the community of migrants. Against this background migrant organizations find new opportunities to transnationalize. Thus, in this round of the migration–development nexus debate, it is important to reconsider some of the established concepts and approaches in the study of migrant transnationalism and the role of the state.

Sub-national levels of government from the receiving side have come to play an important role in the realm of reception and incorporation as well as within the frameworks of decentralized development cooperation. They have now also entered the stage of the migration–development debate, providing new opportunities for the transnationalization of migrant communities and migrant organizations. Thus far, transnational migration scholarship has accounted for the role of the state focusing on the many and active initiatives of states of origin which address migrants' loyalty and engagement with their 'homeland' (Goldring, 2002; Itzigsohn 2000; Østergaard-Nielsen, 2003; Smith 2003). Receiving states have been considered primarily in relation to their function for incorporation into the 'new land'. In contrast, the absence of favourable conditions in the host state and society is found to contribute to further transnationalization and homeland orientation (Koopmans and Statham, 2003; Layton-Henry, 1990). The potential of active contributions from the receiving side to promote transnational engagements has generally been overlooked. In addition, theoretical concepts, methodologies and the corresponding research designs for the most part limit their focus to the national state level, while the role of localities and local governments has seldom been considered, and least of all on the receiving side. The role of local receiving authorities is now coming to the fore in their active promotion of migrants as agents of development. Hence, receiving-side institutions and local levels need to be systematically integrated into the study of transnationalism. In the new immigration cities of Madrid and Barcelona various municipal agencies not only recognize transnational engagements of migrant communities and their organizations, but they also actively promote these initiatives and provide public subsidies to this end. On the basis of the policy concept of co-development, manifold activities are now expanding in the two cities which contribute to more intense engagement in transnational cooperation across and within migrant organizations. There are partial differences between the two cities in the intensity, understandings and measures related to the concept of co-development. This is reflected in the work of migrant organizations located there. While in both cities initiatives aim to bring migrant organizations and the wider migrant community into development cooperation, the city of Madrid is distinctive in its effort to link these activities to the objective of channelling migration.

The observations of the research presented here also require reconsidering assumptions about migrant organizations and their evolution over time. The study of migrant organizations has largely highlighted tensions between local incorporation and transnational engagement for development in places of origin. Supported by more recent research findings, scholars argue that simultaneous engagements exist and may be compatible (Guarnizo et al., 2003; Portes et al., 2007; Smith, 2007). In this respect the transfer of experiences, skills and social capital acquired through transnational activism is an important means for migrant organizations to relate to the work and institutions of incorporation. The analysis presented in this chapter suggests the need to also consider the possibility of transfers of experiences and resources acquired through engagement for reception and incorporation toward transnational action. Among the investigated migrant organizations reception and incorporation occupied the agendas during the first years of their existence. In the meantime transnational engagement and cross-border projects in countries of origin are growing among actors in both cities. For these purposes organizations greatly rely on opportunities and resources which are now provided in the receiving-site localities. Moreover, they make use of their experiences, knowledge and networks acquired in their work for reception and incorporation.

Supported by the early focus of the city of Madrid on co-development and the strength of organizations located there, cross-border projects seem currently more prominent in Madrid than in Barcelona. Further, while initiatives in both cities aim to involve migrant organizations and communities in development cooperation, only among Madrid-based actors do projects also deal with issues of migration, not least because of the city's strong focus on the management of migration flows. In Barcelona no funding for comparable initiatives could be identified so far. Nonetheless, organizations based in the Catalan city also deal with similar issues, but approach them in more informal ways and through collaboration with other institutions, including origin-side municipalities. This brings migrant organizations along with other non-state actors into the politics of development and migration, together with municipal institutions. While the role of local authorities and (migrant) communities today is increasingly acknowledged as crucial to the reception and incorporation of migrants and in many places they are also involved in development cooperation, both now also enter realms related to channelling migration flows, thus far a domain that has been exclusive to the national state and its territorial sovereignty.

Note

1. The material stems from a larger project on migrant organizing in the new immigration contexts of Madrid and Barcelona (Fauser, forthcoming 2011).

References

Primary sources

Ayuntamiento de Madrid (2005a) Plan Madrid de Convivencia Social e Intercultural, Madrid.

Ayuntamiento de Madrid (2005b) Plan General de Cooperación 2005–2008, Madrid.

El Diario [Colombia], 29 December 2009.

Fons Català (2006) *Co-développement Catalogne-Sénégal: leçon de 10 ans d´experience. Évaluation du projet MIDEL* (Barcelona: Fons Català de Cooperació al Desenvolupament).

Fons Català (2007) Fons Català de Cooperació al Desenvolupament, at: www.fonscatala.org (accessed 8 November 2010).

MTAS (2007) *Plan Estratégico Ciudadanía e Integración 2007–2010* (Madrid: Ministerio de Trabajo y Asuntos Sociales [MTAS])

Vomade (2006) Voluntariado de Madres Dominicanas en España, at: www.vomade.net/actual.html (accessed 11 September 2006).

Secondary sources

Agrela, B. and Dietz, G. (2006) 'Nongovernmental versus Governmental Actors? Multilevel Governance and Immigrant Integration Policy in Spain', in T. Tsuda (ed.), *Local Citizenship in Recent Countries of Immigration: Japan in Comparative Perspective* (Lanham: Lexington Books).

Aragón Medina, J., Artiaga Leiras, A., Haidour, M. H., Martínez Poza, A. and Rocha Sánchez, F. (2009) *Las políticas locales para la integración de los inmigrantes y la participación de los agentes sociales* (Madrid: Catarata).

Baraulina, T., Bommes, M., El-Cherkeh, T. and Vadean, F. (2006) *Ägyptische, afghanische und serbische Diasporagemeinden in Deutschland und ihre Beiträge zur Entwicklung ihrer Herkunftsländer* (Eschborn: Deutsche Gesellschaft für Technische Zusammenarbeit [GTZ]).

Çağlar, A. S. (2006) 'Hometown Associations and Grassroots Transnationalism', *Global Networks*, 6 (1), 1–22.

——— (2007) 'Rescaling Cities, Cultural Diversity and Transnationalism: Migrants of Mardin and Essen,' *Ethnic and Racial Studies*, 30 (6), 1070–1095.

Casas Álvarez, F. (2000) 'Emigración, Codesarrollo y Cooperación para el Desarollo. Reflexiones desde una Óptica Española', *Migraciones*, 8, 101–126.

Cordero-Guzmán, H. (2005) 'Community-Based Organisations and Migration in New York City', *Journal of Ethnic and Migration Studies*, 31 (5), 889–910.

Daum, C. (ed.) (1993) *Quand les immigrés du Sahel construisent leur pays* (Paris: Institut Panos).

De Haas, H. (2006) *Engaging Diasporas: How Governments and Development Agencies Can Support Diaspora Involvement in the Development of Origin Countries* (Oxford: International Migration Institute, University of Oxford).

Escrivà, A. and Ribas, N. (2004) 'La investigación sobre migración, desarrollo y transnacionalismo. Contribuciones para un debate desde España', in A. Escrivà and N. Ribas (eds), *Migración y Desarrollo: Estudios sobre remesas y otras prácticas transnacionales en España* (Córdoba: Colección Politeya. Estudios de Política y Sociedad).

Faist, T. (1998) 'Transnational Social Spaces out of International Migration: Evolution, Significance and Future Prospects', *Archives européennes de sociologie/European Journal of Sociology*, 39 (2), 213–248.

——— (2000) *The Volume and Dynamics of International Migration and Transnational Social Spaces* (Oxford: Clarendon Press/Oxford University Press).

——— (2008) 'Migrants as Transnational Development Agents: An Inquiry into the Newest Round of the Migration-Development Nexus', *Population, Space and Place*, 14 (1), 21–42.

Fauser, M. (forthcoming 2011) *Migrants and Cities: The Accommodation of Migrant Organizations in Europe* (Aldershot: Ashgate).

Fernández, J. C. (2009) 'Experiencia de campo. Programas de Cideal en Ecuador y Colombia', in A. Gónzalez Gil (ed.), *Lugares, processo y migrantes. Aspectos de la migración colombiana* (Brussels: Peter Lang).

Fitzgerald, D. (2006) 'Inside the Sending State: The Politics of Mexican Emigration Control', *International Migration Review*, 40 (2), 259–293.

Giménez Romero, C., Martínez Martínez, J. L., Fernández García, M. and Cortés Maisonave, A. (2006) *El Codesarollo en España. Protagonistas, Discursos y Experiencias* (Madrid: Catarata).

Glick Schiller, N., Basch, L. and Blanc-Szanton, C. (1992) 'Transnationalism: A New Analytical Framework for Understanding Migration', *Annals of the New York Academy of Science*, 645, 1–24.

——— and Çağlar, A. S. (2009) 'Toward a Comparative Theory of Locality in Migration Studies: Migrant Incorporation and City Scale', *Journal of Ethnic and Migration Studies*, 35 (2), 177–202.

——— and Fouron, G. (1999) 'Terrains of Blood and Nation: Haitian Transnational Social Fields', *Ethnic and Racial Studies*, 22 (2), 340–366.

Goldring, L. (2002) 'The Mexican State and Transmigrant Organizations: Negotiating the Boundaries of Membership and Participation', *Latin American Research Review*, 37 (3), 55–99.

Grillo, R. and Riccio, B. (2004) 'Translocal Development: Italy – Senegal', *Population, Space and Place*, 10, 99–111.

Guarnizo, L. E., Portes, A. and Haller, W. (2003) 'Assimilation and Transnationalism: Determinants of Transnational Political Action among Contemporary Migrants', *American Journal of Sociology*, 108 (6), 1211–1248.

Intermón-Oxfam (2005) *Estudios intermón oxfam*, 16.

InWEnt (2007) 'Die kommunale Entwicklungszusammenarbeit in ausgewählten europäischen Ländern. Fallstudien zu Frankreich, Norwegen und Spanien', *Material – Schriftenreihe der Servicestelle Kommunen in einer Welt*, 29.

Itzigsohn, J. (2000) 'Immigration and the Boundaries of Citizenship: The Institutions of Immigrants' Political Transnationalism', *International Migration Review*, 34 (4), 1126–1154.

Kivisto, P. (2005) 'Social Spaces, Transnational Immigrant Communities, and the Politics of Incorporation', in P. Kivisto (ed.), *Incorporating Diversity: Rethinking Assimilation in a Multicultural Age* (Boulder: Paradigm Publishers).

Koopmans, R. and Statham, P. (2003) 'How National Citizenship Shapes Transnationalism: Migrant and Minority Claims-making in Germany, Great Britain and the Netherlands', in C. Joppke and E. Morawska (eds), *Toward Assimilation and Citizenship: Immigrants in Liberal Nation-States* (Basingstoke: Palgrave Macmillan).

Lacroix, T. (2005) *Les réseaux marocains du développement. Géographie du transnational et politiques du territorial* (Paris: Presses de la Fondation Nationale des Sciences Politiques).

Layton-Henry, Z. (1990) 'Immigrant Associations', in Z. Layton-Henry (ed.), *The Political Rights of Migrant Workers in Western Europe* (London: Sage Publications).

Levitt, P. (1997) 'Transnationalizing Community Development: The Case of Migration between Boston and the Dominican Republic', *Nonprofit and Voluntary Sector Quarterly*, 26 (4), 509–26.

——— (2001) *The Transnational Villagers* (Berkeley: University of California Press).

Morales, L., González, A. and Sánchez, G. (2004) 'La integración política de los inmigrantes: un estudio sobre las asociaciones de immigrantes en Madrid y Múrcia', *Actes del IV Congrés sobre la immigració a Espanya: Ciutadania i Participació, Girona*.

——— and Jorba, L. (2010) 'The Transnational Links and Practices of Migrants' Organisations in Spain', in R. Bauböck and T. Faist (eds), *Transnationalism and Diaspora. Concepts, Theories and Methods* (Amsterdam: Amsterdam University Press).

Naïr, S. (1997) *Rapport de bilan et d'orientations sur la politique de co-développement liée aux flux migratoires*, Paris, at: www.ladocumentationfrancaise.fr/rapports-publics/984000139/index.shtml (accessed 8 November 2010).

Orozco, M. and Lapointe, M. (2004) 'Mexican Hometown Associations and Development Opportunities', *Journal of International Affairs*, 57 (2), 1–21.

Østergaard-Nielsen, E. (2003) 'The Politics of Migrants' Transnational Political Practices', *International Migration Review*, 37 (3), 760–786.

Pacheco Medrano, K. (2003) 'El Codesarrollo en España: Posibilidades y Desafíos', *Migraciones*, 13, 185–207.

Pájares, M. (2006) 'Las políticas locales en el ámbito de la inmigración', in E. Aja and J. Arango (eds), *Veinte Años de Inmigración en España. Perspectivas Juridícas y Sociológicas (1985-2004)* (Barcelona: Fundació CIDOB).

Park, R. E. and Miller, H. A. (1969[1921]) *Old World Traits Transplanted* (New York: Arno Press and the New York Times).

Petiteville, F. (1995) *La coopération décentralisée. Les collectivités locales dans la coopération Nord-Sud* (Paris: Editions L'Harmattan).

Portes, A., Escobar, C. and Arana, R. (2008) 'Bridging the Gap: Transnational and Ethnic Organizations in the Political Incorporation of Immigrants in the United States', *Ethnic and Racial Studies*, 31 (6), 1025–1055.

Portes, A., Escobar, C. and Walton Radford, A. (2007) 'Immigrant Transnational Organizations and Development: A Comparative Study', *International Migration Review*, 41 (1), 242–281.

Pries, L. (1999) 'New Migration in Transnational Spaces', in L. Pries (ed.), *Migration and Transnational Social Spaces* (Aldershot: Ashgate).

——— (2010) '(Grenzenüberschreitende) Migrantenorganisationen als Gegenstand der sozialwissenschaftlichen Forschung: Klassische Problemstellungen und neuere Forschungsbefunde', in L. Pries and Z. Sezgin (eds), *Jenseits von 'Identität oder Integration'. Grenzen überspannende Migrantenorganisationen* (Wiesbaden: VS Verlag für Sozialwissenschaften).

Pries, L. and Sezgin, Z. (eds) (2010) *Jenseits von 'Identität oder Integration'. Grenzen überspannende Migrantenorganisationen* (Wiesbaden: VS Verlag für Sozialwissenschaften).

Ramos, J. A., Bazaga, I., Delgado, L. and del Pino, E. (1998) *La política para la integración social de los inmigrantes: una perspectiva intergubernamental* (Madrid: Fundación Ortega y Gasset).

Ruiz, I. (2003) *Estratègies Associatives dels Collectius Marroquins a Barcelona. Informe de recera* (Barcelona: Centre d´Estudis Africans de Barcelona).

Ruiz Jiménez, L. (2006) *Información Coordinada. Cooperación Efectiva. Un proyecto Informativo sobre la Cooperación de España y Portugal con América Latina* (Madrid: Instituto Universitario Ortega y Gasset).

Sassen, S. (2002) 'Global Cities and Diasporic Networks: Microsites in Global Civil Society', in M. Glasius, M. Kaldor and H. Anheier (eds), *Global Civil Society Yearbook* (Oxford and New York: Oxford University Press).

Schöneberg, U. (1985) 'Participation in Ethnic Associations: The Case of Immigrants in West Germany', *International Migration Review*, 19 (3), 416–437.

Schrover, M. and Vermeulen, F. (eds) (2005) *Journal of Ethnic and Migration Studies*, 31 (5), Special Issue on Immigrant Organisations.

Sieveking, N., Fauser, M. and Faist, T. (2008) *Gutachten zum entwicklungspolitischen Engagement der in NRW lebenden MigrantInnen afrikanischer Herkunft,* Working Paper 28/2008 (Bielefeld: COMCAD – Center on Migration, Citizenship and Development).

Smith, M. P. (2003) 'Transnationalism, the State, and the Extraterritorial Citizen', *Politics and Society*, 31 (4), 467–502.

——— (2007) 'The Two Faces of Transnational Citizenship', *Ethnic and Racial Studies*, 30 (6), 1096–1116.

Vertovec, S. (2004) 'Migrant Transnationalism and Modes of Transformation', *International Migration Review*, 28 (3), 970–1001.

Waldrauch, H. and Sohler, K. (2004) *Migrantenorganisationen in der Großstadt. Entstehung, Strukturen und Aktivitäten am Beispiel Wien* (Frankfurt a.M. and New York: Campus Verlag).

Zabin, C. and Escala, L. (2002) 'From Civic Association to Political Participation: Mexican Hometown Associations and Mexican Immigrant Political Empowerment in Los Angeles', *Frontera norte*, 14 (27), 1–34.

7
A Sociology of Diaspora Knowledge Networks

Jean-Baptiste Meyer

Diaspora knowledge networks (DKNs) – associations of highly skilled expatriates willing to contribute to the development of their origin countries – emerged in the 1990s. For mobility studies and migration policies, this meant a shift in the existing emphasis on brain drain toward a perspective on brain gain and from the physical return of people to distant though dense and continuous connections. The traditional 'return option' is distinguished from the 'diaspora option' with respect to the potentials of migration for development. Highly skilled migrants were no longer to be seen only as human capital holders to be repatriated but also as accessible social capital mediators who could potentially be mobilized in support of the country of origin (Barré et al., 2003). As new actors in the migration–development arena, DKNs have raised interests and expectations. But they have also been received with some suspicion, doubt and criticism as to their actual ability to perform a development role effectively. This chapter discusses new literature and empirical evidence from different world regions to point to the weaknesses of the DKN but also to the visible strengths. Thus it conceives of the DKN as an essential element of the migration–development nexus.

Several case studies report systematic or anecdotal evidence of DKNs' active involvement in and contribution to science and technology developments in origin countries. The accumulating evidence about DKNs has gradually made possible a more precise analysis of their benefits or shortcomings. A number of academic research or cooperation agencies' works have highlighted a diverse set of case studies which together can be useful for assessing the strengths and weaknesses of the 'brain gain diaspora option': the Colombian Red Caldas network (Meyer et al., 1997; Charum and Meyer, 1998; Chaparro et al., 2006);

the South African Network of Skills Abroad as well as the South African Diaspora Network (Brown, 2003; NRF, 2005; Marks, 2006); the network experiences of Latin America (Lema, 2003), Argentina (Kuznetsov et al., 2006), India (Khadria, 2003; Leclerc and Meyer, 2007; Pandey et al., 2006), the Philippines (Opiniano and Castro, 2006) and Afghanistan (Hanifi, 2006), as well as Armenia (Minoian and Freinkman, 2006) and the huge Chinese diasporas (Guo, 2003; Xiang, 2005). There are also a number of synthetic works compiling some of these contributions and others (Barré et al., 2003; Westcott, 2005, 2006; Kuznetsov, 2006). All these case studies of DKNs refer to initiatives led either by state administrations (primarily those of countries of origin) or by groups of migrants themselves or, quite often, the two combined.

Activities in which the DKNs' contributions have been observed are summarized in the following list:

(a) Exchange of scientific, technical, administrative or political information (contribution to the creation of the new Colombian National S&T system in the early 1990s, by prominent expatriates);
(b) Specialist knowledge transfer (waste management procedures from the Ecole Polytechnique Fédérale de Lausanne, Switzerland, with the Universidad del Valle, Cali, Colombia);
(c) 'Scientific or technological diplomacy' or promoting the home country in the R&D and business communities of the host country (South African medical research in England, Indian IT entrepreneurs in Silicon Valley);
(d) Joint projects, partly on a virtual basis (distant working, simulations);
(e) Training: attending home-country sessions, and meeting/mentoring students abroad (a feature shared by most DKNs);
(f) Enterprise creation (including multinational subsidiaries) to assist the possible return of expatriates on a part-time or permanent basis (Chinese high-tech firms with returnees in science parks);
(g) Ad hoc consultations, for example on research/development projects (peer review, job recruitment, technology assessment).

In contrast to studies which highlight these aspects, some surveys from different areas or disciplines (migration, science policy, economics) have questioned the diaspora option (Gaillard and Gaillard, 2003; Lowell and Gerova, 2004; Lucas, 2004). Their inquiries can be classified in the following four categories:

(a) Those dealing with the magnitude of the phenomenon: are the networks already identified and studied isolated events or a representative sample? Do these examples of strong identification from expatriate talents signify a general dynamic or simply an exceptional form of international socialisation?
(b) Those putting into question the sustainability of the expatriate associations: are these networks technically equipped to last more than a few years? As temporary groupings of highly mobile individuals can they keep a membership stable enough to manage a necessary continuity?
(c) Those criticizing the consistency and extrapolation of activities from internet visibility: are websites really picturing associations with a true social and productive life? Are they not often short-lived individual attempts left as remnants on cyberspace, dead stars sending light of anterior existence? Would the networks not be simply token means responding to the hunger of agencies desperately looking for attractive solutions to the brain drain?
(d) Those expressing strong scepticism about the actual impact of the networks on the home countries' S&T or economic developments: can they really contribute to local scientific communities when these are almost non-existent (in Africa for instance)? Can they compensate virtually for the lack of physical resources in laboratories or enterprises? Can we attribute high-tech or IT developments to these diasporas when the combination of local factors and conditions seems to potentially explain the determinants of change (in India for instance)?

When several of these questions are taken jointly into account, the object of research and of policy – the very diasporic associations themselves – dissolves into thin air. If a group of highly skilled expatriates working officially for the development of their country of origin is an exception, with a very low probability of survival, with an internet window serving as a pretext for inflated international projections and expectations but whose real impact on the country of origin is simply an illusion, there is nothing of substance left in the diaspora option.

In fact, the evidence on which many of the doubts about the networks mentioned above is based is limited. The hunch that highly skilled diasporic initiatives might have been a short-lived postmodern fantasy in the social sciences and a fashionable tool for policy-makers impatient for quick-fix solutions cannot be confirmed. Some of the critiques raised may thus be addressed and answered through a deeper analysis

The experience indeed shows the erratic activities, limited results and precarious life of many DKNs. However, the question of the relationship with and impact on the country of origin is a crucial one. This fact calls for an elaboration of the dynamics of such networks: do they have autonomous effects or are these still dependent on national conditions? What are the market and/or policy impacts on their developments? Do network histories reflect and reproduce states-of-origin weaknesses or can they provide these with unexpected resources such as access to remote facilities or specialized knowledge and expertise?

In order to explain the constitution and dynamics of DKNs, this chapter uses a theoretical framework to interpret the evidence gathered in many case studies. It draws on actor/network sociology (Latour, 1987, 2005) to explore the way that action shapes the context and therefore results of transnational activities and relations in the making. In particular, the concept of translation and interessement (*intéressement*) are used. Both provide an analytical framework to explain the divergent fate of various networks and suggest constructive avenues to deal with such dynamics. The overall argument is that social ties – here diasporic links – are woven through mediations put in place by the actors. By comparing conventional success stories, such as the Indian and Chinese examples, with less successful endeavours from the Colombian and South African cases – the only countries for which detailed evidence was available – some explanatory factors are extracted. They point at differing relational strategies and practices by diasporas, which explain the variations in results. The concepts of translation and interessement provide tools for interpretation in terms of mediation processes and ability to act. Applied to the four diasporic cases, they show the presence of active and decisive mediators in the two Asian diasporas and their absence or weaknesses in the other two cases, which crucially undermined their networks' efficiency.

The chapter consists of three sections: the first deals with the constitution and dynamics of DKNs; the second addresses the question of their impact on developments in the countries of origin; and the third proposes a conceptualization of what explains the success or failure of these developments through the ANT (Actor Network Theory) theoretical framework.

Constitution and dynamics of diaspora knowledge networks

The DKNs are very diverse regarding geographic scope, thematic focus, size, activity and longevity. However, they are all built on the same basic objective: to take advantage of expatriate networks and human resources for the benefit of the origin country. The logic to which they all respond is thus one of connectivity. This is what makes the diaspora option distinct from – though complementary to – the return option. The latter relies on permanent repatriation of individuals' human capital to be physically reinserted in the local environment, while the former mobilizes networks of expatriates through a single actor with whom direct contact is made. There is, thus, a multiplier effect.

What make expatriates particularly valuable, indeed, for their country of origin, is obviously the skills displayed in their cognitive activities and made available at home, but also the path or access to equipment and facilities unavailable locally, the status, credibility and peer recognition attached to formal employment in a firm or lab of international visibility and thus provided to a peripheral actor or local site without any cost, access to major funding programmes (see US-National Science Fund cases in Johnson, 2003; and EU multilateral projects in Granes and Morales, 1998), the introduction to markets especially through the integration of procedures, standards and quality assessments (see Lucas, 2004) and the like.

In the case of the South African Network of Skills Abroad (SANSA), some human capital and social capital indicators have been defined in a reductive though analytical manner (Meyer et al., 2001). The diploma and the socio-professional positions have been chosen as proxies, for human capital and social capital respectively. Both types of capital are very high in the South African diaspora: the rate of PhDs is twice as high as in the equivalent qualified population at home (figures for the year 2000); three out of four expatriate professionals are in executive positions in organizations where they are employed. While the former (human capital) requires the reconstruction of an adequate context in order to be used intensively once repatriated, the latter (extensive social capital) can be made available in a remote manner.

For the governments of the countries of origin, the goal is to tap the expatriate professionals and the resources connected to them. Because of the executive positions and power these professionals hold, their capacity to mobilize significant resources is globally very high, making the potential multiplier effect quite effective. For these reasons, the involvement and commitment of even a small number of expatriates may be decisive, as shown by anecdotal evidence on other diasporas (for instance, on the case of Chile, see Kuznetsov, 2006, pp. 5–6).

The evidence also demonstrates that for the cases observed, a significant number of the highly skilled expatriates are willing to help their countries of origin. The individual motivations may be quite diverse: guilt feelings over having left and 'made their fortune' away from home; activist commitment or sentimental nostalgia; opportunities to keep in touch with relatives; expectations about professional developments; social or entrepreneurial expansion; opportunities for international connections and support granted by cooperation agencies. Diaspora members are, in principle, sensitive to the home country's situation, open to its solicitation and available for cooperation. Even though only a fraction of DKN members may actually respond to its call, the occasional surveys of non-participants in DKNs (South African or Colombian expatriates interviewed about their knowledge of respective DKNs) indicate they are inactive more for reasons of simple ignorance or unawareness than lack of interest in the life of their home countries. The desire for networking usually comes from both sides: the diaspora and the state of origin.

The motivation behind DKN creation, development and members' commitment deserves a more detailed explanation. The mutually reinforcing relationship between human and social capital has been observed (Helliwell and Putnam, 1999; Denny, 2003) and the highly skilled expatriates' propensity to gather and build associations fits with this pattern (Banks and Tanner, 1997; Gibson, 2001). At the same time, however, the opportunity cost for professionals to get involved in non-profit activities is comparatively high (Brown and Lankford, 1992). This also explains why it is difficult for DKNs to retain the highly skilled expatriates – even more so than to recruit them – because their time is relatively less available than for other working or non-active persons. Underproductive endeavours are thus quickly punished with an 'exit' by those who might have embarked on them initially with enthusiasm.

Beyond individual dispositions, however, there is an interesting collective process at work in the constitution of DKNs. As mentioned by Brinkerhoff (2006), expression of identity in such networks plays an important role. Our own research results on Colombian and South African networks have shown that these identity expressions are very much constructed by the actors themselves when they decide to get involved in the network (Meyer et al., 1997; Meyer et al., 2001).

The identification of professional expatriates with their countries of origin is a product of networking through DKNs. However, it does correspond to a rather classical phenomenon in sociology. The labour market, traditionally regulated and bounded by national borders, is a site in which national belonging is visible (Gellner, 1983). This is largely because certain career markets are still relatively closed and access is regulated by certificates prescribed by public authorities, which have been defined by local agreements and negotiations. Though this situation is certainly evolving quickly, values and the evaluation of professional achievements are still tied to national references and therefore to social and personal relations kept there (Dubar, 1991). The professional identification along nationally bounded labour markets strengthens the national origin as a determinant of identity. It is a re-identification through professional motives. This finding points to an important fact: identification processes are dynamic and action-related, and they are tied more to current work activity than to passive cultural remnants. This is especially so for cognitive professional practice. Knowledge production and development are indeed activities in which self-identification processes through collective projection into the future are very high (Meyer, 2006). The new diasporas of scientists and engineers have highlighted this phenomenon in an unexpected manner (Meyer, 2004a). The increasing awareness of the importance of knowledge in the development process, stimulated by the emerging national systems of innovation in developing countries, as well as the opening up of these countries to international influences in the 1990s – Argentina, Chile, China, Colombia and India being good examples – have generated an active re-integration process between the diaspora and the countries of origin. This new integrative perspective implemented by many countries today is part of a wider repertoire of public policies toward emigrants (Gamlen, 2005).

The questionable impact of diaspora knowledge networks

The diaspora option – taken to mean the actions of highly skilled expatriates' networks to foster development in their home countries – originally emerged in Latin America. Of all the Latin American experiences, the Red Caldas network is probably the best known, having been the focus of various studies since its inception in 1991. The network was the outcome of a combination of factors, including a spontaneous initiative on the part of Colombian expatriates to form local associations (mainly in the United States, Spain, France, Britain, Switzerland, Belgium and Germany) and their decision to link up via the Internet, which was booming at the time, just as Colombia was launching its own science and technology system, backed by policies to promote international cooperation (Meyer et al., 1997). The Red Caldas network was a model of its kind owing to its rapid growth, but its subsequent development has been marked by numerous problems. These were brought to light in a recent evaluation report of this network commissioned by the

World Bank, as part of a general study on knowledge inputs within the migration–development nexus (Kutznetsov, 2006). This study looked back over the network's history and highlighted issues such as resource allocation weaknesses, poor organization and technical management on the communication front, a mismatch between administrative structures in Colombia and in the host countries, and the failure to develop the network and its skills in Colombia itself (Chaparro et al., 2006).

A broader historical review of all Latin American networks points to a crucial lack of professionalism. Run by voluntary members with enthusiastic personal commitment but too little time to devote to such work, they are subject to the vagaries of organizations whose staff cannot ensure the regular continuity of projects and activities (Lema, 2003). This lack of professionalism obviously limits any scope for sustainable development. The problem has apparently been overcome by some networks whose expatriates are from a part of the world where government or business can take over from volunteers where necessary, namely Asia (see below).

The second interesting case, the South African Network of Skills Abroad (SANSA), was created in 1998 and turned into a well-studied case in the following years. Before the end of the millennium it managed to gather more than 2000 members in 65 countries, with very high numbers of individuals who were educationally qualified and who held senior positions in all sorts of professional fields (Brown, 2003). Initially highly successful in the mobilization process, like the Colombian Red Caldas, it also faced problems in subsequent developments. A recent evaluation of its activities emphasizes the fact that in spite of being in possession of a sophisticated internet infrastructure, that infrastructure is underutilized and dormant (NRF, 2005).

However, these isolated case studies on the Colombian and South African experience elicited only partial information from specific surveys, ethnographic observation, and personal interviews. Were they representative of a new transnational practice among scientists and engineers? It could not be determined whether such examples reflected a general trend toward a 'brain gain' approach or exceptional and short-lived attempts. Today, the data collected about highly skilled diaspora networks overcome most of the limitations discussed by various authors (Lowell and Gerova, 2004; Lucas, 2004). These data come partly from a systematic analysis of hundreds of websites on the one hand, and from specific studies of Asian diaspora networks on the other hand (Meyer and Wattiaux, 2006; Leclerc and Meyer, 2007). These analyses yielded quantitative evidence and qualitative information about the dynamics, relations and actions of some of these networks. The former study confirmed the existence of many recent diaspora networks working for their members' countries of origin; the latter demonstrated that such networks could have a significant impact on developments at home through effective transnational ties.

The cases of China and India are now well documented and a few lessons may be extracted from their detailed description (Xiang, 2006; Leclerc and Meyer, 2007). Among the points more specific to the Chinese case which explain the magnitude and success of its highly skilled diaspora mobilization, the following five aspects may be emphasized: first, the population of OCPs (Overseas Chinese Professionals) in the world is estimated to be about one million, with high concentration in North America; second, there are more than 200 OCP associations registered by the OCAO (Council for Overseas Chinese Abroad Office); third, a specific policy (*wei guo fuwu*) was set up by the Chinese government in the late 1990s promoting linkages with talents in the diaspora; fourth, at least five ministries and a large number of provincial government agencies as well as quasi-state entities are involved in programmes and activities with highly skilled expatriates; and finally, short-term visits, collaborative projects between OCPs and home academic communities, senior expatriate scientists lectures in China, occasional technical advice, local recruitment through major fairs, or more selective encounters are part of the many activities displayed by the diaspora and counterparts in China.

The role of the associations of OCPs, whose number has increased during recent years, seems a key factor in the expansion of links between formal and informal networks. In addition, the internet happens to be the major medium used by OCPs to stay connected with the country and among themselves.

The Chinese case provides strong confirmation of the great number and current expansion of highly skilled expatriate associations, their intensity of activity, as well as their responsiveness to policy factors. The key question addressed here concerns the transformations these associations generate in the countries of origin and more specifically on the development process – of which it may, or may not, be the impulse. Thus far divergent explanations have been offered, as in the case of India for instance.

The role of the diaspora, particularly in the Indian IT industry's development, has also been discussed during the past few years. Scholars are unanimous in thinking this role has been important, especially in lowering trade barriers, but divergences are recorded with regard to the priority given. Some authors (Lucas, 2004; Kapur and McHale, 2005) subordinate the expatriates' input to local factors in India (mainly cheap, highly skilled labour), while others see the intervention of prominent non-resident Indians (NRI) and associations in the United States as crucial and determining (Saxenian et al., 2002; Khadria and Leclerc, 2006). Overall, as in the case of the underestimated numbers of diaspora networks, the evidence increasingly points to the key role of diaspora entities compared to traditional market factors. Anecdotal evidence of Non Resident Indians Information Technology (NRT-IT) executives and entrepreneurs in the US shows, indeed, their direct involvement in and original contribution to high-level activities geared toward development in Bangalore and other industrial locations (Pandey et al., 2006). Strategic transformation in this field in India with the branch moving up the value chain from low- to highly skilled activities appears to be directly related to diaspora initiatives combined with the return of well-trained IT employees after the slowdown of activities in the US in the early 2000s (Warrier, 2006). Micro-level and historical records of Indian IT firms reveal that a real transfer of technology has taken place, with India capturing knowledge-intensive and competitive parts of the production process from expatriates (Leclerc and Meyer, 2007).

The Indian high-tech sector's development is correlated with the impressive expansion and intensity of professional associations of NRI-IT specialists and engineers in the United States and in California in particular. India ranks first among the countries with DKNs working for the development of the country of origin. To these DKNs with clear transfer and development purposes should be added the many professional associations serving the careers, entrepreneurial and business endeavours, and networking activities of Asian/Indian community members in the US. The profusion of actors and intermediaries makes this milieu extremely dense and fertile. This situation is matched in India where national and local governments as well as universities, technology institutes, professional associations, federations, commissions and chambers of commerce are very present and active. Between India and the US, continuous circulation of human and material agents feeds both poles with complementary tasks and objects. Interactivity in this multiple and dispersed milieu is ensured by a systematic and creative use of computer-mediated communication. It is such a basic existential attribute that the absence of a personal blog is, for instance, sarcastically described by the actors themselves as a prehistoric situation (Leclerc and Meyer, 2007).

These high-tech Asian diaspora success stories are sometimes considered to be exceptional cases. Would such positive impacts be plausible in other sectors and places, where transportability and conditions of re-appropriation would be much poorer? Interesting cases in the health sector in Africa may be mentioned indicating that even in physically grounded activities and resource-deficient receptive communities, the influx of networks could be tangible and significant. One example that has been mentioned is that of a pool of medical surgeons based in France, making themselves available through a simple telephone call and realizing specific on-the-spot interventions in their country of origin, Benin (COCODEV, 2002). Telemedicine has also been referred to as a potential response to health professional outflows and local shortages (OECD, 2007).

While there is no commonly agreed set of indicators of the impact of DKNs on their countries of origin, studies do show that there are impacts and the conditions in which these occur. It is thus possible to conceptualize the socio-logics – logics of association – that make the networks more or less active and productive.

Conceptualizing networks' outcomes

We turn now to the harvest of case studies referred to earlier, to examine them not only in a policy evaluation perspective through comparative analysis of individual experiences with successes and failures, but also by drawing systematic lessons from these many stories and conceptualizing the general dynamics at work in this diasporic scheme.

Almost all of the dozens of networks mentioned were created in the 1990s and 2000s, and cannot be dissociated from the expansion of Arpanet, Bitnet and the Internet. The role of Information and Communication Technologies (ICTs) has been absolutely crucial in the spontaneous emergence of such DKNs in a humanly non-coordinated though convergent manner. Even when traditional associations pre-dated the constitution of the actual DKNs, the introduction of computer-mediated communication boosted their activities. For all the networks registered, the Internet is by far the major way of exchanging information. In specific cases where the development of both the Internet and a single DKN coincided and could be tracked and reported empirically, the dynamics indicate unequivocally that the electronic media have been fundamental in the creation of the social entity (Granes and Meyer, 2000). In the Red Caldas network, for instance, e-mail lists, news groups and institutional nodes have made it possible to identify diaspora members, to contact them for an initial and often successful 'recruitment', to mobilize their own networks, to provide a permanent common space shared by all, and to build on complementarities with the Colombia-based communities.

At the same time, however, the tremendous input of the ICTs in the DKN process had an ambiguous effect. The proliferation of messages of all sorts, sometimes with few matters of substance, occasionally with controversial debates on sensitive issues with respect to the country of origin, led to excessive noise. As in the e-mail list *R-Caldas*, it sometimes exhausted the founding fathers' intentions, squandered their energy by endless and sterile discussions, suffocated members' potential initiatives in useless fora, and generated bitter comments spurring further controversies and acrimony. In that sense, if the ICTs and Internet have, without any doubt, been crucial in the development of DKNs, it may also be said that they caused many of these networks' growth problems. These are no different from traditional problems in communication studies (noise, conflicts, misunderstandings, accusations, echoes, amplification, rumours, and so on). But they expanded precisely because communication happened to be disconnected from action. In the Caldas network, for instance, the coincidence between the proliferation of discussions within the Red Caldas list and the drying up of political initiative from Colciencias (the Colombian national research agency) – initially the major stakeholder – in the network development after the mid-1990s is striking evidence of this.

The South African Network of Skills Abroad (SANSA), though organized in a very different manner, exhibits similar deficiencies. Drawing lessons from the Colombian shortcomings in communication tools, it was thus provided with efficient instruments (website, newsgroups, forum, e-mail list, bulletin board, etc.) for its 2500 members located in 65 countries (Brown, 2003). However, after five years, the agency managing the network concluded that resources were sub-utilized (NRF, 2005). The reason for such under-utilized networking resources may be attributed to a lack of coordination and animation, since human agency in these socio-technical networks is crucial (Turner et al., 2003).

This is where an appropriate theory of action becomes useful, in order to understand what is needed to develop and sustain new forms of association such as the DKNs. The sociology of science and technology or the sociology of innovation provides an appropriate conceptual framework with the actor-network theory (ANT), developed over the last 20 years, which is relevant for such objects of analysis as the DKN. The actor-network theory is based upon four concepts: problematization, interessement, enrolment and mobilization (Callon, 1986; Latour, 1987; Law and Hassard, 1999; Latour, 2005). These concepts constitute the translation process through which socio-technical change may occur. Such a process may be described and made visible through dynamic mapping instruments (see Callon et al., 1991, for the theoretical and methodological approach). In brief, for an innovation to succeed, those who create it (scientist, entrepreneur, R&D department) must reformulate a problem in appropriate terms, capture the interest of entities capable of choosing the new path, enrol the allies (humans and non-humans) who will define the new standard, mobilize, and channel the resources and actors along these new lines, making these gradually irreversible. Thus, the innovation process is not the result of a self-imposing logic or natural diffusion of a superior artefact; it is a struggle between, on the one hand, existing entities and networks and, on the other hand, those trying to achieve relevance and momentum in order to create their own place in the sun. Therefore, in many ways, innovation means a dissociation of a previous configuration, capturing actors, and building a network in which these will hold together in a new manner. Through problematization, interessement, enrolment and mobilization, there is thus a recombination of previous elements and their associations to the benefit of new consortia.

This approach fits with the DKN dynamic. Let us examine more precisely what happens with the diaspora option. In this scheme, the expatriate is an actor-network, condensing his/her connections internally and individually. The DKN's purpose is to capture this actor-network and divert him/her toward the home country, which is itself, at least potentially, a consortium of networks. In this sense, in order to realize the translation process, the DKN must perform the problematization, interessement, enrolment and mobilization operations. In fact, today most of the existing DKNs may be considered as having succeeded in several but not all of these operations, namely: problematization, mobilization and enrolment. The experience shows indeed that the following three steps have often been accomplished (Meyer et al., 1997).

Problematization

The problem of skills circulation has been reformulated, with a paradigm shift, from brain drain to brain circulation, during recent decades. Even though conceptual debate is still going on, the emerging brain-gain approaches left room for a vision in which possible reconnection became a workable and promising option. Today, neither a single country nor an international organization would reject the possibility of networking with expatriates in a systematic manner, and this opens opportunities for many DKNs.

Many expatriates have implicitly or explicitly acknowledged their potential contribution to their country of origin, meaning that they were no longer unreachable and could be available for projects run by their fellows back home. This is an actual, pragmatic, individual brain-gain stance, instead of the previous notion of permanent expatriation that used to prevail in these people's minds. The personal interviews conducted with many network members indeed show this historical reformulation of the concept of mobility: it is mentioned as a moment in one's life experience and not as a definite farewell to the place of birth (Meyer et al., 1997). A crucial shift in this reformulation has been the introduction of Internet communication, as a reconstruction of continuity between separate places and sequences of time, as opposed to the feeling of uprootedness that prevailed previously.

Mobilization

In all cases where networks were successfully set up, a significant number of expatriates could be mobilized. Yet the extent of the mobilization does vary considerably from one network to the other, and from country to country, but the message or call from home have proved to be appealing to many. This message has usually been spread through e-mail lists made up of personal or institutional contacts. Interestingly, many expatriates confess that prior to such a call, they had been removed from any national – especially state-driven – initiative. Appealing to professional and intellectual instincts and interests seems to have fuelled the mobilization process, while political or patriotic channels appear to be more divisive or dissuasive. The new medium of the Internet, being neutral on these aspects and in this particular context, has allowed reconnection on new grounds (Turner et al., 2003).

Enrolment

The numerous DKNs reveal a high degree of formal enrolment into associative structures. The expatriates agree to become members of a collective endeavour with an explicit purpose and in which they play a definite role. The review of websites shows that a number of associations provide their affiliates' personal data and professional attributes (Brown, 2003). They are stored in databases as individual components of the network, to which they agreed to contribute, becoming by the same token accessible to anonymous actors who can access the network for any reason or objective. The actors are thus 'punctualized' (unified in one single entity) in the network, as described by Callon et al. (1986, 1991).

The evidence thus clearly shows that adequate problematization, significant mobilization and actual enrolment have been achieved through the diaspora option in general and by individual DKNs in particular. There is one point, however, on which the results have been for the most part much less satisfactory: interessement. And sustainability depends on interessement.

Interessement is what durably ties the actor to the network. Beyond simple incentives capable of generating psychological motivation, it covers all the intermediaries that stick the actor to a particular network. *Inter-esse* in Latin means to stand in between. The interessement devices (*dispositifs d'intéressement*) are those standing between the actors and nurturing collective action through which they link up. It takes for granted that the actor's situation is in a competitive environment: interessement is what makes him/her select one network instead of others among various possible connections.

In DKNs, as in innovation networks in general, the interessement devices may be diverse: programmes, funding, invitations, meetings, rewards, contracts, information and so on. In a physically scattered group of actors, ICTs play an immense role among these devices. They have the power to extract the individual expatriate from his/her daily local networks and to insert him/her within those of relevance in the origin country. However, this only makes sense for active purposes since involvement in a DKN is not for communication *per se* but for action with regard to developments at home. This explains the weariness brought on by passive general mailing lists expressed by Red Caldas members, for instance, and the importance of interactive *ad hoc* devices. ICTs have the power to attract expatriates to purposeful actions in the origin country's networks; without action this attractive power vanishes into thin air. This dynamic seems to make the case for focused instruments, ones that would take proper institutional or organizational forms on specific projects run jointly by DKNs and home communities' members.

Notwithstanding, there is a very specific feature of DKNs with respect to interessement procedures and one that may explain some of their shortcomings in that regard. In a process quite different from what normally happens in innovation networks, DKNs do not aim at capturing the actor-networks represented by the expatriates, for their exclusive integration. They try instead to do so only temporarily, in such a way that these actors maintain their multiple connections. Removing the expatriate from his/her invaluable networks is the last thing that the DKN would pursue; this feature differs from traditional innovation network processes. A DKN member serves as a bridge between his/her own networks in the host country and the ones of the origin country. This collaborative (as opposed to competitive, in the traditional innovation networks) scheme is theoretically possible and actually successful in a number of cases but the tension does exist. It may result in a withdrawal if the interessement procedure is not strong enough, as has been seen in a number of cases. Existing involvement in other networks may become dissuasive of new relational investments if these latter fail to meet legitimate expectations.

As mentioned above, the expatriate is generally integrated with his/her socio-professional and other networks in the host country, and these generate strong interessement devices locally which tend to keep the actor removed from any non-competitive association proposed from a peripheral place. For instance, why would a prominent geneticist leading international projects from the UK be interested in linking with peers in his native Bangladesh if no demand is relayed, no concrete perspective is given, no support is considered, no information is provided? In spite of his/her awareness of this country's problems (problematization), active personal motivation (mobilization) and initial involvement in tentative actions (enrolment), when called by his/her compatriots at home, he/she may slowly or quickly drop out and even try to protect himself/herself from further useless disturbances in his/her daily work, when it becomes clear that his/her engagement is not being met by investments on the other side.

In fact, many testimonies of DKN members point to the fact that passivity – a generic term for absence of (re)activity – in the country of origin led them to stand aside, sometimes with the feeling of having been first lured and then deceived. A primary reason is time, as time is the currency of the individual's investment in networks, and therefore constitutes the interessement exerted by associations on the actor. Even though the diaspora option is non-exclusive since it combines existing and new associations, time is limited and therefore implies selection by the actor among various alternatives. Then occasionally the expatriate has to choose between alternatives to devote time to – in that particular sense, competing – activities. At the opposite of the return option, in which competition with alternative activities from other associations is cancelled or minimized by the expatriate's physical reintegration, the diaspora option always has to provide attractive conditions for action since mobilization is always partial. Moreover, in some reported instances, the expatriate's investment into a DKN conflicted with his/her professional involvement, when expectations of associations of his/her networks in the host country competed with corresponding ones in the origin country.

DKNs must clearly aim at minimizing conflict of interest and be equipped accordingly. If executives in the diaspora have very little time, even if they may be potentially highly productive because of their networks, then the DKN must provide time-producing (vs. time-consuming) intermediaries; in other words, it must focus on productivity. Technology is a key issue here but policy is no less important. The combination of both is necessary. Rapid access to the actors is only possible if information technology is available but also if these actors have been previously made aware of the option, mobilized, enrolled and 'interessed'.

In many origin countries this effort has not been made. The creation of institutions has recently been proposed as a possible solution (see Kuznetsov, et al. 2006; Chaparro et al., 2006). However, this is only a part of the answer. It unrealistically assumes that diaspora groups will provide their skills and contacts to a governmental agency at the interface with the local communities, as if both the former and the latter were homogeneous entities easily represented by a couple of single actors. In the case of the Colombian Red Caldas network, disengagement and criticisms from the expatriate members coincided with its institutionalization within Colciencias during the mid and late 1990s. Instead of strengthening the response to the diaspora, it weakened its diffusion within and impact upon the social fabric in Colombia.

Actors such as country of origin governments must certainly show the way and boost initiatives, but should also delegate and pass on decisions, measures and negotiations to other entities. The Chinese and Indian cases leave no room for doubt on this point. Erroneously perceived as a paragon of centralized intervention, these countries on the contrary foster tremendous involvement of heterogeneous actors and a multiple mediation process in the development of their S&T diasporas (Xiang, 2006; Leclerc and Meyer, 2007). The central state in these cases has indeed pursued clearly helpful policies – *wei guo fuwu* in China, a high-level committee on diasporas in India – but the initiatives of provincial states, distinct administrative bodies, single institutions, quasi-state organizations, NGOs, academia, firms and individuals have also had a decisive impact. The fact that many different DKNs and programmes developed at the same time for the same country of origin did not have a negative effect. Quite the opposite – it helped multiply opportunities for cross-fertilization. Therefore, instead of – or beyond – institution building, the state's role is rather to suggest, facilitate and coordinate multiple actors' initiatives.

When comparing the two success stories (the Chinese and Indian examples, above) with less positive examples (Colombia, South Africa, above, and Meyer et al., 1997, 2001), a striking difference may immediately be noticed. While the first show large numbers of actors of all sorts involved in the relationship between home and host countries, the second feature a thin population of a few individuals and organizations with little interaction. The Indian and Chinese cases even reveal that there is no single way of governing these networks: the former relies on market, business and essentially private links, and the latter on institutional, academic and mainly public ones. What matters is not status or category but rather plurality and involvement. In this relational economics, efficiency relies more on proliferation of inputs than on the selective optimization of a few links. This contradicts earlier social network and social capital approaches or interpretations by emphasizing the need for sophisticated architectures for network structures to be effective (Burt, 2000). In other words, network efficiency in relational production owes more to actors and actions than to structural ties. An implication of such a constructivist approach is that initiative to shape conditions is more relevant than predefined positions in the elaboration of the transnational field.

In fact, the representative model to follow has more to do with lessons from the recent field of innovation studies (sociology, anthropology and economic geography). The evidence shows that highly innovative *milieux* are made up of heterogeneous networks interweaving increasingly in a reduced space where productive associations tend to concentrate (Callon et al., 1991; Temri and Haddad, 2006). They practically combine a mix of different, complementary, skills in complex production processes. The intensity of exchange is thus correlative to dense though exclusive links where tacit knowledge can flow easily and quickly. Though the literature has focused on the local nature of such spill-over and transfers, it has also shown that in fact geographical proximity is not the decisive factor. It is only a reflection of social relationships facilitated by neighbourhood, and is apparent when physical and relational factors are analytically distinguished (Breschi and Lissoni, 2003). Social propinquity is what matters, more than contiguous presence.

Concluding remarks

This chapter has tried to bring conceptual tools drawn from the actor-network theory to bear upon the contemporary emergence of a particular transnational object: the DKN. It has thus taken a proactive stance in favour of a positive migration–development relationship, with these tools being used not only for interpretation but also for implementation of DKN dynamics. This constructive/constructivist standpoint is not intended, however, to deflect a more critical view. At present, the involvement of national states does not promote only equitable circulatory schemes with regard to development. The vision of a global war for talent (Kapur and McHale, 2005; OECD, 2008), however artificial it might be, reinforces narrow perceptions of national interests, misuse of human resources (skills wasted by indiscriminate attraction), and self-centred developments through polar mobility, instead of mutual benefits through increased cooperation. The migration–development relationship should thus not be taken for granted but should rather be taken in a broader global context (see Delgado Wise and Márquez Covarrubias, Chapter 3 in this volume; Faist, 2007; Guarnizo, 2003; De Haas, 2007; Monsutti, 2008; Raghuram, 2007). In order to deal with such a context, where new social spaces and entities are emerging, new sociological approaches are useful. In particular, taking some distance from *Durkheimian* assumptions of organic relationships between human beings or groups within national borders may help to redefine the scope of relevant sociological analysis. Withdrawing from methodological nationalism is a step away from limited traditional societal conceptions (Glick-Schiller, Chapter 2 in this volume and Glick-Schiller et al., 1992). Emphasis on micro-macro mediations, beyond human ontology, such as with the actor-network approach presented here, is also a useful approach, complementary to the former (Latour, 2005). By adopting a perspective of relational logics (socio-logics) of heterogeneous actors we avoid homogenizing assumptions that are no longer convincing. New empirical studies should strengthen the use of such conceptual tools and contribute to theory-building for a better understanding of transnational networks and dynamics.

References

Banks, J. and Tanner, S. (1997) *The State of Donation: Household Gifts to Charity, 1974–1996* (London: Institute for Fiscal Studies).

Barré, R., Hernandez, V., Meyer, J.-B. and Vinck, D. (2003) *Diasporas scientifiques/Scientific Diasporas* (CD-ROM) (Paris: IRD Editions).

Breschi, S. and Lissoni, F. (2003) 'Mobility and Social Networks: Localised Knowledge Spillovers Revisited', paper presented at 'R&D, Education and Productivity', Paris, August 2003.

Brinkerhoff, J. (2006) 'Diasporas, Mobilization Factors and Policy Options', in Asian Development Bank (ed.), *Converting Migration Drains into Gains, Harnessing the Resources of Overseas Professionals* (Manila: Asian Development Bank).

Brown, E. and Lankford, H. (1992) 'Gifts of Money and Gifts of Time: Estimating the Effects of Tax Prices and Available Time', *Journal of Public Economics*, 47, 321–341.

Brown, M. (2003) 'The South African Network of Skills Abroad: The South African Experience of Scientific Diaspora Networks', in R. Barré, V. Hernandez, J.-B. Meyer and D. Vinck (eds), *Diasporas scientifiques/Scientific Diasporas* (CD-ROM) (Paris: IRD Editions).

Burt, R. (2000) 'Structural Holes versus Network Closure as Social Capital', in N. Lin, C. S. Cook, R. S. Burt and A. de Gruyter (eds), *Social Capital: Theory and Research* (Hawthorn: Aldine de Gruyter).

Callon, M. (1986) 'Some Elements for a Sociology of Translation: Domestication of the Scallops and the Fishermen of St Brieuc Bay', in J. Law (ed.), *Power, Action and Belief: A New Sociology of Knowledge?* (London: Sociological Review Monograph, Routledge and Kegan Paul).

Callon, M., Courtial, J.-P. and Turner, W. (1991) 'La méthode Leximappe: un outil pour l'analyse stratégique du développement scientifique et technique', in D. Vinck (ed.), *Gestion de la Recherche, nouveaux problèmes nouveaux outils* (Bruxelles: De Boeck).

Callon, M., Law, J. and Rip, A. (1986) *Mapping the Dynamics of Science and Technology* (London: Macmillan).

Chaparro, F., Jaramillo, H. and Quintero, V. (2006) 'Promise and Frustration of Diaspora Networks: Lessons from the Network of Colombian Researchers Abroad', in Y. Kuznetsov (ed.), *Diaspora Networks and the International Migration of Skills: How Countries Can Draw on Their Talents Abroad* (Washington, DC: World Bank Institute).

Charum, J. and Meyer, J.-B. (eds.) (1998) *Hacer Ciencia en un Mundo Globalizado; la Diaspora Colombiana en Perspectiva* (Bogotá: TM Editores).

COCODEV (2002) *Restitution des travaux du groupe 'Organisations de solidarité issues des migrations internationales et développement'*, mimeo (Paris: Commission Coopération Développement).

De Haas, H. (2007) 'Migration and Development: A Theoretical Perspective', COMCAD Working Paper 29/2007 (Bielefeld: COMCAD – Center on Migration, Citizenship and Development).

Denny, K. (2003) 'The Effects of Human Capital on Social Capita: a Cross-Country Analysis', Working Paper 03/16 (London: Institute of Fiscal Analysis).

Dubar, C. (1991) *La socialisation: construction des identités sociales et professionnelles* (Paris: Armand Colin).

Gaillard, J. and Gaillard A.-M. (2003) 'Can the Scientific Diaspora Save African Science?', *Science and Development Network (Scidevnet)*, published 22 May 2003

Gamlen, A. (2005) 'The Brain Drain is Dead: Long Live the New Zealand Diaspora', COMPAS Working Paper 10 (Oxford: Oxford University).

Gellner, E. (1983) *Nations and Nationalism* (Oxford: Basil Blackwell).

Gibson, J. (2001) 'Unobservable Family Effects and the Apparent External Benefits of Education', *Economics of Education Review*, 20, 225–233.

Glick Schiller, N., Basch, L. and Blanc-Szanton, C. (eds) (1992) 'From Immigrant to Transmigrant: Theorizing Transnational Migration', *Anthropological Quarterly*, 68 (1), 48–63.

Granes, J., and Morales, A. (1998) 'Las potencialidades y limitaciones de la Red Caldas de Investigadores Colombianos en el Exterior: los Proyectos Internacionales Conjuntos: un estudio de caso', in J. Charum and J.-B. Meyer (eds), *Hacer Ciencia en un Mundo Globalizado; la Diaspora Colombiana en Perspectiva* (Bogotá: TM Editores).

——— and Meyer, J.-B. (2000) 'Globalization of the National Scientific Community through Electronic List: Lessons and Prospects from a Case Study in Colombia', in J. Charum and J.-B. Meyer (eds.) *International Scientific Migrations Today* (CD-ROM). Paris: Editions IRD-COLCIENCIAS.

Guarnizo, L. E. (2003) 'The Economics of Transnational Living', *International Migration Review*, 37 (3), 666–699.

Guo, Y. (2003) 'How Can the Chinese Intellectual Diasporas Bridge their Host and Home Countries as well as Help their Home Country Integrate into the International Community', in R. Barré, V. Hernandez, J.-B. Meyer and D. Vinck (eds), *Diasporas scientifiques/Scientific Diasporas* (CD-ROM) (Paris: IRD Editions).

Hanifi, S. M. (2006) 'Material and Social Remittances to Afghanistan', in Asian Development Bank (ed.), *Converting Migration Drains into Gains, Harnessing the Resources of Overseas Professional*s (Manila: Asian Development Bank).

Helliwell, J. F. and Putnam, R. (1999) 'Education and Social Capital', NBER Working Paper 7121 (Cambridge: National Bureau of Economic Research).

Johnson, J. (2003) 'S&T Resources and Programs in the United States for Networking with Developing Countries', in R. Barré, V. Hernandez, J.-B. Meyer and D. Vinck (eds), *Diasporas scientifiques/Scientific Diasporas* (CD-ROM) (Paris: IRD Editions).

Kapur, D. and McHale, J. (2005) *Give us Your Best and Brightest: The Global Hunt for Talent and Its Impact on the Developing World* (Washington, DC: Center for Global Development).

Khadria, B. (2003) 'Case Study of the Indian Scientific Diaspora', in R. Barré, V. Hernandez, J.-B. Meyer and D. Vinck (eds), *Diasporas scientifiques/Scientific Diasporas* (CD-ROM) (Paris: IRD Editions).

Khadria, B. and Leclerc, E. (2006) 'Exode des emplois contre exode des cerveaux, les deux faces d'une même pièce?', *Autrepart: Revue de sciences sociales au Sud*, 37, 37–51.

Kuznetsov, Y. (ed.) (2006) *Diaspora Networks and the International Migration of Skills: How Countries Can Draw on Their Talents Abroad* (Washington, DC: World Bank Institute).

———, Nemirovsky, A. and Yoguel, G. (2006) 'Argentina: Burgeoning Networks Abroad, Weak Institutions at Home', in Y. Kuznetsov (ed.), *Diaspora Networks and the International Migration of Skills: How Countries Can Draw on Their Talents Abroad* (Washington, DC: World Bank Institute).

Latour, B. (1987) *Science in Action. How to Follow Scientists and Engineers through Society* (Milton Keynes: Open University Press).

——— (2005) *Reassembling the Social: An Introduction to Actor-Network Theory* (Oxford and New York: Oxford University Press).

Law, J., and Hassard, J. (eds) (1999) *Actor Network Theory and After* (London: Blackwell Publishing).

Leclerc, E. and Meyer, J.-B. (2007) 'Knowledge Diasporas and Development: A Shrinking Space for Scepticism', *Asian Population Studies*, 3 (3), 153–68.

Lema, F. (2003) 'Professional Migration from Latin America and the Caribbean; From NGO to Multilateral Organization and Government Involvement: Three Case Studies', in R. Barré, V. Hernandez, J.-B. Meyer, and D. Vinck (eds), *Diasporas scientifiques/Scientific Diasporas* (CD-ROM) (Paris: IRD Editions).

Lowell, L. and Gerova, S. (2004) *Diasporas and Economic Development: State of Knowledge* (Washington, DC: World Bank).

Lucas, R. (2004) *International Migration Regimes and Economic Development* (Stockholm: EGDI).

Marks, J. (2006) 'South Africa: Evolving Diaspora, Promising Initiatives', in Y. Kuznetsov (ed.), *Diaspora Networks and the International Migration of Skills: How Countries Can Draw on Their Talents Abroad* (Washington, DC: World Bank Institute).

Meyer, J.-B. (2001) 'Network Approach versus Brain Drain: Lessons from the Diaspora', *International Migration*, 39 (5), Special Issue 2, 91–110.

——— (2004a) 'Savoirs, diasporas et identités projectives', *Hermès*, 40, 350–54.

——— (2004b) 'Les diasporas de la connaissance: atout inédit de la compétitivité du sud', *La Revue Internationale et Stratégique*, 55, 69–76.

——— (2006) 'Connaissance et développement: un lien à actualiser,' in M. Carton and J.-B. Meyer (eds.) *La société des savoirs: trompe l'œil ou perspectives?* (Paris: L'Harmattan).

———, Charum J., Gaillard J., Granes J., Leon J., Montenegro A., Morales A., Murcia, C., Parrado L-S. and Schlemmer B. (1997) 'Turning Brain Drain into Brain Gain: The Colombian Experience of the Diaspora Option', *Science, Technology and Society*, 2 (2), 285–317.

——— and Wattiaux, J.-P. (2006) 'Diasporas Knowledge Networks. Vanishing Doubts and Increasing Evidence', *International Journal on Multicultural Societies*, 8 (1), 4–24.

———, Kaplan, D. and Charum, J. (2001) 'Scientific Nomadism and the New Geopolitics Of Knowledge', *International Social Sciences Journal/Revue Internationale des Sciences Sociales*, 168, 341–54.

Minoian, A. V. and Freinkman, L. (2006) 'Armenia: What Drives First Movers and How Can their Efforts be Scaled Up?', in Y. Kuznetsov (ed.), *Diaspora Networks and the International Migration of Skills: How Countries Can Draw on Their Talents Abroad* (Washington, DC: World Bank Institute).

Monsutti, A. (2008) 'Migration et développement: une histoire de brouilles et de retrouvailles', *Migration et Développement: un Mariage Arrangé, Annuaire Suisse de politique de développement*, 27 (2), 23–42.

NRF-National Research Foundation (2005), *SANSA Suvey Results* (Pretoria: Icognition, NRF).

Opiniano, J. M. and Castro, A. T. (2006) 'Promoting Knowledge Transfer Activities through Diaspora Networks: A Pilot Study on the Philippines', in Asian Development Bank (ed.), *Converting Migration Drains into Gains, Harnessing the Resources of Overseas Professionals* (Manila: Asian Development Bank).

OECD (2007) 'Immigrant Health Workers in OECD Countries in the Broader Context of Highly Skilled Migration', in *SOPEMI, International Migration*

Outlook 2007 (Paris: Organisation for Economic Cooperation and Development [OECD]).

——— (2008) *The Global Competition for Talent: Mobility of the Highly Skilled* (Paris: Organisation for Economic Cooperation and Development [OECD]).

Pandey, A., Aggarwal, A., Devane, R. and Kuznetsov, Y. (2006) 'The Indian Diaspora: a Unique Case?', in Y. Kuznetsov (ed.), *Diaspora Networks and the International Migration of Skills: How Countries Can Draw on Their Talents Abroad* (Washington, DC: World Bank Institute).

Raghuram, P. (2007) 'Which Migration, What Development: Unsettling the Edifice of Migration and Development', Working Paper 28/2007 (Bielefeld: COMCAD – Center on Migration, Citizenship and Development).

Saxenian, A. L., Motoyama, Y., Quan, X. and Wittenborn, D. R. (2002) *Local and Global Networks of Immigrant Professionals in Silicon Valley* (San Francisco: Public Policy Institute of California).

Temri L. and Haddad, S. (2006) 'Les start-up: un pont entre connaissance scientifique et développement économique', in M. Carton and J.-B. Meyer (eds), *The Knowledge Society: Trompe l'œil or Accurate Perspectives* (Paris: L'Haramattan).

Turner, W., Henry, C. and Gueye, M. (2003) 'Diasporas, développement et TICs', in R. Barré, V. Hernandez, J.-B. Meyer and Vinck, D. (eds), *Diasporas scientifiques/Scientific Diasporas* (CD-ROM) (Paris: IRD Editions).

Warrier, M. (2006) 'Temporary Mobility Schemes and the Indian Software Industry', paper presented at the COMPAS Annual Conference 'International Labour Migration: In Whose Interest?', Oxford, 5–6 July.

Westcott, C., (2005) *Promoting Knowledge Exchange through Diasporas*, Workshop on 'Demographic Challenges and Migration', Sydney, August 2005.

Xiang, B. (2005) *Promoting Knowledge Exchange through Diaspora Networks (The Case of the People's Republic of China)*, COMPAS Report (Oxford: University of Oxford).

Part III
Outlook

8
Academic Knowledge, Policy and the Public Role of Social Scientists

Thomas Faist

> *Practical men, who believe themselves to be quite exempt from any intellectual influences, are usually the slave of some defunct economist. Madmen in authority, who hear voices in the air, are distilling the frenzy from some academic scribbler of a few years back. Not, indeed, immediately, but after a certain interval...* (Keynes, 1970, p. 361)

There is an often mentioned gap between research in the social sciences on the one hand and social action and praxis on the other hand. This alleged disjuncture is particularly pertinent in the migration–development nexus. At first glance, this may seem astonishing because migration studies and development research – both fields are interdisciplinary research sites – are characterized by a high degree of commissioned research; development research perhaps even more so than migration studies. This kind of research is often politically motivated, for example, by the intention to reduce international migration through economic development. To illustrate, over recent years politicians across Europe have often claimed that higher levels of economic development (measured by per capita income and/or increased human development symbolized by lower infant mortality and higher rates of literacy) would eventually lead to a decrease in international migration. Academic analysts of migration, however, insist that – while this expectation may be borne out in the long run, considering demographic transitions and economic transformations – increased economic development correlates highly with increased international migration, expressed in concepts such as the 'migration hump' (Martin and Taylor, 1996). Moreover, while the policy world may be concerned with more efficient means of migration control, ranging from border controls to development cooperation, academic researchers often insist on those endogenous dynamics of international migration which escape blunt efforts at control, such as irregular migration. Thus, even in these fields of migration and development which seem to be strongly immersed in public policy issues and public debates, both practitioners and academic researchers heatedly debate the difficulties of mutual exchange. At its core, the gap hypothesis raises the following question, which has been debated as long as social science research has existed: would social science knowledge be more useful if it could be more easily applied instrumentally? In other words, would we desire a state of affairs in which political action could be systematically based on knowledge about calculable causal relations, as the term 'evidence-based policy' instead of 'dogma' would suggest (cf. Boswell, 2009)? While this may be a fruitful question to begin with, it is ultimately misleading.

Instead, there is a strong coupling of the two worlds of policy-politics and academia, albeit not through direct application of knowledge but rather through ways of thinking and representation in the public sphere. It is in this way that social scientists are brokers bridging 'structural holes' (cf. Burt, 1992) resulting not simply from the absence of social ties but from different systemic dynamics. The public sphere function of academic knowledge goes beyond the 'enlightenment' role (Weiss, 1979) because it designates a 'place' for change to occur. Thus, the proposition advanced here is that social science knowledge, on the one hand, and the system of public policy, on the other hand, are two very different worlds but are linked via the public sphere, the realm of the exchange of ideas, and arguments in publicly accessible forums, ranging from mass media to small circles of debate. The worlds of academic research and public policy work on different assumptions, which in turn provide for different endogenous dynamics concerning views about instrumental usage of knowledge vs. its potential function as ways of understanding and as criticism. The social sciences do not so much produce social technologies but offer world views and lenses which help to categorize observable social facts and to arrive at interpretations. This takes place not through any direct linkage to policy but in the public sphere. The world of public policy-making, by contrast, is structured by its own dynamics, which aim toward advancing interests to shape social life. Social science knowledge is used by policy-makers when it serves the internal dynamics of policy-making, although in fact, quite often, it may not serve this function, as when electoral pressures trump expert knowledge. Politicians are often driven by political exigencies and in such circumstances end up ignoring evidence where it fails to support electorally appealing courses of action – especially in areas susceptible to populist styles of action such as migration. At any rate, the social sciences, including not only sociology but also political science, anthropology and economics, have delivered such lenses galore, in the form of concepts dealing with human, economic and social development.

The very fact that the social sciences usually do not have direct impact on decision-making but are able to influence at best the lenses through which 'social problems' are viewed make it all the more important to look not only at the interaction of social scientists and policy-makers in governments, international organizations, non-governmental organizations, social movement organizations and the like, but also at their role in the public sphere. If it is true that social scientists can usefully provide lenses through which to view and identify issues, topics and problems and not so much be prescriptive, the direct linkage to policy and thus decision-making should not be overrated. Yet the discursive impact then assumes an ever more crucial role. And it is in the public sphere that such lenses are debated. And it is above all in the public sphere that political decisions in democracies, no matter how particularist the interests behind them are, can usually be seen to make and to have been legitimated by reference to both universal norms and plausible conceptual beliefs. The ubiquitous references in policy debates to meta-norms such as human rights, or the gospel of economic growth, are examples that come to mind.

This proposition can be explicated in three issue areas. The first concerns public policy and research agendas, social order, and the organization of research in the specific field of migration and development. In this area we are basically concerned with the (mutual) conditioning and conjunctures of academic research and policy paradigms. The second issue area deals with knowledge production in the social sciences and the public role of social scientists. Finally, the third issue area addresses social science knowledge and its uses in public policy and in the public sphere. But before plunging into these issue areas, however, it is necessary to question the standard account of why the worlds of academic research and public policy supposedly talk past each other.

The standard account: the gap hypothesis and its deficiencies

The standard argument's core is a deficit or gap argument, which states that given the large stock of academic knowledge in various fields of societal life, the de facto usage of this kind of knowledge in politics and by state and non-state policy-makers is widely insufficient. In the field of migration and development, we claim to have knowledge about how financial remittances ameliorate or increase social inequalities in regions of origin and destination of migrants. This knowledge, as the argument goes on, is only insufficiently applied to policies by the respective national governments or international organizations. In this perspective, much more could be done to facilitate the transfer of money by reducing transaction costs in offering channels alternative to Western Union and MoneyGram, or even to 'illegal', viz. informal, routes, such as the Hawala system. Hence, no publication on the subject of remittances fails to mention the Mexican government's '3 for 1' programme in which each 'migradollar' is complemented by an extra dollar from the federal and regional governments. The fact that only a fraction of remittances is channelled into this program is rarely mentioned (cf. Castles and Delgado Wise, 2008).

Usually, three reasons are advanced to account for the allegedly deplorable gap between the plentiful store of research knowledge and its application in decision-making. The first posits that social scientists simply do not yet know enough about certain causal relationships or mechanisms of behaviour. In the case of financial remittances, this refers, for example, to the question how – if at all – remittances sent to family members in regions of origin aggregate from the family level to local communities or even to the national economy. So far, social scientists know very little about these processes of aggregation. The second reason offered relates to the transfer of results from the social sciences to *praxis*. Each of the two worlds uses its own language and particular jargon. One could argue that social scientists write in barely intelligible ways and should strive for greater clarity. This insight suggests that a simple one-to-one transfer is not possible. Instead, the processes and tasks involved could be better described as the mutual translation of different codes characteristic of the social sciences and public policy respectively. Thus, it is not surprising that policy-makers establish expert commissions – such as the Global Commission on International Migration (GCIM) convened in 2005 by the then Secretary General of the United Nations (UN), Kofi Annan – not only to legitimate decisions or delay them but also to translate actual research results. We can observe a similar pattern of knowledge translation in the run-up to the latest Human Development Report (UNDP, 2009), which has placed international migration as its core subject. A third explanation of the gap suggests that those who apply social science knowledge are thought to lack the capacity to interpret research results correctly, or that their readiness to learn is, moreover, also limited. If so, a change in the style of thinking among this group would be warranted. This third argument is highly questionable because we find that many policy-makers in fact have a social science background. While one may quibble with the fact that among social scientists in the field of development those with an economics background predominate, and while one may also plausibly argue that economics as a field has been buoyant and imperial, and perhaps less reflexive about the transfer problem, it is still true that the staff of national and international organizations is filled by academically trained persons. And policy-makers are certainly capable of being influenced.

This standard account needs to be questioned in a fundamental way because of its rationalist prejudice. This mode of thinking is based on a purely instrumental model according to which the social sciences are to be used in applying generalized findings to particular, concrete situations. In abstract terms this perspective says: if A then B, or B as a function of A. The policy-maker then seeks to change B or produce B, and so forth. This formula seems to be rather short-sighted, not least because all knowledge needs to be translated, for example, to consider ceteris paribus conditions. When talking about the effects of a policy, one cannot simply say, when A then B, etc. but one needs to know about consequences of specific and complex sets of factors. Yet such knowledge is not simply stored in the warehouse of the social sciences. There is also no recipe-knowledge in the form of easy rules to follow (Luhmann, 1992). For example, it is plausible to argue that financial remittances may result in the economic improvement of regions of origin. Yet the number of ceteris paribus conditions affecting this formula are legion, and it would take a great deal of specific knowledge other than academic knowledge – such as tacit, 'everyday', and local knowledge – to appreciate the conditions under which financial remittances make a particular impact.

Even more important is that all social science knowledge is value-bound, even that derived under the ideal of value-free objectivity. Concepts have direct and strong relations to values, such as development, evolution, exploitation, social progress, social integration and social inequality. With these notions social scientists produce something of a world view of selected parts of reality, which also implies an urge to act in a certain way. For example, the notions of economic development and social development suggest somewhat different policy action regarding the use and desirability of financial remittances.

Notions of economic development would emphasize the investment character of remittances, such as into education, health or manufacturing. By contrast, notions of social development, such as Amartya Sen's (1984) capability approach, draw upon the idea that persons have a choice in how to employ remittances in aid of certain objectives, for example, geographical mobility, which constitutes one of many possible elements in the individual's well-being and quality of life.

Issue area 1: public policy, social order and research

This issue area concerns a host of questions revolving around how research and policy agendas are set and potentially interact, and especially how public policy agendas impact on actual research undertaken: how have public policies, foundations and other actors influenced research on the migration–development nexus, and in what ways – for example, what are the mechanisms of influence, such as funding and hiring? How have institutions such as the World Bank and state governments set the migration–development agenda? Since the concept of development achieved prominence in the late 1940s how have issues of economic growth and political order been bundled over time? What premises have been underlying policy research agendas, for example neo-liberal or grass-roots perspectives and orientations? How did these agendas reflect the changing or even transformed relationships between principles of social order – that is, state, market, civil society/community? In which institutions has research been undertaken – such as in universities, independent research institutes or research institutes of international organizations?

While it is impossible even to begin addressing these questions here, it is helpful to place them into a discursive-institutional context. In other words, one needs to identify how the research and policy interests in the migration–development nexus have coincided in three consecutive cycles or phases (see Faist and Fauser, Chapter 1 in this volume), and what exactly the (counter-)paradigmatic strands were. The first and the third of these phases undoubtedly were stimulated by public policy interests – the first in the 1950s and especially the 1960s by the OECD. The third and ongoing phase has taken off after the World Bank placed migrants' financial remittances at the core of its annual report (World Bank, 2002). Other agents, national governments and international organizations included, have followed suit. In the phase in between, the second, one also finds a correspondence between public policy interests in the South and the North, and academic concepts – a 'strange bedfellow' arrangement of both restrictive migration control on the one hand and a critical analysis of underdevelopment through reference to such deleterious mechanisms as the 'brain drain' on the other hand. In all three phases research knowledge was and still is scrutinized for its applicability to development, based on different theoretical assumptions and slightly different policy priorities.

In phase 1, during the 1950s and 1960s, with spin-offs into the 1970s, economic policy-makers and most representatives of the discipline of economics held that migration contributes to the development of sending regions. In fact, most research was actually undertaken after restrictive migration policies had been implemented in the early 1970s (for example, Penninx, 1982, on Turkey). Following the 'recruitment halt' in Western Europe public policies aimed to encourage migrants to 'return' to the regions of origin. Financial incentives were offered to those returning. By and large, the theoretical underpinning of the recruitment drive of the 1960s was social modernization theory. International migration, quite apart from the much more massive internal migration in the South, was meant to siphon off excess labour and transfer it to the North, where it could – according to the OECD (Kindleberger, 1967) – fill labour gaps in labour-intensive industries. In this way, international South–North migration (East–West was curtailed by the Iron Curtain) could both contribute to development in the South and the growth of GDP in the post-war reconstruction economies of the West. Although modernization theories covered a great deal more terrain than economic development per se, the focus and terminology of the migration–development nexus was heavily dominated by an economic lens. From a wide array of complex theoretical components in modernization theory, only the economic perspective was chosen to justify public policy choices. Up until the late 1970s, when the first studies were published on the effects of remittances, social scientists and governments alike saw migration as a solution to development obstacles in emigration regions. Empirical results, however, painted a different picture, often concluding that there was little evidence that remittances boosted local, not to speak of national, economic development (for example, Lipton, 1980).

Whereas in phase 1 causal reasoning went from international migration to development, social science thinking during phase 2 largely reversed causality: the line now ran from underdevelopment to migration. Still rooted in modernization theoretical assumptions, dependency and world systems theories questioned the impact of economic modernization on developing regions, now cast as peripheries. Coinciding with such theoretical underpinnings, policy debates also highlighted the deleterious consequences of migration, especially the 'brain drain' of professionals. The debate reached a climax in the context of discussions of the 'New International Economic Order' in which many Southern states in the United Nations system raised their voices. Now international migration as a policy solution became problematic. Instead, the solution itself turned into the problem in this reformulation of modernization theory, leading to the conclusion that migration as such contributes to structural economic heterogeneity and ever increasing social inequalities between South and North and between centres and peripheries within these regions. Needless to say, there was little policy impetus in the North to challenge such assumptions. After all, restrictive immigration policies, implemented in virtually all states in the North/West since the early 1970s, were not accompanied by alternative means to promote development, such as international trade. Thus, restrictive migration controls and the brain drain rhetoric nicely complemented each other in portraying international migration as a social problem. In the contemporary research carried out in phase 2 the emphasis lay even more forcefully than in phase 1 on an economic perspective, this time with a counter-hegemonic political economic drive.

Phase 3 in policy clearly took off with the wake-up call by the World Bank in its report on development finance (2002). Now, concepts such as increasing competitiveness, hunting for the 'best brains', and other key notions dominated the policy debate. In tune with globalization talk, concepts such as 'circularity' assumed greater importance (GCIM, 2005), in addition to efforts at tapping into the benefits brought about by return migrants. Now terms such as 'brain gain', later modified to 'brain circulation', came to replace 'brain drain'. In an interesting twist, non-economic factors were brought in with associated economic language, such as the concept of 'social remittances' (Levitt, 2001). The European Union (EU) itself now declared its aim to compete on par with the United States in attracting the so-called highly skilled. In addition, the second demographic transition in most immigration states renewed discussions about attracting migrants as a means to cushion the hard landing resulting from a rapid decline in the labour force and a concomitant increase in the pensioner population over the coming decades. As a legitimizing strategy to engage in attracting the 'best and brightest' (Kapur and McHale, 2005), this development policy for the North was placed in the context of helping countries in the South to develop their economies – and, again a direct demand by the EU – to build up their migration control infrastructure. This latter issue has been of particular relevance with respect to states such as Morocco and Turkey, bordering on the EU and being transit countries for migrants from further afar.

In all three phases mentioned there was a confluence of policy and research cycles on the migration–development nexus. This is not to say that there were one-way streets between science and policy or public debates. Nonetheless, it indicates that there were elective affinities or even mutual conditionings. What can be said with some certainty is that public policy drew upon research concepts when suitable and that academic research provided suitable models, which were later (indirectly) used to justify a renewed emphasis on remittances. For example, in the transition from the second to the third phase, in the 1990s, approaches such as the New Economics of Labour Migration in economics and the livelihood approach, originating in sociology and anthropology, focused on small collective units such as families and kinship groups as main decision-making sites and realms of action regarding (international) migration. The former approach looks at migration as a form of informal insurance against risks such as crop failure, whereas the latter views migration through the lens of ensuring a living in often adverse circumstances. These mid-range concepts constituted a decisive move away from analytical models that prioritized individuals as the main unit of analysis, as in neo-classical migration economics. The change of perspective from individuals to small groups, and from rational choice to social choice, led researchers to take a more nuanced look at the origins, flows and consequences of financial remittances. For example, in the past the use of remittances to pay bills for health and tuition fees or consumer products had been seen as unproductive. Yet a closer look at how some families or larger collectives pooled resources to cope with risks collectively led researchers to realize that investments into the areas mentioned could be helpful in coping with diverse economic hazards and combatting poverty. Now there was a proliferation of arguments that the effect of remittances in the earlier literature and policies was underestimated. Though it would be difficult to trace the exact route these changing concepts from the social sciences took to find their way into the decision-making and planning of (inter-)governmental organizations, it stands to reason that the changes of analytical patterns used across the three phases of the migration–development nexus is no coincidence. In the third phase, in particular, academia-policy brokers of knowledge, such as authors of the reports by the intergovernmental International Organization of Migration (IOM), played an important role, and tried thus to gain a prominent place among the spate of international organizations dealing with cross-border migration.

The very fact that a reappraisal of the migration–development nexus has been going on for some years now means that perceptions of negative effects of migration upon development, so prevalent in phase 2, have changed. Indeed, the change would not have been possible without a much broader transformation of the social order and the relationships among the underlying principles. Such a sea-change can be identified on the discursive level and in the institutional and policy domains. If for heuristic purposes we define three principles of social order as state(ness), market, and civil society or community, we can trace the shifting emphasis of public policy-making and research agendas over the past several decades since development entered the lexicon of public debate in the late 1940s. Apparent are two discursive and policy shifts, both of them combinatorial forms including civil society or community. The overarching characteristic is a move away from the national state (apparatus) as an engine and coordinator of development. The demise of the national developmental state was accompanied not simply by a rise of the market, as critics of the so-called Washington Consensus would have it. Indeed, the first shift is a combination of stateness and civil society. The national state has not been replaced but complemented by local state and international organizations. Terms such as 'government' have been complemented by 'governance', and 'state' has been extended to 'stateness' (Faist and Fauser, Chapter 1 in this volume). Obvious examples of combinations of local state and civil society are programmes labelled *co-développement*, which often include local states – cities, municipalities – in immigration states and transnationally active migrant associations. The second move is the combination of market(s) and transnational civil society. In our case, this shift is best exemplified by the term diaspora. Both those who advocate the entrepreneurial market citizen, an individual migrant economically active across borders, and those who favour participatory approaches rooted in collectives, have used the term diaspora to indicate a new stage of either individual or civil societal involvement. Those who see diaspora as a form of entrepreneurial activity focus on the role of the 'highly-skilled' living outside their country of origin. These persons are thought to contribute to development via the transfer of knowledge. By contrast, those taken with the notion of cross-border civil society emphasize the role of hometown associations and other small-scale groups in providing collective goods for the regions of origin. Both approaches make far-reaching assumptions about diasporists as brokers. What can be stated with some certainty is that there has been an increasing co-optation of diaspora groups in policy-making and policy-consultancy (cf. de Haas, 2006).

Issue area 2: knowledge production and the public role of social scientists

The second issue area broadly concerns the kind of knowledge produced by academic social scientists and the role these scientists play in the public sphere. The public sphere is much broader than the world of public policy-making, goes beyond decision-making, and relates to the realm of public debate. The questions thus are: what role have social scientists played in the linkage of knowledge production and public policies through participation in the public sphere as experts, advocates, partisans or public intellectuals? What have been the differences among the various social science disciplines, such as economics, political science and sociology? And what have been the differences, if any, between the interdisciplinary fields of migration research and development research? What kind of knowledge production has been propagated by social scientists, for example, instrumental vs. reflexive knowledge? What has been the self-understanding of social scientists involved – professional, critical or policy-based?

Again, this sketch may offer only a partial frame in which to consider these questions. To start with, knowledge gained from research in the social sciences can rarely be condensed into social technologies. The specific objects of the social sciences are not amenable to social engineering. Yet this technological deficit is not an outcome of the inability of most social sciences to devise ever more sophisticated techniques of observation and measurement but is due to the specificity of the objects and the associated normative implications. In societies with high degrees of personal freedom and a high value on individual autonomy a premium is placed on social change. Progress is legitimized by the concept of 'modernity', itself a cultural consciousness of the changeableness of things. A direct consequence of this spirit of modernity is that scientific claims usually allow for various and diverging interpretations. There is a constant debate over results, based in the competing paradigms and the multiple normatively grounded belief systems underlying social scientists' claims. One does not need to adhere to a criticism of the 'strong programme of science' (Barnes, 1974) and thus engage in a social reductionist interpretation of the social sciences to realize that the questions posed by social scientists and the interpretations of research results are guided by normatively bounded ideas. The migration–development nexus in general and the term 'development' as a short-hand for multifarious and even contradictory goals such as 'the good life', economic growth and ecological sustainability lends at least suggestive support to the hunch that such normative ideas need not be very specific and may even have passed their conceptual zenith – as the concept of development in fact has – but still serve as rallying foci.

The crucial point of departure is the linkage between knowledge and the public. Often, two types of knowledge are contrasted, namely, instrumental knowledge which is oriented toward the means to achieve goals, and reflexive knowledge, which is geared toward (normatively desirable) ends. This stark distinction is reminiscent of Kant's moral imperative which argues against using persons as means rather than ends. Both forms of knowledge, instrumental and reflexive, can be found in the various self-understandings of sociology and sociologists. While sociology is selected here as exemplary of the social sciences, it stands to reason that similar distinctions could also be fruitfully applied to other social science disciplines such as political science (but not necessarily for economics). Michael Burawoy (2005) has devised a four-fold typology of sociology and its public role. He distinguishes between professional, policy, critical and public sociology. First, in his view, professional sociology is heavily engaged in knowledge production along a positivist methodological perspective, using both qualitative and quantitative methods. We could classify many contributions to so-called mainstream journals and publications as professional. This kind of sociology has established clear-cut criteria for ranking the quality of knowledge, such as peer review. Second, policy sociology, quite simply, produces knowledge for a client. It is mainly engaged in carrying out commissioned research for government agencies or private end-users. Third, critical sociology incorporates both those researchers who are 'reflexive' – those who openly question the assumptions and underlying politics of the discipline – and people who are politically aligned activists, and who see sociology as a way of confronting injustice or power or elites. We may refer to C. Wright Mills as representative of this branch. Fourth, Burawoy's favourite type, public sociology, speaks directly to 'publics', that is, various kinds of groups, either randomly gathered (such as television viewers) or grouped by common interest (such as experts working on the migration–development nexus). Public sociology engages diverse publics, reaching beyond the university to enter into an ongoing dialogue with these publics about fundamental values.

There are also 'in-between' positions, such as that of 'involved detachment', as claimed by Norbert Elias, which is rooted in professional sociology but reaches out to public sociology. Elias remarked that the role of social scientists' engagement is an issue of 'how to keep their two roles as participants and inquirers clearly and consistently apart, and, as a professional group, how to establish in their work the undisputed dominance of the latter' (Elias, 2007, p. 84). Public sociology also shows some overlap with critical sociology but is not as openly dedicated to advocacy and partisanship as the latter. There are basically two types of public intellectual knowledge, in Antonio Gramsci's terms, 'traditional' and 'organic'. Traditional public sociology speaks to publics from on high as in such works in American sociology as Robert Bellah et al.'s *Habits of the Heart* (1985) and William Julius Wilson's *The Declining Significance of Race* (1978). In Europe, some of Pierre Bourdieu's later works, such as *La Misère du monde* (1998), may fit this pattern. These books generated public debate, and raised public consciousness about socio-political and economic issues. They work through various media – radio, print, film, electronic – that easily distort the original message. Organic public sociology, on the other hand, involves an unmediated dialogue between sociologists and their publics, taking place in the trenches of civil society. Here we find publics that are thicker, more local, more active and oppositional – at any rate, in direct engagement with labour movements, oppressed minorities, prisoners, lawyers, or even transnational or global NGOs.

The division of the four kinds of sociologies already gives an idea of the role of social scientists in public. Yet we need to go beyond the 'intellectual' typology and distinguish more finely the role of social scientists in the public sphere. Essentially, we may distinguish three main types or functions, since an individual social scientist may fulfil various roles successively: social scientists may act or function as experts, advocates, and intellectuals. A prominent function of the first type, the expert, is that of a consultant to political organizations. Expert hearings, commissions for all types of political issues (ethics, migration and integration, and so on abound in democracies). Jürgen Habermas (1968) famously criticized this position of experts in that such politics leads to the division of labour amongst experts who are no longer able to understand the wider context of society. Migration policy, like other policy fields, abounds with experts. The 'Independent Commission on In-Migration' (*Unabhängige Kommission Zuwanderung*) in Germany (2000–2002), for example, consulted about a hundred academic experts in its comprehensive look at Germany's 'in-migration' processes. The second type is the advocate. Advocates take sides. Their self-understanding may correspond to those of Burawoy's critical sociologists who are politically aligned activists and envision their research as contributing to or strengthening the cause in which they are engaged. Not only is the area of migration and development fertile ground for debates on social justice, equality, human rights and other fundamentals; it is also a field in which advocacy is coupled with research. Finally, the third type is that of the public intellectual. S/he corresponds to the image portrayed above of the traditional public intellectual who seeks to change the perspective of the reader or listener by strength of the better argument. We may find relatives of this type in the arts – just think of numerous public artists who have a focus on Africa, such as Bono, the famous lead-singer of the rock band U2. One may surmise that while direct input into public policy-making concerns above all social scientists as experts, the public sphere is primarily the realm of the advocate and the public intellectual. Needless to say, an overlapping of the three types is possible; for example, a mixed type, called partisan, which is a combination of advocate and public intellectual. S/he comes close to the organic public intellectual described above.

Issue area 3: knowledge and its uses in public policy and the public sphere

The third issue brings together the concomitant production of knowledge and policy cycles from issue area 1 and the public role of social scientists from issue area 2: how have research findings made their way into public debates and political decision-making? Under what conditions has this transfer taken place? Which researchers and research institutes have been influential, directly or indirectly? What kind of knowledge was used and on which level of abstraction? Has theoretical abstraction left room for human agency? What has made a difference – direct knowledge such as concrete research results and suggestions for policies, or indirect impacts such as the spread of concepts, ways of thinking, approaches to problems from the social sciences outward? Which bodies of research, concepts/theoretical guidelines, empirical results and the like have been picked up, which have been neglected or discarded, and on which occasions?

It is of utmost importance to start any analysis of linkages between research and public policy and the public sphere by considering the inherent systemic rationalities of the different worlds. Political decision-making has its own rationality. The instrumental application of social scientific knowledge does not by any means lie at the centre of political decision-making for public policy. Politically, knowledge derived from research is a tool but not necessarily an aid to or requirement for problem-adequate solutions. Academic knowledge may serve three functions for decision- and policy-making: a legitimizing, a substantiating, and a symbolic function.

First, social science knowledge may serve to legitimate decisions already taken or to delay decisions deemed undesirable. In this way, policy-making authorities in government can gain 'epistemic authority' in defining what the public knows, in our case, about migration and development. The fields of immigration and asylum are highly contested policy areas and are characterized by a high degree of methodological uncertainty, as can be seen most dramatically in the field of irregular migration. By definition, it is impossible to arrive at a reliable estimate of the number of irregular migrants, for example. Expert estimates can sometimes show an enormous range: for instance, experts estimate the number of irregular migrants in the US to lie somewhere between 2 and 20 million. Clearly, and most important, there is a huge asymmetry in the usage of knowledge in that political decision-makers may tap social science knowledge at their will, largely unencumbered by the intentions of social scientists. Policy-makers can select a particular voice from the social sciences to listen to and endorse. For example, in phase 2 of the migration–development nexus discussed above, a report by the International Organization of Labour (IOM), written by authors from the Hamburg Archive for World Economy (HWWA), drew on standard trade theory which argued that trade should substitute for migration (Hiemenz and Schatz, 1979), that is, instead of migrating to work in garment shops in New York, Bangladeshi workers should produce shirts in Dhaka to be exported to the Americas. In practice, this does not work since the rich countries usually keep protecting their own inefficient industries while forcing the developing countries to drop their import tariffs. Yet, precisely because the paper mirrored a standard economic argument in migration policy, it was used in such a way as to legitimate very restrictive immigration policies.

Second, academic knowledge may have a substantiating function in that it can strengthen the position of an organization, a political party, or politicians vis-à-vis rivals, contending parties, and positions. The World Bank, for example, emphasized the magnitude of financial remittances sent by migrants compared to Official Development Assistance (ODA) in the early 2000s in order to position itself as a regulator of international financial flows. After all, in those days fewer and fewer developing countries were taking out loans from the World Bank. The World Bank thus used the migration–development link to reposition itself among international players in the field of finance. In taking the lead among international organizations addressing the abovementioned migration–development nexus, the IOM falls into the same category.

Third, knowledge sometimes fulfils a symbolic function by contributing to the credibility of politicians and public authorities. To illustrate, one has only to call to mind the spate of academic working papers usually commissioned or invited by organizations such as the United Nations Development Program (UNDP) for its latest Human Development Report on international migration and the push to connect migration to capabilities (UNDP, 2009).

Whatever the specific function knowledge from research plays in policy-making and public debates, political decisions have to be legitimated by referring to universal values and norms although they may be guided by particularist interests. For example, restrictive immigration clauses in the EU regarding asylum-seekers are not simply legitimated by referring to potentially tight labour markets or the burden upon social welfare systems. Rather, such policies are discussed jointly with 'positive' normative goals, such as policies addressing the so-called 'root causes' of migration in the regions of origin – most prominently, African countries of origin. Further, the EU has taken vigorous measures to link cooperation with African countries beyond clear exchange packages – migration control in exchange for development aid, as in the cases of Albania, Morocco, Senegal and Nigeria.

Beyond looking at various instrumental linkages between social science knowledge and the world of policy it is important to consider that the main self-declared task of the social sciences as academic disciplines is diagnosis, not guiding social action and generating remedies (Mayntz, 1980). Social science knowledge may thus be most effective in publicly disseminating concepts, notions and associated arguments. In this way social science knowledge can make a difference in defining the relevant policy targets and the indicators to measure social problems. The use of knowledge involves attribution of meaning, interpretation of events, and (re)definition of situations. Where public policy in the public sphere is concerned, it is indirect influence that counts, that is, those crucial notions and concepts which guide societal perception and interpretation of societal processes and not the actual stock of empirical findings. The definitions of social – economic, political, cultural – situations are highly relevant for defining and framing issues and questions, not decision-making as such. A prominent example is Amartya Sen's work with the United Nations Development Program (UNDP), in which he advanced his capability concept as an alternative to notions of development built solely around economic growth. Sen argued that the main criterion for development is the availability of choice for persons to pursue certain goals they regard as essential (Sen, 1984). Moreover, Sen developed indicators which were then concatenated into the Human Development Index (HDI) currently used by the UNDP. In sum, the social sciences give ever new concepts and meanings to the changes of objects in societies. Ultimately, this influence increases the reflexivity of societal conditions.

A decisive and close analysis of how social science concepts spread in the public sphere and in public policy-making necessitates a look at the secondary effects of social science knowledge and more specifically a study of feedback loops. How sociological knowledge in the broadest sense is received depends very much upon structures of plausibility in public discourse. While social science concepts may be received favourably under certain conditions, these situations themselves may be propelled to keep changing, also as a result of the diffusion of sociological knowledge. The latest and third phase of the migration–development nexus re-emerged at a time when the development industry was casting around for new target groups, when international financial institutions, most prominently the World Bank, was searching for new areas of activity. The re-combination of statehood-civil society and market-civil society principles allowed for the emergence of a new development actor: migrants and migrant associations. Once the associated ideas of migrants as development agents started spreading across Europe, (local) administrations turned to the social sciences for help in framing issues. Thus, the transnationalist paradigm, for example, is now strongly embedded in various institutions in countries such as France and Spain. Such imports from the social sciences prefigure the engagement of public authorities through the funding of NGOs and migrant associations engaged in development cooperation with regions of migrant origin.

The proposition that the most important effect of social science knowledge is its potential for creating (a new) public perspective on social issues is borne out by the conclusions of researchers who look at the policy implications of the migration–development nexus (de Wind and Holdaway, 2008). Virtually all studies conclude that it is the analytic (research to determine the impacts of policies) and the explanatory (research to explain why governments adopt the policies) functions that loom largest and are most effective, whereas the prescriptive function (recommendations, based on research, regarding policies governments should adopt to attain particular goals) is usually not very successful in finding direct entry into public policy.

Conclusion: production of orientation and meaning

We are now able to return to the original question: would social science knowledge be more useful if it could be more easily applied instrumentally? In other words, would we desire a state of affairs in which political action could be systematically based on knowledge about calculable causal relations? The answer given here is: not really. What applies to societies in general would also be true for the social sciences. There is a difference between formal and material rationality, between instrumental rationality and reason (Max Weber). In other words, while knowledge about causal relations may make political action more rational in a formal sense, it may also be put to service to do normatively undesirable things. Eventually, social scientific knowledge is *'welt-anschaulich'* (ideological) and thus has a function for producing orientation and meaning. These results suggest going further and examining the role of social sciences and social scientists beyond the realm of consultancy and policy-making. While much ink has been spilled over writing about academics as consultants and advisors, less has been said about the role of researchers in the public sphere. Yet it is here that their functions in providing patterns of orientation and meaning have potentially the strongest impact – and, in the long run, on political decisions and public policies.

References

Barnes, B. (1974) *T. S. Kuhn and Social Science* (London: Routledge & Kegan Paul).

Bellah, R., Sullivan, W. M., Swidler, A., and Tipton, S. M. (1985) *Habits of the Heart: Individualism and Commitment in American Life* (Berkeley: University of California Press).

Boswell, C. (2009) *The Political Uses of Expert Knowledge: Immigration Policy and Social Research* (Cambridge: Cambridge University Press).

Bourdieu, P. (1998) *La Misère du monde* (Paris: Seuil).

Burawoy, M. (2005) 'For Public Sociology', *American Sociological Review*, 70 (1), 4–28.

Burt, R. S. (1992) *Structural Holes: The Social Structure of Competition* (Cambridge, MA: Harvard University Press).

Castles, S. and Delgado Wise, R. (eds) (2008) *Migration and Development: Perspectives from the South* (Geneva: International Organisation for Migration [IOM]).

De Haas, H. (2006) *Engaging Diasporas. How Governments and Development Agencies Can Support Diaspora Involvement in the Development of Origin Countries*, a study for Oxfam Novib, Oxford: International Migration Institute, James Martin 21st Century School, University of Oxford.

De Wind, J. and Haldoway, J. (eds) (2008) *Migration and Development within and across Borders: Research and Policy Perspectives on Internal and International Migration* (Geneva: International Organization of Migration [IOM]).

Elias, N. (2007) *Involvement and Detachment. The Collected Works of Norbert Elias*, Vol. 8, Stephen Quilley (ed.) (Dublin: University College Dublin Press/Dufour Editions).

GCIM (2005) *Migration in an Interconnected World: New Directions for Action*, Report of the Global Commission on International Migration (GCIM) (New York: United Nations).

Habermas, J. (1968) *Technik und Wissenschaft als 'Ideologie'* (Frankfurt a.M.: Suhrkamp).

Hiemenz, U. and Schatz, K.-W. (1979) *Trade in Place of Migration: An Employment-oriented Study with Special Reference to the Federal Republic of Germany, Spain, and Turkey* (Geneva: International Labour Organization [ILO]).

Kapur, D. and McHale, J. (2005) *'Give Us Your Best and Brightest': The Global Hunt for Talent and Its Impact on the Developing World* (Washington, DC: Center for Global Development).

Keynes, J. M. (1970) *The General Theory of Employment, Interest and Money*, reprint of the 1936 edition (London: Macmillan).

Kindleberger, C. P. (1967) *Europe's Postwar Growth: the Role of Labour Supply* (Cambridge, MA: Harvard University Press).

Levitt, P. (2001) *The Transnational Villagers* (Berkeley: University of California Press).

Lipton, M. (1980) 'Migration from Rural Areas of Poor Countries: The Impact of Rural Productivity and Income Distribution', *World Development*, 8 (1), 1–24.

Luhmann, N. (1992) *Die Wissenschaft der Gesellschaft* (Frankfurt a.M.: Suhrkamp).

Martin, P. L. and Taylor, J. E. (1996) 'The Anatomy of a Migration Hump', in J. Edward Taylor (ed.), *Development Strategy, Employment, and Migration: Insights from Models* (Paris: Organization for Economic Cooperation and Development [OECD]).

Mayntz, R. (1980) 'Soziologisches Wissen und politisches Handeln', *Schweizerische Zeitschrift für Soziologie*, 6 (3), 309–320.

Penninx, R. (1982) 'A Critical Review of Theory and Practice: The Case of Turkey', *International Migration Review*, 16 (4: Special Issue: International Migration and Development), 781–818.

Sen, A. (1984) *Resources, Values and Development* (Oxford: Blackwell).

UNDP (2009) *Human Development Report – Overcoming Barriers: Human Mobility and Development* (Washington, DC: United Nations Development Programme [UNDP]).

Weiss, C. H. (1979) 'The Many Meanings of Research Utilization', *Public Administration Review*, 39 (5), 426–431.

Wilson, W. J. (1978) *The Declining Significance of Race: Blacks and Changing American Institutions* (Chicago: University of Chicago Press).

World Bank (2002) *Globalization, Growth, and Poverty* (Washington, DC: The World Bank).

9
Modernization, Development and Migration in a Sceptical Age

Peter Kivisto

While we can debate whether or not something called development in the 'underdeveloped nations' actually took off in the post-World War Two era, there is no debating the fact that the construction of models of development wedded to the regnant structural functionalist paradigm of that period can trace their origins to precisely that time. Such theories clearly took off. It's not surprising why this should be the case. Theorizing development began in earnest once the European colonizing nations confronted the imperative of relinquishing their colonies. The end to a century of European colonialism was brought about by the stark realities these powers confronted in the wake of the devastation they experienced on their respective home fronts during the war. The post-colonial world emerged in part as a consequence of the colonial powers' economic inability to sustain colonial control. A further impetus took shape at the ideological level, for in challenging the racist underpinning of Nazi ideology during the war years, it became difficult to sustain the myth of moral and material uplift of tradition-bound regions of the world to which devotees of the 'white man's burden' view of history subscribed.

That being said, however shaken the former centres of empire were, they worked hard to prevent a radical rupture with the immediate past, instead seeking to articulate new ways of connecting to their former colonies, with a goal being to reinvent a new political relationship while ensuring that the economic benefits of the past would continue into the future, a fact missing from the earliest formulations of development theory. While in a literal sense, the sun now did set on the British Empire, the Commonwealth nations created a new, looser but nonetheless interdependent and asymmetrical relationship between the centre and the periphery. A similar alliance would be formed by France and its former colonies, and to a lesser extent with the lesser European colonial powers. But beyond the economic objective for the centre combined with the geopolitics of the Cold War, whether or not there were other objectives for such alliances often remained a rather murky topic.

This transition to the post-colonial era transpired during the age of Pax Americana. Spared the direct devastation of war, the United States emerged from World War Two as the unchallenged superpower among nations – the largest, most economically vibrant and politically and militarily powerful nation on earth. Having only dipped its toes lightly into the waters of colonialism, it could with some reasonable justification claim to be a Western nation free from the taint of colonial oppression. Indeed, such a formidable intellectual figure as Seymour Martin Lipset (1963) could make a rather compelling case for viewing the United States not as a latter-day variant of the colonial powers, but rather as the 'first new nation', the first country in the modern world to have successfully cast off the yoke of colonial oppression. From this claim, he was able to suggest that the United States could, and indeed should, be seen as a model of development for the nations of what would quickly become known as the Third World.

Development and the early optimism of modernization theory

Deeply embedded in the history of sociology is a view of the general dynamics of broad patterns of social change, which are typically cast in terms of a transition from an earlier period to a new one – a movement from the past to the present. Sociology was firmly committed to exploring the present, while not only history, but also the parallel science of anthropology was tasked with plumbing the depths of the past. One can find this case being made in such varied thinkers as Henry Sumner Maine's depiction of the shift from status to contract, Herbert Spencer's military to industrial society, Ferdinand Toennies' community to society, and Émile Durkheim's mechanical to organic solidarity. In various ways, all of these, but especially Durkheim's formulation, filtered into the synthetic work of the preeminent theorist of structural functionalism and the grand theorist of modernization theory in the middle of the 20th century, Talcott Parsons, who opted to cast this binary in terms of 'traditional' and 'modern' societies. With the United States always serving – whether explicitly or implicitly – as the model for the movement from traditional to modern patterns of social and cultural life, he contended that in modern societies, particularism would give way to universalism, ascription to achievement, collective identity to individualism, role diffuseness to specialization, while the primacy of affective relationships would be superseded by a premium placed on instrumental relationships, at least in public life (Parsons, 1966, 1971).

While Parsons did not articulate his own version of development in the Third World, a cadre of like-minded scholars operating under the big-tent theory of structural functionalism focused their attention on those countries that had not yet made, were in the process of making, or had been stymied in the process of making the transition from tradition to modernity. Perhaps the most influential work in development theory to emerge out of this camp was Walt Whitman Rostow's *The Stages of Economic Growth: A Non-Communist Manifesto* (1960). The subtitle of the book serves to remind readers of the Cold War context in which it was written, for here one has a clear example of the fusion of scholarship and partisanship. The West is held up as the exemplar of economic growth in contradistinction to the alternative Soviet-bloc model. The stages of growth describe various preconditions for take-off from traditional society, the elements intrinsic during the take-off period itself, which included translating scientific and technological advances into productive functions, the expansion of the general education of the population, along with the growth of the banking industry and a concomitant increase in investment. This was followed by take-off and what he calls the 'drive to maturity'. Central to these three stages is the unleashing of the productive capacities of a capitalist industrial society, leading to an age of high mass consumption. He assumes that this is an apt characterization of the economic state of the United States by the middle of the 20th century, speculating that in the future the society might move into a stage 'beyond consumption'.

Rostow didn't ignore the role of politics, but he concentrated primarily on economic factors. In this regard, political scientist A. F. K Organski's *The Stages of Political Development* (1965) can be read as a complement to Rostow's work. Organski offered an account of the development of the modern nation-state from the 16th century up to and beyond the present. He offers an operational definition of political development, defining it 'as increasing governmental efficiency in utilizing the human and natural resources of the nation for national goals' (Organski, 1965, p. 7). Identifying four sequential stages of development, he contends that efficiency increases with each shift, from the earliest stage of 'primitive unification' to industrialization, followed by the move to national welfare and ultimately to the stage of abundance. Organski was but one of a number of development theorists who were particularly keen on analysing the potential for former colonies, many carved up by the colonial powers without regard to cultures on the ground, to successfully become functioning nation-states with both the necessary institutional apparatus to act like a state and the legitimacy granted to it by the populace to permit it to do so (for examples of important case studies, see David Apter on Ghana [1972] and Lucien Pye [1962] on Burma). While Organski described two alternative routes to industrialization besides the liberal approach of most Western nations – which he referred to as Stalinist and fascist – it was clear among development theorists that the political objective of development was to establish multi-party liberal democratic regimes.

The often implicit assumptions about the culture of modernity and the personality type that best accords with it was made explicit in two influential works, Daniel Lerner's *The Passing of Traditional Society* (1958) and Alex Inkeles and David H. Smith's *Becoming Modern* (1974). Both books describe 'modern man' as placing a premium on rationality, science, efficiency, instrumental activity, individual autonomy and an achievement orientation, along with openness to new experiences, a heightened capacity for trust and respect for others. Lerner assumed that the general thrust of history would lead to the virtually inevitable move from traditional to modern societies across the globe. Inkeles and Smith concurred, contending that wherever people encountered modernization, typically by moving from rural to urban areas and shifting employment from traditional agriculture to industry, the transition to a modern personality commenced. Critics have been quick to point out the Eurocentric presuppositions of these works (Peet and Hartwick, 2009, p. 126), along with their ideological implications for development policies, as witnessed, for example, in the Agency for International Development that was created during the Kennedy administration (Latham 2000, pp. 46–59).

Development would occur if and when particular societies succeeded in becoming modern. Development policies during this epoch called for large-scale schemes created by experts in the metropole designed to promote the transition from tradition to modernity, often implemented with the assistance of Western-educated local elites. The assumption was that it was possible to create programme prototypes that could be replicated in place after place. This was thought possible because however varied the manifestations of traditional culture might be, all were capable of yielding to the universalizing character of modern society. Financing various programmes would be the responsibility of major Western institutions, none more significant than the World Bank and the International Monetary Fund, but also including private sources such as the Ford and Rockefeller Foundations. Particularly important in the European context is the role played by the respective national development cooperation organizations.

Dependency theory and beyond

Several decades of experience on the ground has proven to be disappointing. David Apter (1987, p. 13), who can be read as an internal critic of development theory (see his earlier, more favorable analysis: Apter, 1969), characterized the policy achievements as 'meager', while more recently William Easterly, former World Bank economist and now Co-director of New York University's Development Research Institute, contends that despite the fact that $2.3 trillion has been spent on foreign aid during the past half century, 'there's surprisingly little to show for it' (interview in Kling and Schulz 2009, p. 166).

At the theoretical level, the major critiques of modernization theory's approach to development can be found in various articulations of dependency theory, an expression of which can be found in Raúl Delgado Wise and Humberto Márquez Covarrubias' chapter (3) in this volume. The shared premise of these critiques revolves around the claim that the central theoretical shortcoming of modernization theory concerns its failure to consider development in relational terms – particularly in terms that seek to analyse the nature of the economic and political connections between the centre and periphery. Nina Glick Schiller's chapter (2) herein is reflective of a general call for an epistemological shift that moves beyond a singular focus on the nation-state to a consideration of the networked or interlocking character of relations at the intra-state level, whether it is described as a global or transnational perspective.

Arguably the most influential version of dependency theory was that produced by the late André Gunder Frank (1966), who argued that to the extent that the nations of the periphery are linked to the nations of the centre, they inevitably and invariably enter into a relationship of dependency, one, moreover, that serves to prevent them from developing. Frank and like-minded theorists such as Samir Amin, Theotonio Dos Santos and Fernando Henrique Cardoso (before 'charting a new course' during and after the years he served as President of Brazil, see Cardoso, 2001) acquired a substantial audience among the left intelligentsia in both the nations of the core and the periphery during the 1970s and 1980s. In making his case for 'the development of underdevelopment',

Frank (1966, p. 18) argued that 'historical research demonstrates that contemporary underdevelopment is in large part the historical product of past and continuing economic and other relations between the satellite underdeveloped and the now developed metropolitan countries. Furthermore, these relations are an essential part of the capitalist system on a world scale as a whole'. This last sentence indicates the affinity that dependency theory would have with the world-systems perspective that Immanuel Wallerstein would develop during the 1970s – both being not necessarily faithful to Marxist theory, but nonetheless very much shaped by it, including the tradition of theorizing imperialism during the era of colonialism.

How do dependency theorists define underdevelopment, as opposed to a state of being undeveloped? In the latter case, potential resources – land, natural resources, technology, labour — are either not being utilized or are underutilized. In contrast, in a state of underdevelopment such resources are being used, but the chief beneficiaries are the nations of the centre at the expense of the nations at the periphery. Thus, the countries of the periphery are not poor because they lag behind the countries of the centre in terms of making the transition from tradition to modernity, but rather because of the asymmetrical nature of the relationship between centre and periphery. The former benefits when the latter can serve as a continuing source of cheap labour and raw materials, with no prospect of transforming the zero-sum game to a non-zero-sum game.

If the problem of underdevelopment is a result of the linkages with the core capitalist countries, the solution might appear to be to free the states of the periphery from those dependent relationships. The evidence in favour of this approach is not encouraging. The collapse of global communism in the waning years of the past century revealed that the Soviet Union and its allies were abject failures. What was once seen as a society that had managed to achieve industrialization outside the capitalist orbit, the Soviet economy looked in retrospect more like a shell game. Other cases tell a similar story. Witness in the not-so-distant past China's Great Leap Forward and the mass starvation that resulted and for a similar outcome focus on North Korea today. Moreover, the poorest countries on earth – most located in sub-Saharan Africa – are those least connected economically to the most powerful capitalist nations.

Given the shortcomings of modernization theory's account of development, it isn't difficult to find efforts to write its obituary, as can be seen in Colin Leys' *The Rise and Fall of Development Theory* (1996). For its part, particularly in the wake of the collapse of communism and the failures of socialist revolution in the Third World, dependency theory was understandably viewed in some quarters as offering an accurate diagnosis, but with capitalist hegemony unchallenged, incapable of offering a cure. Leys (1982) views dependency theory as constituting a response to what clearly proved to be the unwarranted optimism (and, one might add, hubris) characteristic of development thinking among Western policy elites during the 1950s and 1960s – operating, as they did, with a lack of theoretical reflexivity that masked their Eurocentric and economistic presuppositions. He further argues that the pessimism of dependency theorists was both a reaction to the excessive optimism of development theory and a reflection of the fact that implicit in most versions of dependency theory was the assumption that there 'is an alternative, and preferable kind of development... when this alternative does not in fact exist as an available historical option' (Leys, 1982, p. 104). Moreover, he faults dependency theorists for assuming that any significant development is impossible in capitalism's periphery (Leys, 1982, p. 105).

Contemporary thinking about development emerges out of this now decades-long debate, with more than a few calls being made for 'rethinking development' (Apter, 1987). While 'big push' approaches to jump-starting development are no longer in vogue, one can still find optimistic proponents of development, the most influential being Jeffrey Sachs, who argues in *The End of Poverty* (2005) that we can end poverty within the next two decades. Sachs, known earlier for his support of neo-liberal shock therapy approaches to transforming former communist nations from Eastern Europe into capitalist market economies, continues to embrace a view that places a premium on the impact of competitive markets, but in his current work he also sees the need for the developed nations to provide substantial amounts of foreign aid. More to the point, he advocates large-scale projects that are capable of replication, and are primarily top-down in approach.

On the other hand, critics such as William Easterly (2007, 2001) contend that the lack of results is due to the fact that 'Planners' at institutions such as the IMF and World Bank believe they possess the conceptual tools to create workable programmes, despite decades of evidence to the contrary. However, rather than concluding that development is impossible, Easterly makes a case on behalf of what he refers to as 'Searchers', who proceed with the assumption that those on the ground, operating from the bottom up, are in the best position to ascertain what works and what doesn't. As far as the major funding institutions go, Easterly contends that the best plan is no plan – that developing nations that establish democratic political systems and competitive markets will have the necessary conditions for figuring out what sorts of development schemes are best suited to their situation.

The differences between Sachs and Easterly reflect the fact that there is at present a lack of consensus about the theoretical grounding of development policies. Compounding the problem, according to MIT economist Esther Duflo, is the fact that too often in the past insufficient data has been brought to bear in exploring competing approaches to development. Her alternative is to conduct in-depth case studies in order to begin to establish a substantial empirical base upon which to shape future thinking about development (Parker, 2010). It is within this larger context of thinking about development that the more specific concern with the relationship between development and migration needs to be located.

Development and migration

In a report sponsored by the International Organization for Migration (IOM) and the Social Science Research Council, Frank Laczko (2008, p. 9) wrote in the preface that '[r]esearch and policy interest in the linkages between migration and development is probably at an all-time high ...'. While this is an accurate assessment, such an interest was not absent in previous decades. As Thomas Faist and Margit Fauser point out in the introduction to this volume, the impact of migration on development was addressed earlier, and as might be expected it was differentially interpreted during the heyday of modernization theory compared to the subsequent era when dependency theory's influence peaked. However, what they didn't stress was the fact that for the major theorists of development and its subsequent critics, migration appears to have been viewed as a phenomenon of relatively minor impact – a view not necessarily held by theorists of migration.

The earlier period shaped primarily by neo-classical economics had a favourable assessment of the impact of migration – seen without much reflection as temporary or circular migration. The underlying premise of neo-classical economic theory was that out-migration was beneficial to the sending country because it provided a solution to surplus labour, while meeting the labour demands of receiving nations. The result would be an increase in productive capacity in the latter and an increase in wage levels in the former. The improved labour situation in the sending country would over time encourage investment, which would reduce levels of emigration and in the best of circumstances lead to the return migration of some of the émigré population (Lewis, 1959). Stephen Castles (2008, p. 4) has referred to this perspective as a 'virtuous circle', whereby migration stimulates development, which in turn leads to a reduction in levels of migration.

In contrast, dependency theorists, operating from what Castles (2008, p. 4) calls 'the historical-institutional approach' to economics, portray the linkage between migration and development as a 'vicious circle'. Dependency not only retards development, it facilitates the development of underdevelopment, which in turn serves as a trigger for migration. This depresses local wages in the sending country, which further impoverishes the nation and exacerbates the income gap between haves and have nots.

As Faist and Fauser point out (see also Portes, 2009, pp. 12–17), another deleterious impact stressed by dependency theorists is that of 'brain-drain' migrants. The loss of individuals with high levels of human capital is seen as undermining development. While this can include the loss of engineers, scientists and people with a variety of technical skills, one especially significant component of this phenomenon involves the health care sector and the so-called 'care drain'. This can be seen in the exodus of physicians from India and nurses from the Philippines, or the large losses of health care workers from sub-Saharan Africa. For example, a United Nations report reveals that there are currently more Malawian doctors practising medicine in England than in Malawi (United Nations, 2006, p.8).

These two opposing stances regarding the migration–development nexus serve as the historical backdrop to current efforts to explore that linkage, and during the first decade of the 21st century a rather substantial body of work from both the migration and development sides of the equation have been published (for a relatively early review, see Nyberg-Sørensen et al., 2002; for more recent overviews, see Davis, 2007; Castles, 2008; and Faist, 2009). A cursory review of that current literature reveals that it offers a far more complex picture of the linkage, reflective of what Hein de Haas (2010, p. 227) in perhaps the most detailed overview yet to appear, refers to as an appreciation of 'the heterogeneity of migration impacts' on development – positive, negative and neutral.

Four types of potential migrant-driven development

At the moment that a migrant–development nexus became a topic of keen interest, particularly on the part of development agencies and institutions such as the World Bank and the International Monetary

Fund, sceptics appeared questioning the likelihood that this so-called 'third way' or civil society approach to development could actually yield substantial positive results. In an oft-cited article on 'the new development mantra', Devesh Kapur (2005, p. 339) asked if this presumed nexus was simply the latest fad to catch on in development circles, while Ferruccio Pastore (2006) wondered if much of the current discussion amounted to little more than 'hot air'. This volume seeks to address the often inflated enthusiasm but also the substantive issues relating to the migration–development nexus. In doing so, it is evident that four types of migrant engagement with the homeland have become the focus of scholarly attention during the past decade, and any assessment of this nexus needs to separate them analytically: (1) individual remittances; (2) the activities of hometown associations and collective remittances; (3) business networks; and (4) professional/knowledge networks.

It's also clear that given the global dimensions of these phenomena, distinct case studies need always to be seen, not only for what they tell us about specific examples, but also for what they do and do not suggest when trying to generalize. Thus in Chapter 4 of this book, Nicholas Van Hear focuses on the particular characteristics of conflict-ridden societies, countries such as Somalia and Sri Lanka that have experienced long-term civil wars, where the impacts of remittances may not be the same as in nations that don't suffer from such conflict. Lothar Smith's research on transnational business ventures in Ghana (in Chapter 5) similarly opens a window on the possibilities and constraints of such undertakings, but from the vantage of a particular poor sub-Saharan African country whose experience may not be quite the same as in countries that are not as poor. Margit Fauser's study in Chapter 6 of co-development in two major Spanish cities is, likewise, a unique case that may not reflect many of the features of collective remittances in other contexts. In her chapter and in Jean-Baptiste Meyer's study of diaspora knowledge networks (Chapter 7), we enter territory where the body of research to date is quite sparse, and thus in both instances their work can be read as contributions to early efforts intended to help shape a research agenda.

What are the basic issues for research agendas for each of the four types of migrant engagement noted above? We turn briefly to this question.

Individual remittances

Migrants past and present have often sent money and goods to family members who remained in the homeland – and they frequently have done so over relatively extended periods of time. At the same time, it appears that in the long term, if migration levels decline and subsequently as the offspring of immigrants become settled in their new homeland, remittances taper off. There are presumed to be differences between temporary labour migrants and those who have opted for more permanent resettlement, the former having greater incentives in the long run to remit than the latter. We know all this, but until fairly recently, it had to be conceded that data on remittances was fragmentary and imprecise.

With considerably improved methods for measuring remittance levels, it is widely known that prior to the global recession, individual remittances represented the second largest source of finances in poor countries after direct foreign investment (Maimbo and Ratha, 2005, p. 2). According to World Bank data, the rate of increase of global remittances in recent years grew annually at a rate often exceeding 20 per cent per year. Thus, while the remittance figure for 2004 was reported as $125 billion, the figure for 2008 was $338 billion – a dramatic increase over a very short period of time. Moreover, economists working for the World Bank estimated that the annual declines in remittances as a result of the recession would be in the 6–7 per cent range, thus concluding that overall levels would remain very high despite precarious economic circumstances. These estimates are based on data obtained by remitters working through formal channels, and thus they don't include remittances derived from those that opt for more informal channels typically based on religious or ethnic affiliations such as the Islamic *hawala*, the South Asian *hundi*, the Chinese *fei chien* and the Thai *phoe kuan*. Regional disparities in the number of dollars flowing in are quite pronounced, with the largest amounts going to East and South Asia, followed by Latin America and the Caribbean, with by far the smallest amounts entering sub-Saharan Africa (Ratha et al., 2009, p. 14).

Broadly speaking, remittances can be used for two purposes: for consumption and for investment. Consumption involves a range of things from providing basic human needs by assisting people to obtain food, housing, medical care and so forth, to the purchase of luxury items. Investment likewise entails a range of activities, including the use of remittances to purchase land for economic purposes, to invest in business ventures, or to enhance the recipients' human capital by financing educational pursuits. Sometimes these two activities are difficult to untangle, as when immigrants build homes for themselves in their hometowns, assuming that they will return at some time in the future, perhaps after retirement.

One position has it that when remittances are used solely or primarily for consumption, they are not to be viewed as tools for development. Indeed, to the extent that the recipients of remittances become dependent on financial infusions from migrants, it can actually undermine development. Unfortunately, the research to date on the uses of remittances is limited and, moreover, there is a lack of consensus about the extent to which it is directed toward investment. Those most suspicious about the investment potential of remittances contend that virtually all remittances go to consumption, in many instances amounting to an economic safety net – or what is sometimes referred to as 'social insurance'. However, several case studies challenge this pessimism, finding in specific locales evidence that at least a percentage of remittances is in fact invested and thus has development potential. A survey of that literature makes clear that there is no consensus about the role that remittances are playing in development, though there appears to be tacit agreement that remittances are used primarily for consumption purposes.

To complicate the picture, what might be good for individuals and families might not be good for the communities in which they reside. Thus, while individuals may have more disposable income, if their community is losing population due to migration, and those left behind are older and less capable of functioning in the labour market, investment opportunities decline. Likewise, some families may have more resources to invest in education, but the schools in the locality struggle due to declining enrolments (Kapur, 2005, p. 348).

A recent paper on 'Remittances, Consumption, and Investment in Ghana' prepared by economists at the World Bank was based on a survey of 4000 households in the country, some of which received no remittances while others received either internal or international remittances. The authors concluded that recipients of remittances treated this income no differently than other sources of household income, and thus don't proportionally change spending habits by either increasing spending on consumption or investment (Adams et al., 2008). Why spending habits remain the same is not clear, but it may be that Ghana is a poor country and the amounts involved are not sufficiently large to make a difference, although one could make an equally reasonable counterclaim that in a poor country even small amounts make a big difference.

While the need for additional research is obvious, one conclusion can appropriately be drawn: while individual remittances benefit the recipient households, there is little evidence to support the contention that this has spillover effects in terms of reducing levels of poverty at the community level, a conclusion appearing in the United Nations' Human Development Report 2009 (UNDP, 2009). Moreover, although the overall size of remittances is quite remarkable given the limited economic means of most immigrants, there are serious limitations to the amounts they are capable of contributing. Finally, it is unclear what happens after the passing of the immigrant generation and the more acculturated children and grandchildren experience their ancestral homeland with a greater sense of social distance.

Hometown associations

Hometown associations (HTAs) have become the subject of increasing scholarly attention in recent years. The fact that such voluntary organizations can be found in so many different national settings – Mexican hometown associations, Jamaican returnee associations, charitable foundations in Egypt and Turkish hometown associations, to list but a few – has led policy specialists to consider their development potential. However varied these organizations, their members share a common transnational interest in maintaining ties with the community they left by providing assistance in the form of collective remittances intended to improve aspects of local infrastructure. Thus, money has often been raised to build or renovate hospitals, schools, churches, sports and recreation centers, and other public buildings and spaces; to pave roads and highways; to install or improve water and sewage systems; to provide street lights; to offer educational scholarships; and to respond to natural disasters (Kivisto and Faist, 2010, pp. 154–156).

While in many instances, hometown associations function independently of states and INGOs, in other instances they engage in partnerships. Perhaps the most well-known example of a private-public partnership with the sending state is Mexico's 'three for one' programme, wherein for every dollar remitted by an HTA three dollars are contributed, one each by the local, state and federal governments. In some instances, receiving states have initiated programmes, sometimes pilot programmes, to similarly contribute matching funds. Examples can be found in Norway's support of Pakistani immigrant organizations' development projects in Pakistan and with the Canadian International

Development Agency's work with an association of Canadian-Haitian HTAs (Somerville et al., 2008, pp. 11–12).

In France and subsequently in Spain, the idea of migrants as agents of development became the basis for the policy concept of co-development, which is the focus of Fauser's analysis in Chapter 6 of this volume, examining how the strategy has taken shape in Madrid and Barcelona through the workings of members of REDCO and similar immigrant organizations (see also Østergaard-Nielsen, 2010 for co-development activity in Catalonia). The initial statement laying out this strategy is usually attributed to Sami Naïr (1997) when he served as an advisor to the French Ministry of the Interior during the 1990s. Compared to the workings of hometown associations elsewhere, co-development was distinctive in two ways. First, it was more state-oriented, reflecting France's unwillingness to embrace neo-liberalism's anti-state orientation with the same level of enthusiasm found, for example, in the US. Second, development was far more explicitly linked to policies aimed at not only migration control but at encouraging return migration. It was predicated on a conviction that France would best meet its labour needs by bringing in temporary workers, not permanent settlers.

One can readily point anecdotally to successful development projects, and this can be used as evidence for the potential virtues of an expanded role for organized collective remittances. However, in terms of systematic research on the impacts of HTAs, many working in this field stress that we are only at the earliest stages of a sustained research agenda on the long-term prospects of this type of development (Østergaard-Nielsen, 2010, p. 15). Without a doubt, the most sustained study to date of both the developmental potential and the challenges confronting hometown associations is found in Robert Courtney Smith's ethnographic study, *Mexican New York: Transnational Lives of New Immigrants* (2006). It can be read as a cautionary tale where the involvements of the immigrant leaders of the hometown association frequently took a toll on marriages and family relations, while also resulting in often strained relationships with political leaders in Mexico. Moreover, there was little indication that a second generation was in the wings being groomed to take over the organization.

Smith's work is a reflection of the fact that it is important to consider that there are a number of limitations to factor into any critical assessment of the development potential of HTAs. First, many immigrants may not have the requisite organizational and technical skills to successfully translate good intentions into concrete programmes.

Second, the levels of financing that immigrants are capable of providing, especially those who are in the bottom tiers of the receiving country's economy, are quite modest. Third, conflict and contestation appear to be inevitable, and they can undermine the long-term prospects of transnational development schemes (Waldinger et al., 2008). Fourth, as Ferruccio Pastore (2006) has pointed out, over time immigrants may well experience 'the temptation to assimilate', which can result in a reduction in their enthusiasm for such activities, reducing the likelihood that they are prepared to invest over the long term in their country of birth. This can be exacerbated in situations where immigrants, for whatever reasons, lose faith in the potential for the home community to be transformed positively – which can include such factors as high levels of crime and corruption or political instability. Finally, in the case of co-development, where a primary – if not *the* primary – objective involves migration control and finding incentives to stimulate return migration, policy-makers may find themselves in a situation where their goals are out of sync with the aspirations of migrants, who may well want to settle permanently (Khoudour-Castéras, 2009).

Business networks

Immigrant businesspersons in the past have often served as key sources for investment and for transfers of financial capital to their countries of origin. As a number of frequently cited examples indicate, such as northern Europe's Hanseatic League, the African Hausas, and Overseas Chinese in Southeast Asia, business networks have been a vital aspect of previous periods of migration. During the migratory wave out of Europe in the 19th century and early part of the 20th, the literature on migrants included attention to what became known as middleman minorities. Today, as Ivan Light has pointed out, traditional middleman minorities compete with transnational businesspersons and one of the consequences of globalization is that the English language has increasingly become the language of international business. The result is that:

> Today, Chinese business travelers in Eastern Europe speak English with their Polish trading partners. There is no need now to find translators who speak and read both Polish and Chinese. That said, the low-level Chinese merchants in eastern Europe continue to acquire local languages, and to function in them following classic strategies of a middleman minority. Thanks to the dominance of the English

> language, Chinese, Peruvians, and Poles now have a common language, which jeopardizes though it does not exclude the earlier linguistic advantage of middleman minorities. (Light, 2010, p. 9)

In some migrant sending countries, governments have recently initiated programmes designed to encourage their business expatriates to play a role in either directly investing in their country of origin or serving as brokers for foreign investments. For example, Indian immigrants who have become successful entrepreneurs in Silicon Valley's hi-tech industry have played major roles in developing the hi-tech industrial zones in Bangalore and Hyderabad. In this particular case, the investors benefited from the available local skilled workforce that had been trained by foreign companies that had previously established data processing and computer programming operations in India. Similar examples can be found in China. What both countries share in common is that among their respective émigré populations are a large number of well-educated emigrants with both marketable technical skills and entrepreneurial expertise.

To what extent the Indian and Chinese cases can be seen as typifying a more general trend or are rather unusual is an open question. Suffice it to say that Lothar Smith's Ghanaian study in Chapter 5 of this volume would suggest that the differences between Ghana and both India and China are more pronounced than the similarities. The subjects of his study do not appear to have the levels of technical and entrepreneurial skill to match their Indian and Chinese counterparts. Nor do they possess comparable levels of investment capital.

While immigration scholars have long studied ethnic entrepreneurs, focusing, for example, on the merits and drawbacks of enclave economies in receiving countries (see, for example, Light and Gold, 2000), it is only with the emergence of the transnational optic that attention has turned to the impacts of immigrant entrepreneurs on sending nations. This, thus, is clearly an emergent field of research. When one then calls for exploring the developmental potential for such entrepreneurial ventures, the emergent character of such work is all the more obvious. If remittances, both individual and collective, can be seen as 'third way' or civil society approaches to development, business networks constitute a more explicit example of a neo-liberal market approach to development.

While Smith's Ghana study may in many respects represent a unique example, there is one recurring concern voiced by his subjects that ought to be considered in other national contexts: the role of trust. There appears to be a trust deficit among Ghanaians, and kin networks don't overcome that deficit, but instead may contribute to it. Connected to this general concern are issues related to the investment climate of particular countries. Is there a labour force with sufficient human capital to serve as an investment incentive? To what extent does a country operate according to the rule of law? How endemic are levels of corruption? Is the country politically stable? Does the existing infrastructure – everything from roads and communication systems to educational institutions – represent an incentive or deterrent to investment? These are examples of some of the core questions that will need to frame research agendas, as recent calls for such an agenda attest (Patterson, 2006).

Professional/knowledge networks

The idea that the most highly educated professionals in poor countries have a decided tendency to succumb to the temptation to migrate to rich countries where they can best translate their high human capital into financial success has been a longstanding concern in development circles. However, more recently the view that the outmigration of skilled workers is a net loss for the sending country has been questioned. Oded Stark (2004), for example, has argued that the incentive to emigrate in the right circumstances can actually have a beneficial impact on the poor country, enhancing rather than reducing human capital levels. The general consensus at the moment is that the exodus of highly trained professionals can have different impacts, some negative, some neutral, and some positive – depending on circumstances on the ground and migration policies. In some cases, the exodus of the highly educated is a result of the poor country's inability to absorb their talents, as, for example, with a theoretical physicist in Lesotho or Haiti. Beyond the significance of the exodus of talent at the individual level is the potential for those individuals to become part of networks that are designed to stimulate development in their homelands.

Professional and knowledge networks constitute a clear parallel to business networks and in many concrete cases, though an analytical distinction can be made, the two types blur considerably into each other. This is evident in the Indian IT example cited above. The emergence of such networks is seen in some quarters as a potential response to the negative impact of 'brain-drain' migration. What Jean-Baptiste Meyer refers to in Chapter 7 as 'diaspora knowledge networks' (DKN) are organizations, sometimes formal, sometimes informal, that attempt to affect knowledge and skill transfers from the centre to the periphery. As his chapter indicates, the sorts of activities that fall under this general rubric are varied, including longer-term partnerships between expatriate knowledge elites and counterparts in their homeland or short-term consultancies. It can involve projects requiring sustained interpersonal connections or a less personalized process of knowledge transfer.

A survey of the literature on this phenomenon reveals considerable debate about brain drain/brain circulation/brain gain. There is no consensus about how best to approach the topic conceptually and theoretically, and the empirical evidence is limited. Thus, as with business networks, this is most definitely an area of inquiry at the cusp of formulating and setting the groundwork for a sustained research agenda.

Concluding remarks

Given the preliminary character of research on the migration–development nexus, a conclusion to this chapter – and indeed, to this book – cannot possibly amount to a pulling together of the strands and the offering of a general summary of what the state of the field is at the moment. The state of the field, quite simply, is inchoate. As someone who comes at this 'nexus' from the migration side of the equation, I know one thing: during the past two decades, a considerable body of solid and compelling work on international migration has been produced. Theoretical advances have been made, complemented by quality empirical research. Given the controversies that inevitably surround such fields, the quality of this work is all the more impressive. To large extent this is because a majority of the key scholars in the field have managed more successfully than many suspect of maintaining a healthy distance between scholarship and partisanship. The debates and controversies have, in most respects, been handled in ways that have served to advance this subfield of sociology rather than fragmenting and undermining it. One conceptual development in particular has served to create the climate for the emergence of an interest in the relationship between migration and development: transnationalism. As this concept has evolved during its short history, it has set the stage for what has been heretofore ignored – a sociology of *emigration* – to complement the well-established sociology of immigration. Down the road, this may serve to facilitate advancing what John Urry (2000) has called for: a 'mobile sociology'.

Coming at development studies as an outsider, my impression is that its recent history has not been as sanguine as that of immigration studies. On the contrary, it appears that the polarized debate between modernization and dependency theorists has resulted in a critique of both poles without yet coming to terms with a synthesis or alternative theoretical model that can serve as the basis for tomorrow's research agenda. I will be the first to admit that my knowledge of the history of development studies is sufficiently limited to be prepared to concede that this may amount to an oversimplification of a more complex – and possibly more optimistic – sense of where things actually stand. What is clear is that scholars working in development studies occupy a space much closer to political and policy action and to the funding sources that often determine research agendas. This is a mixed blessing, for while there is indeed money on offer to do large-scale research projects, development studies is also far more intellectually dependent on non-scholarly research agendas than is immigration studies.

This contrast can well serve as a parting remark for this collection of papers because it is clear that the migration–development nexus constitutes a research site that is as important as it is untapped. There is a significant post-World War Two history to support those who are critical of positions that embrace an unreflective optimism about this nexus. However, there are also good reasons to be suspicious of those who advocate an unbridled pessimism. The proper attitude, it seems, is to view the potential of migration to facilitate development in poor countries with a healthy dose of scepticism: being critical of empirically unsupported enthusiasms, continuing to be open to the possibility of unexpected positive outcomes, while always understanding that migration cannot be a panacea for the problems confronting the nations of the South and East.

References

Adams, R. H., Cuccuecha, A. and Page, J. (2008) 'Remittances, Consumption, and Investment in Ghana', *World Bank Policy Research Working Paper* 4515 (Washington, DC: World Bank).

Apter, D. (1969) *The Politics of Modernization* (Chicago: University of Chicago Press).

Apter, D. (1972) *Ghana in Transition*, 2nd rev. ed. (Princeton: Princeton University Press).

Apter, D. (1987) *Rethinking Development: Modernization, Dependency, and Postmodern Politics* (Newbury Park: Sage).

Cardoso, F. H. (2001) *Charting a New Course: The Politics of Globalization and Social Transformation* (Lanham: Rowman & Littlefield).

Castles, S. (2008) 'Development and Migration – Migration and Development: What Comes First?', unpublished paper, International Migration Institute, Oxford University.

Davis, R. (2007) 'Reconceptualizing the Migration–Development Nexus: Diasporas, Globalisation, and the Politics of Exclusion', *Third World Quarterly*, 28 (1), 59–76.

De Haas, H. (2010) 'Migration and Development: A Theoretical Perspective', *International Migration Review*, 44 (1), 227–264.

Easterly, W. (2001) *The Elusive Quest for Growth: Economists' Adventures and Misadventures in the Tropics* (Cambridge, MA: MIT Press).

Easterly, W. (2007) *The White Man's Burden: Why the West's Efforts to Aid the Rest Have Done So Much Ill and So Little Good* (New York: Penguin).

Faist, T. (2009) 'Transnationalization and Development: Toward an Alternative Agenda', *Social Analysis*, 53 (3), 38–59.

Frank, A. G. (1966) 'The Development of Underdevelopment', *Monthly Review*, 18, 17–31.

Inkeles, A. and Smith, D. H. (1974) *Becoming Modern: Individual Change in Six Developing Countries* (Cambridge, MA: Harvard University Press).

Kapur, D. (2005) 'Remittances: The New Development Mantra?', in S. M. Maimbo and D. Ratha (eds), *Remittances: Development Impact and Future Prospects* (Washington, DC: World Bank).

Kivisto, P. and Faist, T. (2010) *Beyond a Border: The Causes and Consequences of Contemporary Immigration* (Thousand Oaks: Pine Forge Press).

Khoudour-Castéras, D. (2009) 'Neither Migration nor Development: The Contradictions of French Co-development Policy', Paris, unpublished paper.

Kling, A. and Schulz, N. (2009) *From Poverty to Prosperity: Intangible Assets, Hidden Liabilities, and the Lasting Triumph Over Scarcity* (New York: Encounter Books).

Laczko, F. (2008) 'Migration and Development: The Forgotten Migrants', in J. DeWind and J. Holdaway (eds), *Migration and Development Within and Across Borders: Research and Policy Perspectives on Internal and International Migration* (Geneva and New York: International Organization for Migration and The Social Science Research Council), 9–13.

Latham, M. (2000) *Modernization as Ideology: American Social Science and 'Nation Building' in the Kennedy Era* (Chapel Hill: University of North Carolina Press).

Lerner, D. (1958) *The Passing of Traditional Society: Modernizing the Middle East* (New York: Free Press).

Lewis, A. (1959) *The Theory of Economic Growth* (London: Allen & Unwin).

Leys, C. (1982) 'African Economic Development in Theory and Practice', *Daedalus*, 111 (2), 99–124.

Leys, C. (1996) *The Rise and Fall of Development Theory* (Bloomington: Indiana University Press).

Light, I. (2010) 'Transnational Entrepreneurs in an English-Speaking World', *Die Erde*, 141 (1–2), 1–16.

Light, I. and Gold, S. (2000) *Ethnic Economies* (San Diego: Academic Press).

Lipset, S. M. (1963) *The First New Nation: The United States in Historical and Comparative Perspective* (New York: Basic Books).

Maimbo, S. M. and Ratha, D. (2005) 'Remittances: An Overview', in S. M. Maimbo and D. Ratha (eds), *Remittances: Development Impact and Future Prospects* (Washington, DC: World Bank).

Naïr, S. (1997) *Rapport de bilan et d'orientation sur al politique de codéveloppement liée aux flux migratoires* (Paris: Premier Ministre).

Nyberg-Sørensen, N., Van Hear, N. and Engberg-Pedersen, P. (2002) 'The Migration-Development Nexus: Evidence and Policy Options', *International Migration*, 40 (5), 49–73.

Organski, A. F. K. (1965) *The Stages of Political Development* (New York: Alfred A. Knopf).

Østergaard-Nielsen, E. (2010) 'Codevelopment and Citizenship: The Nexus between Policies on Local Migrant Incorporation and Migrant Transnational Practices in Spain', *Ethnic and Racial Studies*, iFirst article, 1–20.

Parker, I. (2010) 'The Poverty Lab: Transforming Development Economics, One Experiment at a Time', *The New Yorker* (May 17), pp. 78–89.

Parsons, T. (1966) *Societies: Evolutionary and Comparative Perspectives* (Englewood Cliffs: Prentice-Hall).

Parsons, T. (1971) *The System of Modern Societies* (Englewood Cliffs: Prentice-Hall).

Pastore, F. (2006) 'Transnationalism and Co-Development: Are They Just "Hot Air" or Are They Useful Concepts?', Discussion Paper to the project 'Development and Migration Circuits' (Rome: Centro Studi di Politica Internazionale [CesPi]).

Patterson, R. (2006) 'Transnationalism: Diaspora-Homeland Development', *Social Forces*, 84 (4), 1891–1907.

Peet, R. and Hartwick, E. (2009) *Theories of Development: Contentions, Arguments, Alternatives* (New York: Guilford Press).

Portes, A. (2009) 'Migration and Development: Reconciling Opposite Views', *Ethnic and Racial Studies*, 32 (1), 5–22.

Pye, L. (1962) *Politics, Personality, and Nation Building: Burma's Search for Identity* (New Haven: Yale University Press).

Ratha, D., Mohapatra, S. and Silwil, A. (2009) 'Migration and Remittance Trends 2009', *Migration and Development Brief*, 11 (Washington, DC: World Bank).

Rostow, W. W. (1960) *The Stages of Economic Growth: A Non-Communist Manifesto* (Cambridge: Cambridge University Press).

Sachs, J. (2005) *The End of Poverty: Economic Possibilities for Our Time* (New York: The Penguin Press).

Smith, R.C. (2006) *Mexican New York: Transnational Lives of New Immigrants* (Berkeley: University of California Press).

Somerville, W., Durana, J. and Terrazas, A. M. (2008) 'Hometown Associations: An Untapped Resource for Immigrant Integration?', *MPI Insights*, No. 8 (July) (Washington, DC: Migration Policy Institute [MPI]).

Stark, O. (2004) 'Rethinking the Brain Drain', *World Development*, 32 (1), 15–22.

UNFPA (2006) *The State of World Population* (New York: United Nations Population Fund [UNFPA]).

UNDP (2009) *Human Development Report 2009* (New York: United Nations Development Programme [UNDP]).

Waldinger, R. Popkin, E. and Magana, H. A. (2008) 'Conflict and Contestation in the Cross-border Community: Hometown Associations Reassessed', *Ethnic and Racial Studies*, 31 (5), 843–870.

Urry, J. (2000) 'Mobile Sociology,' *British Journal of Sociology*, 51 (1), 185–203.

Index